# Taking Our Country Back

Oxford Studies in Digital Politics

Series Editor: Andrew Chadwick, Royal Holloway, University of London

*News on the Internet: Information and Citizenship in the 21st Century*
David Tewksbury and Jason Rittenberg

*The Digital Origins of Dictatorship and Democracy: Information
Technology and Political Islam*
Philip N. Howard

*The MoveOn Effect: The Unexpected Transformation of
American Political Advocacy*
David Karpf

# Taking Our Country Back

## THE CRAFTING OF NETWORKED POLITICS FROM HOWARD DEAN TO BARACK OBAMA

DANIEL KREISS

OXFORD
UNIVERSITY PRESS

# OXFORD
## UNIVERSITY PRESS

Oxford University Press, Inc., publishes works that further
Oxford University's objective of excellence
in research, scholarship, and education.

Oxford    New York
Auckland    Cape Town    Dar es Salaam    Hong Kong    Karachi
Kuala Lumpur    Madrid    Melbourne    Mexico City    Nairobi
New Delhi    Shanghai    Taipei    Toronto

With offices in
Argentina    Austria    Brazil    Chile    Czech Republic    France    Greece
Guatemala    Hungary    Italy    Japan    Poland    Portugal    Singapore
South Korea    Switzerland    Thailand    Turkey    Ukraine    Vietnam

Published by Oxford University Press, Inc.
198 Madison Avenue, New York, New York 10016

www.oup.com

Oxford is a registered trademark of Oxford University Press

Library of Congress Cataloging-in-Publication Data
Kreiss, Daniel.
Taking our country back: the crafting of networked politics from Howard Dean to Barack Obama /Daniel Kreiss.
    p.    cm.—(Oxford studies in digital politics)
ISBN 978-0-19-993678-6 (paperback: alk. paper) 978-0-19-978253-6 (hardcover: alk. paper)
1. Internet in political campaigns—United States—History. 2. Campaign management—
Technological innovations—United States—History. 3. Political campaigns—Technological innovations—
United States—History. 4. Political participation—Technological innovations—United States—History.
5. Presidents—United States—Election—2004—Technological innovations. 6. Presidents—United States—
Election—2008—Technological innovations. 7. Political consultants—United States—History—21st century.
8. Internet—Political aspects—United States. 9. Digital media—Political aspects—United States. I. Title.
JK2281.K74    2012
324.70973—dc23        2011048012

Printed in the United States of America
on acid-free paper

# Contents

# Acknowledgments

Many individuals and institutions shaped this book. I conducted the research for the early chapters on the Howard Dean campaign while writing my dissertation in the Department of Communication at Stanford University. I would like to thank the members of my dissertation committee, James Fishkin, Doug McAdam, Clifford Nass, Walter W. Powell, and Fred Turner, as well as the faculty of the department, especially Jeremy Bailenson, Theodore Glasser, Shanto Iyengar, and Jon Krosnick, for their immeasurable guidance in my research and thinking around new media and politics. Fred Turner has been a true mentor and friend since the beginning of my academic career, and I am deeply indebted to his scholarship and teaching. I could not have conducted this work at Stanford without the generous financial support of Rowland and Pat Rebele and the Nathan Maccoby family, as well as the incalculable administrative support of Susie Ementon and Barbara Kataoka.

The dissertation became a book during my time as a postdoctoral associate at the Information Society Project at Yale Law School. I am deeply thankful for the opportunity to research and write in such a rich intellectual environment. Jack Balkin and Laura DeNardis were supportive interlocutors as this book took shape, as were fellows Nicholas Bramble, Bryan Choi, and Seeta Peña Gangadharan. The book also benefited greatly from the insightful comments of those who encountered it as a work in progress at workshops and conferences during the past two years. In particular, I thank Michael Schudson, Richard John, Marshall Ganz, Jim Katz, Beth Noveck, Caroline Lee, Edward Walker, Patrick Lynn Rivers, Jeffrey Alexander, Nina Eliasoph, Jeremy Shtern, Fenwick Mckelvey, Aaron Shaw, Christina Dunbar-Hester, and Colin Agur for their comments on this work.

My colleagues in the School of Journalism and Mass Communication at the University of North Carolina at Chapel Hill have been immensely supportive through the final stages of research, writing, and revisions. I would particularly like to thank Rhonda Gibson, Sriram Kalyanaraman, Daren Brabham, Daniel

Riffe, Cathy Packer, JoeBob Hester, Jane Brown, Seth Noar, Anne Johnston, Ferrel Guillory, Paul Jones, Jean Folkerts, and Dean Susan King for their advice, insightful critiques, and assistance in making the transition to such a wonderful public institution. I also thank Lisa Barnard, my research assistant during the 2011–2012 academic year, for her invaluable help in preparing this manuscript. In addition, my colleague Terence Oliver was incredibly generous with his time and expertise in developing the infographic for this book. I thank Alexis Gargagliano for her insight into the book publishing process and Elizabeth Bauman for her transcription services.

I would like to thank my editor at Oxford, Angela Chnapko, for her skillful guidance through the review process and comments on this manuscript. Andrew Chadwick, the series editor, has played a large role in my scholarship over the years, supporting my work since I was a doctoral student. Andrew has also made many of the scholarly contributions that this book aspires to build upon.

I owe a great deal of gratitude to my colleagues who have commented on drafts and debated the ideas in this book endlessly over cocktails in Brooklyn, at dawn and late at night on the Metro-North Railroad, in pubs at Oxford, and virtually in e-mails: Chris Anderson, Dave Karpf, and Rasmus Kleis Nielsen. The book is much stronger because of their tough critiques and continual inspiration. I could not have asked for a better group of scholars as fellow travelers. I also thank Philip Howard for his support and guidance over the years, as well as his foundational contribution to scholarly understanding of new media campaigns that this work hopes to extend.

Most importantly, I am grateful for the access I have had to many of the leading practitioners in the field and whose work of world-making continues to be an inspiration to me. In addition to all those who sat for interviews, I would especially like to thank the many who devoted hours to helping me understand their work: Jerome Armstrong, Michael Bassik, Larry Biddle, Andrew Bleeker, Gray Brooks, Jim Brayton, Will Bunnett, Bobby Clark, Zack Exley, Jascha Franklin-Hodge, Judith Freeman, Teddy Goff, Sam Graham-Felsen, Marshall Ganz, Chris Hughes, Aldon Hynes, Neil Jensen, Clay Johnson, Patrick Michael Kane, Nicco Mele, Amanda Michel, Adam Mordecai, Aaron Myers, Kelly Nuxoll, Tamara Pogue, Zack Rosen, Joe Rospars, Mike Sager, Michael Silberman, Dan Siroker, Neil Sroka, Zephyr Teachout, Scott Thomas, Kevin Thurman, and David Weinberger. I would also like to thank Ben Self, Michael Slaby, and Mark Sullivan for both sitting for interviews and for taking the time to read chapter drafts.

And to my wife, Destiny Lopez, and daughter Carmen Stella Kreiss, who have endured many early mornings and long nights of my research and writing—this book would not have been possible without your patience, care, and inspiration.

# Key Political Staffers and Consultants and Relevant Electoral Work Mentioned in This Volume[1]

Jerome Armstrong
Founder, MyDD blog
Consultant, Dean for America

Larry Biddle
Deputy national finance director, Dean for America

Jeremy Bird
Congressional district director, New Hampshire, Dean for America
South Carolina state field director, 2008 Obama primary campaign
Maryland state field director, 2008 Obama primary campaign
Pennsylvania state field director, 2008 Obama primary campaign
General election director, Ohio, 2008 Obama general election campaign
National field director, 2012 Obama campaign

Andrew Bleeker
Internet advertising, John Kerry general election campaign
Internet advertising, Hillary Clinton primary campaign
Director of Internet advertising, 2008 Obama general election campaign

Jim Brayton
Web developer and systems administrator, Dean for America
Cofounder and chief technology officer, EchoDitto
Internet director, Obama Hope Fund political action committee

Gray Brooks
Staff specialist, Dean for America
New media ombudsman, 2008 Obama primary and general election
campaigns

Jon Carson
    Illinois state director, 2008 Obama primary campaign
    National field director, 2008 Obama general election campaign

Bobby Clark
    Director, Internet fund-raising, Dean for America
    Executive director, ProgressNow

Peter Daou
    Online communications advisor, John Kerry general election campaign
    Internet director, Hillary Clinton primary campaign

Neil Drumm
    Participant, Hack4Dean
    Cofounder, CivicSpace Labs

Zack Exley
    Organizing director, MoveOn
    Consultant, Dean for America
    Director of online communications and organizing, John Kerry general election
        campaign
    Cofounder, New Organizing Institute

Jascha Franklin-Hodge
    National systems administrator, Dean for America
    Cofounder, chief technology officer, Blue State Digital

Judith Freeman
    Internet organizing, John Kerry general election campaign
    Cofounder, New Organizing Institute
    New media field manager, 2008 Obama general election campaign

Steve Geer
    Director of e-mail and online fund-raising, 2008 Obama primary and general
        election campaigns

Scott Goodstein
    External online director, 2008 Obama primary and general election
        campaigns

Teddy Goff
    E-mail staffer, 2008 Obama primary campaign

Director of new media—battleground states, 2008 Obama primary and general election campaigns

Digital director, 2012 Obama campaign

Sam Graham-Felsen

Director of blogging and blog outreach, 2008 Obama primary and general election campaigns

Matthew Gross

Director of Internet communications, Dean for America

Senior advisor for online communications, 2008 John Edwards primary campaign

Josh Hendler

Manager of software development, John Kerry general election campaign

Director of technology, Democratic Party

Karen Hicks

New Hampshire state director, Dean for America

Senior advisor, Hillary Clinton  primary campaign

Chris Hughes

Director of Internet organizing, 2008 Obama primary and general election campaigns

Clay Johnson

Lead programmer, Dean for America

Cofounder, Blue State Digital

Tom Matzzie

Director of online organizing, John Kerry general election campaign

Nicco Mele

Webmaster, Dean for America

Cofounder, EchoDitto

Amanda Michel

Director, Generation Dean, Dean for America

Organizer, MediaCorps, John Kerry general election campaign

Cofounder, New Organizing Institute

Markos Moulitsas Zúniga
Founder, Daily Kos blog
Consultant, Dean for America

Adam Mordecai
Internet director, Iowa at Dean for America
Cofounder, Advomatic

Aaron Myers
Senior web producer, Al Gore primary and general election campaigns
Director of Internet operations, 2004 John Edwards primary campaign
Director of Internet development, John Kerry primary and general election
   campaigns
Internet director, 2008 John Edwards primary campaign
Director of online communications, 2008 Democratic National Convention
   Committee

Kelly Nuxoll
E-mail manager, Dean for America

David Plouffe
Campaign manager, 2008 Obama primary and general election campaigns

Tamara Pogue
National field director, Dean for America

Zack Rosen
Founder, Hack4Dean
Web developer and technical volunteer coordinator, Dean for America
Cofounder, CivicSpace Labs

Joe Rospars
Writer, Dean for America
Cofounder, Blue State Digital
Internet director, Democratic Party
New media director, 2008 Obama primary and general election campaigns
Chief digital strategist, 2012 Obama campaign

Josh Ross
Director of Internet strategy, Kerry primary and general election campaigns
Cofounder, Mayfield Strategy Group

Ben Self
  Data architect, Dean for America
  Cofounder, Blue State Digital
  Technology director, Democratic Party

Michael Silberman
  National MeetUp director, Dean for America
  Cofounder, EchoDitto

Dan Siroker
  Director of analytics, 2008 Obama general election campaign

Michael Slaby
  Deputy director of new media, 2008 Obama primary campaign
  Chief technology officer, 2008 Obama general election campaign
  Chief integration and innovation officer, 2012 Obama campaign

John Slabyk
  Art director, 2008 Obama primary and general election campaigns

Neil Sroka
  New media director, South Carolina, 2008 Obama primary campaign
  New media director, Ohio, 2008 Obama general election campaign

Mark Sullivan
  Cofounder, Voter Activation Network

Scott Thomas
  Design director, 2008 Obama primary and general election campaigns

Zephyr Teachout
  Director of Internet organizing, Dean for America

Kevin Thurman
  Internet director, Tom Vilsack primary campaign
  Deputy Internet director, Hillary Clinton primary campaign

Joe Trippi
  Campaign manager, Dean for America
  Senior advisor, 2008 John Edwards primary campaign

Aaron Welch,
  Web developer, Iowa at Dean for America
  Cofounder, Advomatic

Buffy Wicks
  Iowa field staff, Dean for America
  California field director, 2008 Obama primary campaign
  Missouri state director, 2008 Obama general election campaign

# Taking Our Country Back

# 1

## Innovation, Infrastructure, and Organization in New Media Campaigning

On February 10, 2007, Barack Obama's presidential exploratory committee posted a video of the candidate on BarackObama.com. In it, Obama declared that he was formally entering the race for the presidency and that "tomorrow, we begin a great journey. A journey to take our country back." Obama echoed Howard Dean's announcement speech nearly four years earlier, on June 23, 2003, in which the former Vermont governor declared that "we stand today in common purpose to take our country back." Obama, of course, ascended to the presidency—an achievement of which Dean had only dreamed.

More than rhetoric links the campaigns of the two men. Dean's run came up short, but the insurgent, outsider candidate was stunningly successful at mobilizing his supporters. While ultimately short-lived, Dean's success was in large part due to the campaign's embrace of the Internet. The Dean campaign took up an extraordinary array of tools to spur supporters to action and to coordinate their efforts. The campaign was the first to routinely and systematically use e-mail for fund-raising and to deploy a blog to gather supporters. The campaign was also a remarkable site of technical innovation, as staffers and volunteers modified existing technologies to meet their needs and built entirely new tools, including an early social networking application that enabled supporters to find one another and thus coordinate their electoral efforts. The campaign's organizational innovations were as important as its technical work. Dean's staffers crafted new and effective practices for mobilizing and coordinating the efforts of supporters online. As a result of this work, the campaign set records for fund-raising, drew tens of thousands of supporters to events, and moved thousands of volunteers to contact voters months in advance of the Iowa caucuses.

With these tools in hand, and with the knowledge and skills gained over the course of an election cycle, a new generation of political staffers and consultancies specializing in new media campaigning emerged from the ashes of Dean for America and helped rebuild the infrastructure of the Democratic Party. Through these staffers and firms, the tools and practices for online campaigning, first honed during Dean's run, spread across Democratic politics. One of these firms, Blue State Digital (BSD), played a particularly important role in rebuilding the party's technical infrastructure after John Kerry's devastating defeat.[1] Jascha Franklin-Hodge, Clay Johnson, Joe Rospars, and Ben Self, four young veterans of the Dean effort who got their start in politics during that campaign, launched BSD soon after the candidate withdrew from the race. It was a time when the phones of Dean's Internet staffers rang with opportunities, despite their candidate's collapse. The four found their services in high demand, and quickly built their business of providing tools and strategy for online campaigning. In the process, they contributed to a number of Democratic electoral victories. Among dozens of campaign clients, the firm's founders provided the technology and online strategy for Dean's political action committee Democracy for America and contributed to the effort to get Dean elected party chair. Soon after, working for the new chairman, they rebuilt the party's technological systems, implemented a new online campaign platform, and led the effort to create a national voter file and database system.

The morphing of Dean for America into Obama for America was more than a metaphor for a style of politics. Through their work between the 2004 and 2008 presidential elections, BSD's founders refined the technologies and organizing practices first crafted during the Dean campaign and made them more powerful. They then applied their tools and skills to the 2008 Obama campaign. BSD provided the campaign's electoral platform, and Rospars served as its new media director. (Rospars later became the chief digital strategist for the president's re-election campaign.) The 2008 Obama campaign's tools and new media strategy were not responsible for the extraordinary mobilization around the candidate. Tools and organization translated the efforts of millions—mobilized by Obama's charisma, rhetoric, and the political opportunity to elect a Democrat and African American to the presidency—into the concrete electoral resources that formed the mantra for the campaign's New Media Division: "money, message, and mobilization."[2] Michael Slaby, the 2008 campaign's chief technology officer and the 2012 campaign's chief integration and innovation officer, relates, "We didn't have to generate desire very often. We had to capture and empower interest and desire. . . . We made intelligent decisions that kept it growing but I don't think anybody can really claim we started something."[3]

As this collective outpouring took shape, the campaign had much of the staff, practice, and tools in place to convene and harness it for electoral ends. As they did so, new media staffers helped the campaign build a massive electoral operation that rivaled the partisan mobilization during the era of strong party politics more than a century ago.[4] Supporters across the country used online calling tools to make over 30 million phone calls to voters in battleground states.[5] Millions made small donations online and donned Obama merchandise purchased through the campaign's online store. Over 2 million citizens created accounts on the campaign's electoral platform, My.BarackObama.com, where they used tools to independently host tens of thousands of volunteer and fund-raising events for Obama and set up over 35,000 geographic- and affinity-based groups of supporters. The campaign, through e-mail and online advertising, mobilized tens of thousands to drive hundreds of miles to volunteer for the candidate in states stretching from Washington to Florida.

This book reveals the previously untold history of how the individuals and innovations of the Howard Dean campaign came to play a starring role in the effort to elect the nation's first African American president. In doing so, it tells the history of new media and Democratic campaigning over much of the last decade, documenting key moments of electoral innovation, charting the dissemination and evolution of tools and techniques as they moved across politics, and chronicling the organizations that shape the ways in which candidates use new media.

In addition to providing a rich look at the tools and practices that make up contemporary campaigning, this book contributes to scholarly understanding of new media and politics. Over the decades of the Internet's development and popularization, the medium has inspired reams of books and articles that speculate about its effects on the American political process.[6] In recent years, many scholars have turned to a classic body of work on the cost of participating in and organizing collective action to explain phenomena such as the Dean and Obama campaigns.[7] These scholars analyze the effects of "Web 2.0 information environments" on political organization and citizen participation.[8] Scholars argue that networked digital media dramatically lower the cost of producing and disseminating political information and enable new forms of large-scale, networked collective action to occur entirely independently of formal organizations.[9] Meanwhile, scholars argue that through their use of new media, resource-poor campaigns and political organizations have new opportunities to engage in strategic communications and to organize collective action, ultimately extending their ability to influence the political process.[10]

Despite this large body of work and the insights that it offers, we lack answers to some important questions about new media and politics, which frame this book. If, as many accounts of new media and politics suggest, technologies are "out there" for campaigns to use as needed, why was the Dean campaign the site of the campaign innovations that many document?[11] How did the social and technical innovations of the campaign spread to other sites in politics so that by 2006 Democratic campaigns routinely deployed many of the same tactics and tools used by Dean? What explains the enormous growth in online fund-raising and voluntarism between 2004 and 2008, and why was the Obama campaign the widely regarded leader in using new media during the presidential cycle?

In answering these questions, this book explores three central themes that are largely absent from accounts of new media and politics: *innovation, infrastructure,* and *organization.* A central claim of this book is that information environments do not simply emerge and change on their own through an inherent technological logic. Information environments are actively made by people, organizations, and the tools they create and wield. The most taken-for-granted forms of online electoral collective action, such as donating money and contacting voters, are premised upon years of technical development, infrastructure building, and knowledge creation, as well as enormous investments of financial and human resources.[12] Strategic political actors draw on these social and technical resources to create the work and communication practices and organizational processes that shape and support online collective action. As such, this book argues that much of the scholarly literature in the electoral domain has the wrong object in view in focusing on the outcomes of this work, rather than the processes that create information environments.[13]

In the following pages of this chapter, I discuss the importance of looking at innovation, infrastructure, and organization to understand the form of networked politics. I use the idea of "networked politics" in a dual sense. On one level, networked politics refers to electoral activities that take shape through the technical infrastructure of interlinked computer networks. On another, I refer to networked politics as a mode of organizing electoral participation. Networked politics involves sustained and coordinated collective action that occurs outside of direct managerial relationships and is premised on the voluntary contributions of supporters.[14] I map my exploration of the concepts of innovation, infrastructure, and organization chronologically onto the history that this book will present in the following chapters. This chapter then discusses the import of the history here for evaluating networked politics in democratic terms, and concludes by providing a brief discussion of my methods and an overview of subsequent chapters.

## Technical and Organizational Innovation on the Dean Campaign

In early 2002, Howard Dean, then in his sixth term as governor of Vermont, took his first exploratory steps toward running for the presidential nomination. The decidedly second-tier candidate began to attract attention during the summer and fall for his opposition to the Iraq War authorization, which passed Congress in October with the support of the leading Democratic presidential candidates

Kerry and John Edwards. Disaffected Democratic activists, frustrated with their party's capitulations to Republicans, began to promote Dean's candidacy online, even though the caucuses and primaries were still a year and a half away. In the winter of 2002, Jerome Armstrong, the founder of the blog MyDD (which then stood for "My Due Diligence"), coined and subsequently popularized the term "netroots" (a portmanteau of "Internet" and "grassroots") to refer to these online supporters of Dean's candidacy.[15] By early 2003, a network of blogs, including MyDD, Daily Kos, and the independent, supporter-run Howard Dean 2004, were routinely delivering funds and volunteers to the campaign, becoming the candidate's de facto web presence. These blogs also began encouraging supporters to use a new tool called Meetup, a commercial application that facilitated offline gatherings.

These independent efforts by supporters working on behalf of Dean are the key to understanding the innovations of the campaign, defined in terms of staffers taking up new media tools, creating new ones, and crafting new organizing practices around them. In January 2003, Joe Trippi, who was then consulting for the campaign, in consultation with Armstrong and Markos Moulitsas Zúniga, the founder of Daily Kos, worked out a strategy to convene these online efforts so as to be better able to coordinate them. In Trippi's eyes, the Internet offered the potential to solve the key problem of the Dean campaign. Dean lacked the financial and volunteer resources that candidates such as Kerry and Edwards commanded through strong institutional party and national advocacy group support, given their careers in the Senate.

To coordinate the efforts of the growing numbers of supporters gathering around blogs and on Meetup, Trippi created an autonomous Internet Department on the campaign after he became Dean's campaign manager in April 2003. Trippi then tasked these staffers with developing the tools and practices that would convene supporters and direct their energies toward the fund-raising and volunteering that the campaign needed to make Dean a viable candidate. One of the campaign's innovations lay in this decision to make the Internet a central organizational tool and an explicit part of the candidate's electoral strategy.

Previous campaigns offered models for using the Internet to gain electoral resources, although they were largely experimental. During the 2000 primaries, Bill Bradley and John McCain demonstrated the potential of small-dollar online fund-raising.[16] McCain raised record amounts of money online after his New Hampshire primary victory over George W. Bush.[17] During that electoral cycle, political staffers also began to recognize for the first time that the primary users of candidate websites were supporters, not undecided voters seeking detailed policy statements.[18] To take advantage of this, campaigns began encouraging supporter participation instead of just presenting "brochureware" designed to persuade those who sought out information on the candidate.[19] For example, campaigns began using the Internet to involve supporters in actions such as pro-moting the candidate's visibility. To do so, campaigns provided printable litera-ture and signs for supporters to distribute in their communities, as well as tips for contacting local news outlets to promote the candidate.[20]

In 2000, candidates also increasingly used the Internet to fashion supporters into the conduits of strategic communications and to foster engagement around the campaign. On one level, campaigns sought to take advantage of existing social networks to create a new "digital two-step flow" of political communication.[21] Al Gore's campaign, for instance, enabled supporters to create their own customized webpages based on template policy content so that they could present them to their friends and family. On another, campaigns designed spaces where supporters could create new networks for political engagement. Gore's campaign, for example, provided discussion spaces for supporters in the hopes that they would build rela-tionships with one another, create feelings of social attachment and solidarity in the face of attacks by rivals, and ultimately motivate each other for fund-raising and volunteering during a long campaign season.

The was little carryover in Internet staff between the 2000 and 2004 election cycles, however, and little in the way of a developed industry providing online services to campaigns outside of strategic communications and voter targeting.[22] In part, this was because, at the time, campaigns generally devoted few resources to Internet operations.[23] Nicco Mele, Dean's webmaster who had worked for a number of Democratic advocacy organizations, including Common Cause, and had set up the video streams for the online "Shadow Conventions" in 2000, describes the state of online campaigning when he joined Dean in 2003:

> When I went to work for Howard Dean I don't think the Internet was taken very seriously as a tool. . . . It was at best an afterthought and it certainly was never a product of any campaign manager's explicit strategy. It was something like "I guess we have to do that." If you were a hot shot political operative you did not go into the Internet side of the business. It was a backwater in politics.[24]

As a consequence, there was little in the way of best practices for online cam-paigning or dedicated tools for campaigns up through the 2004 cycle, such as robust customer relations management (CRM) platforms that could handle the scale of a presidential campaign.

Although Dean's staffers looked to what came before in 2000, the 2004 cycle also unfolded in a different sociotechnical context that presented new opportu-nities and challenges for campaigns.[25] Despite the eventual bust, the "dot.com boom" helped more Americans use the Internet and become familiar with things such as online credit card transactions. Communications technologies such as blogs, while not new, had growing user bases and public visibility. There were also a host of new commercial online applications, such as Meetup and the early social networking platform Friendster, that did not exist in previous electoral cycles.

The Dean campaign took shape in, but was not determined by, this sociotechnical context. While much of the scholarly literature on new media and politics generally views technological change as something that happens *to* campaigns, the Dean campaign was a significant organizational and technical achievement. Staffers appropriated existing and created new tools and practices to forge a new mode of online campaigning. The title of this book refers to the active "crafting" of the Dean, and later Obama, campaigns. Staffers of each effort actively labored to construct the technologies and practices that would help them achieve their electoral goals. Unlike the finance and communications professionals on the Dean campaign who had access to developed best practices and ready-to-hand tools for managing and evaluating their work, in 2004 Internet staffers had little to turn to.[26] Indeed, even the legality of much of the campaign's online volunteerism was not clear, given the absence of Federal Election Commission (FEC) rulings on such things as supporters setting up their own websites for Dean. Internet staffers had to continually consult with the campaign's lawyers, and even postponed technical projects, to puzzle through what complied with election law.

With the incentive to innovate, and with the organizational autonomy to experiment provided by Trippi, Dean's staffers assembled their work from a hybrid set of knowledges, practices, and skills in the extraordinarily dynamic and fluid context of a presidential primary run.[27] Attracted to Dean by the candidate's ideology and promise to reinvigorate Democratic and participatory politics, as well as the technological vision that the campaign encoded, these staffers drew on skills honed in careers and interests outside electoral politics.[28] Many of the campaign's Internet and technical staffers came from the technology industry, having worked for start-ups that failed with the market downturn. Others came from college campuses, part of a new generation comfortable with taking social and symbolic political action online.

Many individuals with careers outside electoral politics were attracted to the Obama campaign for similar reasons. Even with a New Media Division led by a veteran of Dean's run, staffers on the Obama campaign came from the leading firms of Silicon Valley, such as Google and Facebook, and helped bring new forms of technical practice to the campaign. Kevin Thurman, an early BSD staffer who also worked for both Tom Vilsack and Hillary Clinton's presidential campaigns, describes his rival's campaign: "They did some ingenious things I hadn't even seen because they built a good team, brought in some people from the outside, from the corporate world. They were doing what Dean also did, drew talent from outside of politics into the campaign. We [the Clinton campaign] weren't the exciting person, so we were not getting a lot of people."[29]

In a shifting technological context and with skills from outside electoral politics, Dean's staffers incorporated and modified a number of existing tools and built a host of new tools for the campaign. Facing data management and capacity issues as the campaign grew through the independent efforts of supporters, staffers used a customer relations management platform built for the nonprofit sector. When faced with the limitations of the platform, staffers modified it to meet their electoral needs, such as developing a fund-raising application so that supporters could raise money independently of the campaign. Staffers launched the first blog in presidential politics and created entirely new campaign tools that stood as innovations even in the commercial market of the time. These tools included DeanSpace, an open source content management system that enabled supporters to set up their own websites for Dean, and DeanLink, a social networking application modeled on Friendster.

These technologies were only as effective as the practices of online organizing that staffers developed around them, which took shape over time and through much trial and error. As Nicco Mele describes: "In the beginning we were very reactive, we were trying to figure this out on the fly. . . . There were very few tried and true strategies." In contrast, later in the primaries the campaign was "a much tighter operation—it's better run, it's better organized."[30] The campaign's use of e-mail, for instance, was largely reactive until individuals from MoveOn, the online progressive advocacy organization, helped staffers think proactively about their communications. Dean's staffers began to develop goals, to think about narrative, and to use metrics to track the most effective appeals and to better target supporters. In the process, the campaign helped carry MoveOn's innovations in the advocacy sector into electoral politics and developed the genre of the campaign e-mail, with its optimized format of mobilizing content and embedded action links.

As importantly, Dean's staffers created practices to effectively coordinate the work of supporters far outside the campaign's formal boundaries and field campaign. Much of the work of Dean's staffers involved "network building," or the creation, cultivation, and maintenance of ties with supporters that staffers could mobilize for collective social and symbolic action. Networked social action entailed distributed, often project-based actions around fund-raising and voter outreach, conducted by supporters gathering on blogs and Meetup. Networked symbolic action involved the campaign leveraging its relationships with supporters to fashion them into conduits for the campaign's communications, mobilizing them to influence other actors such as the professional press.

Dean's staffers sought to create effective practices for coordinating this action online. In doing so, they faced the dilemma of "under- and overorganizing" that the organizational sociologist Katherine Chen has described as a feature of voluntaristic organizations in her study of Burning Man, the annual arts and engineering festival in the Nevada desert.[31] As Chen argues, the challenge of voluntarism lies in the need to craft hybrid organizational forms that mix "collectivist and bureaucratic practices, but avoid exercising coercive control."[32] While organizing mass rallies and canvassing operations have long been a feature of campaigns, the scale and nature of Dean's online participation resulted in new challenges to striking this balance.[33] In traditional field campaigning, allied intermediaries such as advocacy organizations and unions typically mobilize and manage volunteers who have ties to the organization.[34] Even more, much of field operations is an embodied practice coordinated in physical space, with organized teams of volunteers assigned to precincts with clear chains of command. Despite this, in field operations volunteers and paid part-time staffers often have divergent ideas of how campaigns should be run and varying commitments and goals. Online campaigning significantly compounds this problem. During the Dean campaign, the Internet enabled much more distributed forms of collective action, with supporters organizing independently across the nation and with little connection to local field offices. There were no intermediaries to manage these supporters, given that they directly communicated with the campaign using new media. This resulted in a problem of control. Dean's staffers needed to work with supporters outside the boundaries of the campaign organization who were gifting their efforts to the campaign, while simultaneously ensuring that their efforts were coordinated towards the campaign's electoral priorities.

Dean's staffers developed a host of techniques and tools to guide supporters toward needed actions. One way was to communicate the campaign's priorities, such as using the blog as a central messaging vehicle and providing detailed agendas for the supporter-organized Meetups. Another was to delegate the task of coordination to technologies themselves through what scholars call the designed "affordances" of the campaign's applications.[35] The campaign expressly created its online tools with the end of convening and centralizing the independent supporter efforts that were taking shape around the campaign. Through what I call "structured interactivity," Dean's applications provided supporters with some ways to participate in the campaign (such as donating money) while not supporting others (such as formally contributing to the campaign's policy statement on the embrace of open source technologies).[36] In this sense, technologies stood in for a managerial relationship between the campaign and its supporters, setting expectations for volunteer roles and guiding supporter involvement so staffers could garner the money and volunteer labor needed for an effective electoral run.

While these innovative tactics proved effective at generating resources for Dean's run, staffers' work was ultimately constrained by having to develop these practices and technologies while actively campaigning. As detailed above, the campaign's Internet operations evolved reactively to the efforts of its online supporters, particularly at the beginning of the campaign. This meant that there was little in the way of comprehensive planning for the staffing and organization of the campaign's Internet operations. This was not ideal from the campaign's standpoint, with staffers working to define their responsibilities, craft goals and effective practices, develop metrics, and create routines for working with supporters while their organizational roles were in flux. Many staffers only stabilized their work well after the summer of 2003. Furthermore, the campaign's leadership could not anticipate, and did not have the resources early in the campaign to address, the rapid scaling of the online mobilization around Dean's candidacy. As a result, the campaign's underlying technical systems were poorly integrated and lacked the capacity that staffers needed. The contribution system was continually strained under the weight of Dean's online donations, staffers had to use multiple logins and passwords to access the campaign's hastily built applications, and there were numerous incompatible databases on the campaign.

Despite staffers' success in developing new tools and in organizing supporters online for massive fund-raising and voter outreach efforts, the campaign ultimately suffered from the lack of a strong field effort in Iowa and a senior leadership that woke to the problem too late and nearly bankrupted the candidate in a last-ditch attempt to salvage a victory through television advertisements. In the wake of a disastrous concession speech, Dean's electoral fortunes were largely finished. However, even as Dean was making his last stand, his staffers were already creating, and were being recruited for, new ventures such as political consultancies that specialized in new media. Through these ventures, Dean's former staffers carried many of the campaign's electoral innovations to other Democratic campaigns and advocacy organizations (see Figure 1.1). In doing so, they helped to create a robust infrastructure for Democratic new media campaigning that included dedicated political tools, codified online organizing practices, and organizations that trained new online campaigners. This meant that when Obama formally announced his run for the presidency, the campaign had staff and tools in place that Dean's staffers could only dream of. As Andrew Bleeker, a veteran of the Kerry, Hillary Clinton, and Obama general election campaigns, describes:

> There were no technology platforms out there for political campaigns [in 2004] so we had to develop them all from scratch. 2004 was 100% the bedrock. It not only created the tactics . . . but it built the staff. The firms that came out of 2004 were the firms that built the strategy for '08. . . . Those were the keys. That's what drove most of the strategy and tactics in '08.[37]

**Political Movement:** Circulation of select Dean staffers, consultants, and technologies across political organizations and electoral cycles.

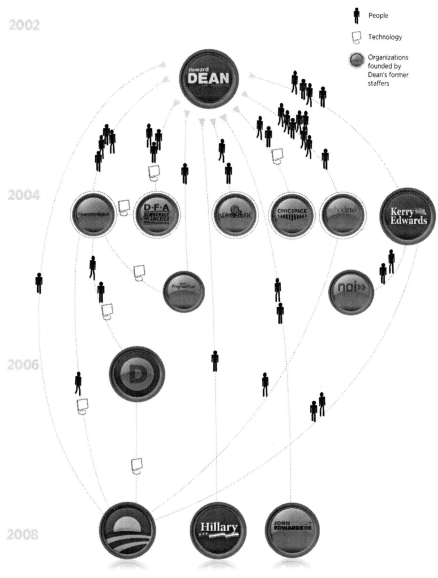

Graphic by: Terence Oliver

*Figure 1.1*

# Infrastructure for New Media Campaigning

After Dean's defeat, the consultancies and other ventures launched by his former staffers helped to formalize many of the practices and to standardize the tools of online organizing that they had crafted during the campaign.[38] Taken together, these consultancies and the best practices, dedicated tools, and trained staffers that they produced served as an infrastructure for online campaigning that a number of Democratic candidates drew from in 2006 and 2008. As sociologist of information Susan Leigh Star detailed, infrastructure "is both relational and ecological—it means different things to different groups and it is part of the balance of action, tools, and the built environment, inseparable from them. It is also frequently mundane to the point of boredom involving things such as plugs, standards, and bureaucratic forms."[39]

In Star's sense, infrastructure encompasses the technical artifacts, organizational forms, and social practices that provide background contexts for action.[40] Despite its importance, the academic literature on new media and politics has generally overlooked the role of infrastructure in campaigning.[41] There are a number of reasons for this. Infrastructure forms the invisible background context for social action and as such is rarely open to scrutiny. Infrastructure building projects, from developing new technical systems to training online campaigners, occur in the years between elections, when there is little public or scholarly attention to electoral politics. Furthermore, infrastructure is often the mundane work object of the database managers, systems administrators, new media trainers, and consultants who operate in the recesses of parties and consultancies.

Moreover, practitioners themselves seldom talk about infrastructure. There is a deeply rooted value of "self-organization," particularly in the context of narratives about online collective action. The stories that many practitioners tell about their work often portray a world where online collective political action is leaderless, decentralized, and authentically "grassroots," pursued by citizens themselves taking action into their own hands. These stories echo influential popular and academic accounts of new media politics, perhaps best captured in media theorist Clay Shirky's empirical claim for and celebration of "organizing without organizations."[42] There is a deep valuation of seemingly spontaneous collective action. As the social movement scholar Francesca Polletta shows, participants in the civil rights movement described their involvement in collective action for racial equity in terms of a "fever."[43] This story emphasized spontaneous action driven by moral outrage, a powerful account of motivation that helped participants situate their experience while distinguishing their activism from that of an older generation. And yet, even as narratives characterized actions in this way, in actuality they were often the product of meticulous planning. Civil rights organizations such as the NAACP organized many protest actions, and their members were often participants. A strategy often determined where civil rights actions occurred, and trained organizers coordinated their on-the-ground execution. In this example, culture and organization go hand in hand—one helping to mobilize participants and enabling them to make sense of themselves and their struggle, the other translating that commitment into effective political action.

In a similar way, the stories that new media campaign staffers often tell of their work claim moral authority and reveal a deep valuation of participatory politics, even as they elide the hard work of infrastructure and organization building that goes on behind the scenes. The rhetoric publicly articulated by Dean and Obama, as well as their staffers, situated their campaigns as the products of authentic expressions of political commitment and moral values among citizens. Trippi's embrace of the metaphor of "open source politics" to describe Dean's campaign, and the quote from candidate Obama that graced the banner of BarackObama. com ("I'm asking you to believe not just in my ability to bring about real change in Washington . . . I'm asking you to believe in yours") exemplify both their very real participatory ethos and the rhetoric that these campaigns deployed to mobilize supporters.[44] These public narratives are firmly rooted on the front stage of what cultural sociologist Jeffrey Alexander calls the "performance of politics" in his study of the Obama campaign.[45] This is the discursive space for the articulation of pure civic ideals. Staffers value these narratives in their own right, and they help them situate their own work and justify their faith in their candidate. At the same time, these narratives also offer candidates the rhetorical advantage of framing their campaigns as a social movement.

While this book addresses the role of rhetoric and design as cultural resources that staffers used to craft and make sense of their work and to mobilize supporters, it focuses closely on the myth-defying backstage that consumes much of the working lives of those active in politics. Building infrastructure requires extensive planning and organization, often with an eye to returns that are years away from being realized. Even more, the infrastructural backstage shapes much of the form that politics takes.

After the primaries, Dean's former staffers helped to create the technical systems and organizational practices that provided an infrastructure for subsequent Democratic online campaigning. While a number of Dean's former staffers went to work for Kerry's general election campaign, others launched political consultancies specializing in developing new media tools and strategy for Democratic candidates and advocacy organizations. Among these firms, Blue State Digital was at the center of these infrastructure projects, including the standardization of existing tools and the development of new ones, the creation of best practices, and the training of new online campaign practitioners.

The massive infrastructure projects undertaken by the party once Dean was elected chair in February 2005 reveal these tools, practices, and practitioners.

While in recent years there has been much scholarly attention to the organizational structure of parties, comparatively little work has focused on how they create the basic infrastructure for much of electoral campaign practice.[46] As chair, Dean orchestrated two complex, large-scale, and complementary sociotechnical projects: the creation of a national voter file and the implementation of a new online electoral platform called PartyBuilder.[47] Dean hired two of his former staffers, Self and Rospars, to coordinate these projects and to overhaul the ways in which the national party conducted its elections and worked with the state parties and supporters.

As the technology director for the party, Self led the effort to create a national voter file. This proved to be a deeply challenging undertaking that involved both rebuilding the technical infrastructure of the party and negotiating data-sharing agreements with all the state parties. Building this national voter file was a priority for Dean, given widespread failures in state voter files and database technologies during the 2004 general election. Looking ahead to 2008, Dean and Self worked out a deal in which the national party assumed the costs of improving and maintaining the state voter files and building a new database to house them, in exchange for permission to aggregate and access them. Self commissioned the firm Voter Activation Network (VAN) to customize its online interface so that party and campaign staffers could continually access and update the voter file database.[48] The system that resulted is called "VoteBuilder," which the national party provides free of charge to the states. "VoteBuilder" refers to the Democratic Party's data (the state voter files as well as commercial data) and the VAN interface system around it. As a key piece of infrastructure for Democratic campaigning, VoteBuilder extended the ability of the party and its candidates to contest elections and to target the electorate. It enabled Democratic candidates for offices from state senate to president to share data across campaigns and election cycles, while ensuring that the voter file was continuously uploaded with quality data. All of the major Democratic presidential candidates' field campaigns used VoteBuilder in 2008.

As Self worked on the voter file project, Rospars, as the head of a newly reconstituted Internet Department, implemented Blue State Digital's campaign platform for the party. After Dean's withdrawal from the primaries, BSD brokered a deal to receive the intellectual property in the campaign's tools in exchange for integrating, rebuilding, and implementing them for Democracy for America (DFA), the organization that Dean created to sustain the mobilization of supporters around his candidacy and platform. After its work for DFA, BSD adopted what is known in the industry as a "software as a service" (SaaS) licensing model, which enabled the firm's platform to serve as infrastructure for a number of Democratic political campaigns and advocacy organizations. BSD's software delivery licensing model works as a partisan version of what economists refer to as a "club good."[49] The firm owns the intellectual property in its technologies, yet manages them as a partisan resource to benefit all its paying Democratic clients that invest and commission modifications in the platform.

Through licensing agreements with its clients, the BSD platform became the most powerful in electoral politics and benefited dozens of candidates and advocacy organizations over the years. The platform provides campaigns and advocacy organizations with customer relations management software, database and e-mail services, customizable fund-raising pages for supporters, and social networking, blogging, group organizing, and event planning applications. While most academic work tends to view technological change as something that happens exogenously to electoral politics, BSD's platform developed in response to many of the concrete challenges that Dean's former staffers faced on the campaign and in their subsequent electoral work. The platform's integration, for instance, grew out of BSD's founders' frustration with the proliferation of separate applications and databases during the Dean campaign. The firm built its group-organizing tools to provide a technical solution to the problem of campaign staffers losing data when Dean's supporters used commercial applications such as Yahoo! Groups to organize. BSD extended the capacity of its platform and built these and other tools through its work with organizations such as DFA, MoveOn Student Action, and ProgressNow, a multistate progressive advocacy organization, among other organizations. The national Democratic Party invested in the platform's capacity and implemented it as PartyBuilder for the midterm elections in 2006. BSD provided this platform to a number of the 2008 presidential campaigns, including that of Barack Obama.

At the same time, BSD's founders learned many strategic and organizing lessons from the Dean campaign. The campaign's innovation was to conceptualize supporters as potential participants and to use new media tools to coordinate their efforts. After witnessing much of the necessary reactivity of the campaign and the ongoing struggle to create best practices for this online organizing, Rospars helped to strategize with clients to create clear goals and expectations for supporter engagement. As Rospars describes it, the firm's approach was to ensure that "those relationships that people have laterally are in the service of the outcomes that the organization seeks," outcomes that need to be strategized and planned.[50] At the party, Rospars worked to integrate online and field operations for the midterm elections, developing practices that he later deployed on the Obama campaign. These included creating internal work practices that led to collaborations between new media and field staffers, using geo-targeted e-mails to turn supporters out at field offices and field events, and creating online systems to further supporters' ability to engage in their own voter canvasses.

The party and its allies also invested in training new staffers to specialize in new media campaigning and created opportunities to keep political practitioners

employed and active between election cycles. The staffers of new training organizations such as the New Organizing Institute (NOI), as well as the party and
the consultancies BSD and EchoDitto, a firm also founded by former Dean
staffers, helped to codify best practices for online organizing and trained hundreds of individuals in them.[51] These included techniques for creating narrative
and optimized e-mails, setting goals for online campaigning, and working with
supporters using new media.[52] In addition to the extensive training that these
organizations offered, they also provided employment opportunities for many
of the staffers of the 2004 and 2006 campaigns to help keep them in politics. As
Franklin-Hodge, a cofounder of BSD and the firm's chief technology officer,
relates: "We were much better at saying 'ok, the campaign is over so come back
home to the party. We will pay your salary, we will keep you in play, we might
send you to this state or that state, but recognize that a lot of what we're doing is
keeping you on path for the next big race when we really need the top talent.'"[53]

The development of the organizational and technical infrastructure for online
electoral campaigning in the years between elections meant that the Obama campaign had access to tools and knowledge for harnessing the mobilization around
his historic candidacy that simply did not exist in 2004. While the Dean campaign
built many of its tools as needs arose over the course of the primaries, the 2008
Obama campaign launched the BSD platform for the candidate's announcement
speech approximately a week after hiring the firm. This meant that the campaign
had a robust online platform in place to immediately translate supporter interest
into electoral resources. The platform, hosted at My.BarackObama.com (MyBO),
featured many of the tools first used on the Dean campaign, including event planning and group organizing tools, personalized fund-raising applications, and social
networking capabilities. At the back end, the campaign had the most developed
content and customer relations management system in politics and access to the
party's voter file through VoteBuilder. Even more, the campaign drew on the deep
knowledge and experience of its new media director, Joe Rospars.

It was this combination of tools and strategy developed in 2004 and honed
between elections that helped Obama gain concrete electoral resources in 2007
and 2008. As Kevin Thurman describes the success of his rival's campaign:

> There is an untold story of the Obama campaign. The technology was phe-
> nomenal ... but it is a misnomer that the social networking is what raised
> Obama a ton of money. It's wrong. It was the kernel of the concept of how
> you raise that much money, how you get people involved in the campaign
> on a grassroots level. That comes from the Dean campaign. But the way
> that it was polished and molded at Blue State Digital for our clients made
> a big difference for what they did at the DNC [Democratic National Com-
> mittee] when Dean was in charge. Then Obama was able to use it.[54]

# Organizational Contexts of New Media Use

Historian Richard John described the wonder and dread that the 1820s public felt toward the functioning of the U.S. post office as a "bureaucratic sublime."[55] The public marveled at the organization of the post office, the large-scale, coordinated human activity that created a communications link between the hinterlands of the American wilderness and the nation's metropolitan environs. During the last century, however, much of the awe of human organization has seemingly been displaced by a "technological sublime" directed at the artifacts of our own creation.[56]

The American technological sublime is readily apparent in the fascination that many journalists and scholars had with the technological dazzle of the Obama campaign. Technology guru Tim O'Reilly expresses this sublime perfectly in his description of the campaign's "Houdini Project," a real-time system of monitoring when voters went to the polls. In language that recalls social theorist Lewis Mumford's classic work on the "megamachine," O'Reilly argues that we should:

> Consider *My.BarackObama.com* as a kind of vast machine, with humans as extensions of the programmatic brain. . . . Inside the machine, programmers are tuning the algorithms, while top campaign staffers are making key decisions to adjust the resource mix. . . . The "explicit" social media elements of *My.BarackObama.com* paled in impact compared to the development of a next generation electronic nervous system, in which volunteers were trained, deployed, and managed by a web application who used them, in Sean McMullen's memorable phrase, as "souls in the great machine."[57]

O'Reilly's narrative neatly captures the technologically sublime response to the Obama campaign. Other accounts of the campaign express similar emotions toward the "online nervous system" of the campaign, from My.BarackObama.com to the Facebook application, although they tend toward the celebratory.[58] In focusing on the technical, however, these accounts overlook the bureaucratic objects that were part of the imaginary of the nineteenth century: the social organization, management structures, large-scale coordination, and meticulous planning that were behind Obama's successful run. As detailed above, networked technologies alone did not produce the enormous energy around Obama's candidacy, nor were they the determinants of electoral success. The presidential campaigns of Bill Richardson and Tom Vilsack also hired BSD early in 2007 and had essentially the same functionality of MyBO and the firm's strategy services. Moreover, as Chapter 6 details, the Houdini Project never worked as planned, for a host of technical and organizational reasons, and was largely abandoned.

The Obama campaign was first and foremost an achievement of organization, the hard work of its staffers to bring people, tools, and practices into alignment and in accord with electoral strategy.[59] The sophistication and polish often associated with the Obama campaign was generally unrecognizable in the moment to staffers as they engaged in the work of crafting the practices, tools, and systems behind the new media operations. Even with a powerful campaign platform in place and the political knowledge and skills of the division's leadership, organizing the Obama campaign was a significant sociotechnical accomplishment.

A key reason for the success of the campaign was a senior leadership that invested in new media early in the primaries, created the organizational structure that made the New Media Division a central part of the campaign, and helped to integrate its work with the finance, field, and communications operations. Similar to the Dean campaign, early in the primaries Obama's senior leadership believed that the campaign needed to make new media central to the candidate's electoral strategy. Obama enjoyed a prominent national profile, given his electrifying speech at the Democratic National Convention in 2004. But, as the junior senator from Illinois with less than one term in office, he lacked the institutional resources of Hillary Clinton. Obama did not have the deep fund-raising networks or turn-out resources of the local party organizations commanded by state Democratic leaders, many of whom backed Clinton. Staffers also describe how campaign manager David Plouffe saw a need for the campaign to expand the electoral map.[60]

Given the need for financial and human resources to compensate for these shortfalls, the leadership invested in new media, making a number of early consequential decisions that shaped the way in which the campaign unfolded. The campaign's leadership created a New Media Division with an organizational role equal to that of the other divisions of the campaign such as field, finance, and communications. In January 2007, the campaign hired Joe Rospars as its new media director, a senior staff position. Rospars took a leave from BSD, and after a vetting process the campaign hired the firm to provide the platform for My. BarackObama.com.[61] Unlike the Dean campaign, Rospars had the luxury of having a robust electoral platform in place, which meant that he had comparatively more time to negotiate the division's responsibilities, plan its structure, and create the strategy for his staffers' electoral work. As a result, the division's role in the larger campaign organization and staffing structure was better defined early in the primaries. For example, the senior leadership clarified the responsibilities of the campaign's divisions in the winter of 2007. While on the Dean campaign it was never quite clear which department handled what, given that everyone used the Internet, Rospars negotiated for authority over specific areas of campaign practice such as e-mail that other divisions also tried to lay claim to. Clear organizational domains meant that staffers of different divisions were not working at cross-purposes or duplicating their efforts. The advance planning and organizing conducted by Rospars enabled the division to adapt to the rapid growth of the campaign and its new media operations as the primaries unfolded.[62]

Meanwhile, New Media Division staffers' work accorded with the overall electoral strategy of the campaign and was integrated with, albeit imperfectly, the operations of the field effort.[63] New media staffers steered supporters coming to the campaign's online platform into field offices, built applications that enabled citizens to register to vote and find their polling places online, and used their massive e-mail list to mobilize volunteers to travel to battleground states. The campaign used Facebook to organize young voters in Iowa, setting up Obama groups for all the local high schools—which organizers then used to recruit students to work in campaign offices. The centerpiece of the campaign's new media effort, however, was organizing the efforts of supporters using MyBO to plan events and canvass voters. Chris Hughes, a cofounder of Facebook and director of Internet organizing for the campaign, describes how, at first, new media staffers' strategy of interacting with supporters on MyBO was simply characterized by the attitude of "don't wait for us; don't wait for somebody to tell you what to do."[64] As time went on, however, division staffers more actively coordinated the work of supporters to further the field goals of the campaign. This involved staffers reaching out to volunteer leaders on MyBO, responding to their many queries, and setting expectations and goals. As Hughes describes, "As 2007 progressed, it was [our job to] really help these grassroots activists structure their activities and what they do to help us win."[65]

This organizing paid dividends on "Super Tuesday." The Obama groups that supporters set up on MyBO were a significant asset for field organizers hitting the ground in advance of the 23 state contests held on February 5. Field staffers were able to rapidly deploy volunteers from these groups for voter outreach, helping the campaign overcome the logistical challenges of setting up ground operations in these states. In part as a result of the use of new media, Obama more than held his own against Clinton on Super Tuesday, a crucial test of organization and viability after the split results of the four early contests.[66] Neil Sroka, the state new media director for South Carolina, describes how Hughes's team:

> helped the grass grow and provided the fertilizer, so to speak, so that literally when the first organizer hit the ground they had a list of people that were committed and had already knocked on doors for Obama and had already started building an organization. And, that is why you hear these stories and see these pictures online writing about the first organizational meetings there were 200 people at them. It is because the grassroots have already cultivated, the sod had already been laid down and fertilized over the previous summer.[67]

The Obama campaign was also adept at managing its technical development. Reflecting the campaign's need for resources, Plouffe told staffers that they needed to run an exceptionally well-managed campaign and innovate in their respective domains to have a chance of winning. As Slaby describes, this opened a space for experimentation that permeated the campaign: "The willingness of people like Plouffe to say 'question all sorts of things' made room for us to innovate as a campaign. And that meant field strategy, that meant organizing strategy, and of course that means that there is room for innovation in new media."[68]

Organizational dynamics shaped these new media innovations. The technical work of the campaign required intradivision collaboration and coordination. Staffers from across the campaign needed to agree on electoral priorities and work together to develop tools that were integrated with work processes. These tools, meanwhile, needed to be aligned with other technical systems, some of which were developed by outside organizations such as the party. This collaboration among staffers across the campaign's divisions was a hard won organizational achievement, and never perfect from the campaign's perspective, but it resulted in some innovative efforts. To coordinate technical work, the New Media Division hired liaisons who worked with staffers in the Field, Communications, and Technology Divisions. For example, staffers in the New Media Division built the campaign's "Vote for Change" voter registration application and its polling place look-up tool with an eye towards the priorities of the field effort. The campaign also coordinated large-scale development projects with the party and BSD. The campaign hired developers whom BSD housed and managed, with the campaign's chief technology officer managing relations with the firm and its liaison to the campaign, Franklin-Hodge. The campaign, for instance, spent much of the general election working with the DNC and BSD on Neighbor-to-Neighbor (N2N), an online calling tool integrated with the voter file. The goal of N2N, which the party commissioned BSD to build for the eventual nominee in 2007, was to further the field campaign by moving "the line between staff and volunteer a lot higher on the organization chart."[69] This meant providing supporters with opportunities that were once the responsibility of paid staffers, such as entering data from canvass calls.

The campaign struggled throughout the general election to integrate the back ends of its various databases, especially the BSD online database and VoteBuilder for N2N, which ultimately limited its utility as a tool. But the application demonstrates how staffers built tools to maximize the electoral participation of supporters. The N2N calling tool lowered the cost of electoral participation by enabling supporters to contribute to the campaign from the comfort of their own homes. N2N also enabled the campaign to more easily access and leverage the resources of a pool of volunteers located in "blue states" where there was little active campaigning taking place. In using N2N, volunteers working online had more information at their fingertips than they would have with conventional walk lists, including basic information on members of their neighbors' households (e.g., ages, party affiliation, registration status, and the results of prior canvasses). At the same time, the online system provided the campaign with more control over these voter contacts. The campaign developed and tested a number of different scripts, depending on the category of the voter in question, and the system encouraged supporters to follow these scripts exactly and to read them in their entirety. Meanwhile, the automated online system enabled the campaign to better control the quality of data being entered into the system, forcing volunteers to conform to particular categories and not enter extraneous information.

The New Media Division was also innovative in its use of data. Rospars developed what I refer to as a "computational management" style in which staffers delegated key managerial, allocative, and design decisions to the results of rigorous and ongoing data analysis. For example, staffers used computational management as an internal tool to make staffing and budgetary decisions. The division routinely evaluated questions such as whether hiring additional e-mail or online advertising staffers would net more money or volunteers for the campaign. This is but one example of how the division calculated the "return on investment" (ROI) for each additional dollar invested in a domain of new media practice versus other potential expenditures. This rigorous analysis of the ROI of every new media expenditure enabled the division to be efficient both in its own work and to demonstrate its effectiveness to the larger campaign in order to garner resources. The division's computational management practices enabled staffers to report exactly what acquiring an e-mail address cost, as well as its value in terms of donations, and to use these figures to justify their expenditures on staff and technology. Staffers cited with pride how the New Media Division was actually in the black, profiting the campaign. Even more, these computational management practices had predictive power, enabling staffers to anticipate resource flows down to the minute.

Staffers also used data as an external management tool to generate the actions they desired from supporters. As supporters interacted with the campaign's media, data rendered them visible to staffers. Transforming user actions into data enabled staffers to create abstract representations of supporters that they then used to produce resources for the campaign. For example, the campaign engaged in what the industry calls "A/B testing" of its e-mail and webpage content and design. Prevalent in commercial settings, A/B testing enabled the campaign to target the content and design of e-mail and webpages to specific supporters to increase the probability of desired actions, such as contributions.[70] The campaign continually ran experimental trials of e-mail subject heads to find the ones most likely to increase "click through" rates. The actions that staffers sought to induce were contingent upon both electoral strategy and the characteristics of the targeted individual. If an individual was a first-time subscriber to the e-mail list, for instance, they received a different request from the campaign than a long-time volunteer.[71] The campaign could generally predict the aggregate outcome of each e-mail solicitation for money and volunteers, and the optimal targeting and design to achieve it, given detailed supporter data and sophisticated systems that tracked when individuals opened e-mails and took online action. The same data practices carried through to the campaign's design work. Site administrators generated different webpage designs, often altering only small details such as the color and shape of the donation button, and tested their click through rates by sampling users. Staffers then analyzed the data to determine which design features were optimal. In these practices, the New Media Division of the Obama campaign functioned as a "computational object," basing much of its communication, coordination, and design practice on the data that continually rendered, and helped produce, an ever-shifting reality of supporter engagement.[72]

Not everything was the subject of rigorous data testing, however. Even as the campaign spent the bulk of its resources on broadcast and cable advertising, networked technologies were an essential part of the symbolic repertoire of the Obama campaign.[73] Staffers used the blog and website design to represent the campaign and to mobilize supporters.[74] Much of contemporary political communication takes place through digital media, so the networked interfaces that connect citizens to candidates, campaign organizations, and one another served as sites for the propagation, diffusion, and co-creation of the meaning of Obama's run. They also produced the emotions that helped inspire and sustain collective action.[75] The affordances of networked communications tools offer qualitatively new opportunities for this cultural work. The interactivity of Obama's web presence enabled supporters to gather around the candidate and to communicate with one another in highly social and participatory ways.[76] As they did so, supporters moved through the symbolic worlds that staffers designed to help create an "experience" of Obama's candidacy, the moment in history, and the stakes for America.[77] The New Media Division had marked autonomy to craft and control this experience within the larger campaign's messaging strategy (i.e., no negative attacks) and with only informal coordination with the Communications Division.

For example, staffers used the blog to portray the campaign as a grassroots movement and to provide a venue for supporters to forge solidarity, make public commitments to the campaign, and defend Obama from the attacks of other candidates and the news media. Staffers also utilized design extensively to create and impart the meaning of Obama's candidacy, a departure from recent political campaigns.[78] While the crafting of the content of television advertisements and speeches has long been a part of political practice, campaigns have historically paid less attention to design, other than logos.[79] This has been true even over the past decade and a half of Internet campaigning, where design is often an out-sourced afterthought for political staffers. In contrast, Obama's staffers conceived of design, from candidate placards to the splash (or landing) page of the website, as a symbolic resource to help construct and reinforce the meaning of the campaign.

Staffers used design to try to create an alternative, expansive, and meaning-laden "political horizon" among supporters that would impart a sense of political efficacy.[80] For example, Scott Thomas, one of the campaign's in-house designers, sought to "communicate the excitement that this candidate offered the United States of America and that this election season really offered to the country."[81] Designers developed what Thomas referred to as an "aesthetic of Obama" intended to help supporters and staffers alike imagine the candidate as a trans-formational figure and the campaign as a participatory movement that could change America.[82] As part of this aesthetic, designers created a number of dif-ferent "brand groups," or themes, intended to convey particular understandings of the campaign and candidate. The general "campaign brand" featured the iconic Obama blue, campaign logo, and standardized typeface—the very consis-tency of which designers used to suggest that the candidate was efficient and experienced. Designers pored through historical documents and photographs of iconic American events, such as scenes from the civil rights movement, to stylize images of Obama in ways that would conjure up associations between the candi-date and these events. Designers also created a brand group that consisted of official-looking documents in order to help the public imagine Obama as presi-dent. Finally, staffers utilized a "supporter" theme which involved customized versions of the campaign's logo for different demographic and affinity groups.

## New Media, Electoral Campaigning, and Democracy

In his first speech to the nation as president-elect, Obama attributed his historic victory to "the millions of Americans who volunteered, and organized, and proved that more than two centuries later, a government of the people, by the people and for the people has not perished from this Earth." Much popular and scholarly discourse has followed Obama's lead in analyzing the extraordinary participation around the campaign and new media's role in facilitating new ave-nues for political expression and engagement. Asking instead how campaigns strategically use new media necessarily provides a more nuanced perspective of contemporary electoral campaigning. The structured interactivity of the Dean and Obama campaigns and computational management practices of the Obama campaign suggest the extent to which these organizations focused on the tradi-tional metrics of electoral success. Indeed, the mantra of Obama's New Media Division was "money, message, and mobilization"—which have long served as the staple resources of electioneering. For campaigns, electoral politics is highly transactional, with very clear metrics that define success. Creating opportunities for supporters to have what many theorists would consider higher order participation in these campaigns, such as providing input into policy positions, detracts from the work that needs to be done, given the ruthless electoral math of fund-raising deadlines and canvass targets.[83]

As such, the history presented here suggests that new media have not brought about a qualitatively new form of politics. In keeping with institutional perspectives detailed by Philip Agre, among others, the book shows that new media have dramatically amplified some forms of political participation.[84] Campaigns' use of new media has significantly lowered the cost of making small-dollar contributions online. Supporters have more opportunities to volunteer, and it is far easier to do so than it once was, as phone banking, event planning, and fund-raising have gone online. What new media have not done is to necessarily make candidates more responsive to their mobilized supporters, as the "Get FISA Right" (Foreign Intelligence Surveillance Act) protests around the Obama campaign, detailed in Chapter 6, suggest.[85] Despite predictions to the contrary, the book shows that the use of new media in *campaigning* has seemingly not brought about fundamental changes in the levers of accountability, forms of political representation, quality of democratic conversation, or distribution of power in the American polity.

This is not to say that campaigns need to play a transformational role in democratic life. New media tools in campaigning work best as coordinating machinery when we are enthralled with a vision of transformation, and sure of our ends—and willing to work for them.[86] While scholars such as Jeffrey Alexander have persuasively shown how candidates, filtered through mass media, rhetorically articulate civic values to win the consent of citizens, new media staffers generally focus on mobilizing preexisting selves who bring their ideological commitments to the public sphere.[87] Campaigns use new media to mobilize sheer numbers of individuals to deliver financial, human, and political resources. While at times they may be the by-products of campaigns, the forms of mediated electoral participation documented here are not designed for the ends of psychological growth, the development of civic skills, discovery of the public interest, achieving democratic legitimacy, or community building— claims historically made for increased participation in civic life.[88]

It is in this sense of the endurance of electoral mobilization that I offer the book's title, *Taking Our Country Back*. The phrase long predates Dean's presidential run. The archconservative Pat Buchanan used the slogan for his own presidential bid in 1992.[89] Buchanan, of course, wanted to take the country back from very different people. As such, the slogan reveals continuities in electoral politics in the face of considerable technological change. Insurgent candidates seek to mobilize supporters for money and volunteers, and use all the tools at their disposal to do so. This is a time-honored phenomenon, particularly in an era when parties are more diffuse, candidates more autonomous, and the news media exert a more influential role in the process since the electoral reforms implemented in the wake of the 1968 Chicago Democratic National Convention.[90]

At the same time, however, this book suggests that new media use in campaigning is far from the professionally "managed" polity that many have feared, given the proliferation of data that enable the "narrowcasting" of persuasive political communication to small segments of the electorate.[91] While these practices certainly occur in staffers' use of e-mail and the probabilistic control that optimization and online advertising offers, narrowcasting is only one aspect of contemporary political campaigns. The Dean and Obama campaigns genuinely respected supporters and sought to empower them for electoral ends. Indeed, voluntaristic collaboration requires relationships that are not solely transactional; supporters need to feel that their contributions are valued and worthwhile and that they are listened to, or they will not participate.

Weighing the balance between supporter desires and expectations and the resource needs of electoral campaigns is difficult. As campaign staffer Teddy Goff, who oversaw Obama's state-level new media teams during the general election and is now the digital director of the president's reelection bid, describes, there was always a tension between "the desire to be authentic and the desire to be super duper effective."[92] Former new media staffers on the Obama campaign often used the word "authentic" to describe their work. These staffers prided themselves on thinking about supporters and striving to live up to the participatory ideals that they believed the campaign was about. These individuals did not just pay lip service to supporters; these values actively shaped new media practice. For example, staffers set limits on how much they would automate their tailored e-mails, given that they wanted to maintain a degree of authenticity in their relationships with supporters. As Goff explained:

> Had we been confronted by data that showed that an automated e-mail program would have raised twice the amount of money that we were raising, that would have been a crisis. I guess we would have had to go do that, but it is just not what we wanted to do. . . . It is a fairly constant tension between this almost crusader-like mentality of focusing on the user. . . . We didn't want to base too much on that [automation] operation. We wanted enough to be able to maximize returns to the degree we are comfortable with, but I am sure we could have raised a lot more money had we pursued things in a different way. . . .[93]

It is in this context that technical design and the abstractions made possible by data helped staffers manage this balance. Staffers delegated the challenge of coordination to technical design, such as building in certain affordances to the electoral platform. Data and analytics enabled the campaign to create abstract representations of its supporters that were then managed more transactionally. Meanwhile, the stories of supporters that came from other campaign channels, such as the blog and the video team, provided a picture of users that much of the data elided.

Supporters, meanwhile, wanted to feel like their contributions and input were valued by the campaign, even as they wanted staffers to maximize their time and donations. Supporters wanted Obama's opponents to be defeated, and were generally willing to serve in that effort as best they could. As a result, Obama's supporters accepted the conditions of their participation, so long as the goals of the individuals taking distributed electoral action and those of the campaign were aligned. This was the norm for most of the campaign. Yet, as detailed in Chapter 6, this balance between supporter desires and staffer needs broke down at times when supporters felt as though they were not being heard, such as when they organized using the campaign's own tools against the candidate's changed position on the Foreign Intelligence Surveillance Act.[94] During this moment of crisis, the transactional elements of the campaign came into full view, and supporters exercised their "voice," expressing frustration and disappointment on the campaign's blog, though they ultimately remained loyal.[95]

## Methods and Chapter Outline

The historical research presented here spans nearly a decade and includes a number of different sources of data, including interviews, analysis of published works, and fieldwork. The core of the research that animates this book consists of open-ended interviews with more than 60 Internet and new media staffers, consultants, and volunteers active across the 2000, 2004, and 2008 election cycles. I interviewed individuals who had worked on a number of different campaigns, including those of Al Gore, Howard Dean, Wesley Clark, John Kerry, John Edwards (2004 and 2008), Barack Obama, Tom Vilsack, and Hillary Clinton. I also interviewed individuals who worked for organizations that support campaigns, such as the Democratic Party, the New Organizing Institute, and Voter Activation Network, as well as consultancies such as Advomatic, Blue State Digital, EchoDitto, and Trilogy Interactive.

Given that the Dean and Obama campaigns were the focus of this study, I interviewed nearly the entire Internet Department of the Dean campaign and the principals of the New Media Division of the Obama campaign, as well as other individuals who played key roles in the technical operations of these campaigns, including systems administrators and technology officers. I also interviewed staffers on both of these campaigns who worked in other organizational divisions, such as field and finance.[96] In addition, many staffers who worked on the Obama campaign also worked for the presidential transition and Organizing for America (OFA). I used interviews with staffers on other campaigns to verify information and to compare practices across campaigns and electoral cycles. All interviews were "on-the-record," although participants could declare any statement "off-the-record," "not for attribution," or "on background" at their discretion. This happened very rarely in practice. No individuals whom I contacted explicitly declined to participate in this study, although scheduling challenges did not permit me to interview everyone of interest to the history here. I purposively selected interviewees on the basis of their positions in these campaign organizations, as revealed by Federal Election Commission organizational filings, including those compiled on websites such as the George Washington University elections project, and through public data on the organizations and consultancies launched after the 2004 elections.[97]

This book also draws on the accounts of a number of campaign staff and volunteers, practitioners, and journalists who reflected on the Dean and Obama campaigns in books, talks, and articles. In relation to the Dean campaign, these works include Joe Trippi's influential autobiographical account *The Revolution Will Not Be Televised* and Thomas Streeter and Zephyr Teachout's edited collection *Mousepads, Shoe Leather, and Hope*. For the Obama campaign, I draw on practitioner Colin Delany's *Learning From Obama* and campaign manager David Plouffe's *The Audacity to Win*, as well as talks by campaign staffers such as Dan Siroker, director of analytics, and Scott Thomas, design director. This book extends these accounts by weaving them together into a single chronological history, while analytically bringing questions of innovation, infrastructure, and organization to the fore.

I also engaged in participant observation as a California-based volunteer for the Obama campaign during the primaries and general election. I extensively used the suite of tools hosted on My.BarackObama.com and the campaign's voter database over many months as a precinct captain in San Francisco. As a precinct captain, I went door to door canvassing for the candidate in the Mission District, was trained on and used the campaign's tools to deploy volunteers to contact targeted voters, and made hundreds of phone calls in the months before the California primary. I also served as a "Virtual Precinct Captain" of a district in Laredo, Texas, using online databases to call hundreds of voters in advance of the primary and caucuses. During the general election, I travelled to the electorally important county of Washoe, Nevada to walk alongside other Obama volunteers as they went door to door to canvas for their candidate.

## CHAPTER OUTLINE

This book provides a rich look at the history of the staffers, organizations, and technologies that have shaped new media and Democratic campaigning over the last decade. It focuses especially closely on the Dean and Obama campaigns, the structures of these organizations and the tools they deployed, and the technological and institutional contexts in which they took shape. As a work of history, the book proceeds chronologically. The story begins in 2002, with initial independent blogger efforts taking shape around the Dean campaign, and concludes with the president-elect's speech in Grant Park.

Chapter 2, "Crafting Networked Politics," begins in the summer of 2002, when many now-prominent bloggers began promoting Dean's candidacy and Trippi started plotting the online strategy of the campaign. The chapter details the political climate and primary field at the time and the growing importance of these political blogs and new commercial services, such as Meetup, as organizational vehicles for independent supporter efforts. Chapter 2 shows how these efforts delivered key monetary, organizational, technical, and human resources to the fledging campaign. It then reveals how the campaign took shape as an organization and chronicles the efforts of its Internet staffers to craft goals, strategies, and practices for coordinating the work of online supporters to help routinize these resources. The chapter ends with consideration of the role of MoveOn staffers in helping Dean's Internet team develop new practices around e-mail and tools for event planning. With strong fund-raising and increasing journalistic attention, Dean emerged as the front-runner for the nomination after the second quarter, so much so that the candidate graced the covers of both *Time* and *Newsweek* in mid-August.

Chapter 3, "Dean's Demise and Taking on Bush," begins with Dean's "Sleepless Summer Tour" and ends with Kerry's defeat at the hands of George W. Bush. Dean's eight-city tour drew tens of thousands to rallies, revealing the extent of the candidate's national support and the power of staffers' use of the Internet to mobilize supporters across the country. The success of Sleepless Summer provides a revealing contrast to the field efforts on-the-ground in Iowa, which the campaign's leadership began to realize were seriously flawed in the fall. Despite the campaign deploying staffers to Iowa during this time, the caucus effort was fatally under-organized. Staffers on-the-ground in Iowa faced significant data issues and lacked very basic tools for organizing volunteers and contacting voters, even as national campaign staffers faced extensive data and systems issues of their own at the time. The campaign also had a series of missteps leading up to the caucuses. Journalists found footage of Dean making disparaging comments about the caucuses, which became a big controversy in Iowa. The campaign also ran ineffective television advertisements that practically bankrupted the campaign.

In the end, Dean had little hope for a better outcome than third. Dean's highly publicized "scream," endlessly replayed on national television, effectively ended his candidacy, despite a strong field effort in New Hampshire that enabled him to finish second. The chapter concludes by following a number of Dean's staffers and consultants to the campaign of John Kerry, where they worked on Internet operations and found a very different ethos and organization.

Chapter 4, "Wiring the Party," reveals how, in the wake of Dean's defeat, a number of his former staffers stayed in politics, founding political consultancies and other ventures. Through these organizations Dean's former staffers carried their tools and practices to other Democratic campaigns and advocacy organizations and trained political staffers. The chapter tells this story through the lens of the history of Blue State Digital, detailing the founders' work for Democracy for America, the transfer of ownership of tools from the Dean campaign to the fledgling firm, the efforts to help Dean get elected chair of the party, and subsequent development of the electoral platform through work with clients such as ProgressNow. It then follows the work of two of BSD's founders on two massive and extraordinarily challenging sociotechnical projects that made substantial contributions to subsequent electoral victories: rebuilding the party's voter file, and implementing a new online platform and practices for electoral campaigning.

Chapter 5, "Organizing the Obama Campaign," follows the Obama campaign from the winter of 2007 to the eve of the Iowa caucuses. In doing so, it tells the story of how the Obama campaign drew from the infrastructure for online Democratic campaigning that had been created between election cycles. The campaign hired Joe Rospars as the campaign's new media director and BSD to provide the online electoral platform. The chapter details how the campaign made a number of key organizational decisions that shaped the role that new media played in the campaign, including hiring Rospars as a member of the senior staff, and giving him a voice in all the key strategic decisions. Chapter 5 then provides an extensive discussion of the "money, message, and mobilization" approach of Rospars and his new media team, detailing the campaign's strategy behind its use of e-mail, the blog, and design. All these tools were backed by extensive use of computational management practices that calculated the returns on investment for nearly all this new media work.

Chapter 6, "Mobilizing for Victory," looks closely at how the Obama campaign integrated its new media and field efforts for the primaries and the general election. While Dean's campaign collapsed in part because of the large disconnect between the national campaign and what was taking place on-the-ground in Iowa, Obama's staffers worked to ensure that new media efforts furthered the field efforts. To this end, the campaign's online organizers worked with supporters on the MyBO platform and on Facebook, creating distributed supporter operations that furthered the campaign's field efforts in the primaries, especially the 23 state contests that took place on Super Tuesday. As field staffers hit the ground in these states, in some cases only 24 hours after the South Carolina primary, they had access to hundreds of willing volunteers who were already mobilized and active in their communities. The chapter also shows how online organizing efforts played a crucial role in supporting field operations during the general election, as did a number of tools that the division launched, including Neighbor-to-Neighbor and Vote for Change.

The book's conclusion opens with staffers rushing to send out a final "thank you" e-mail before racing to catch the last bus (or just running) to hear Obama's victory speech in Grant Park. It then discusses the analytical insights that emerge from the historical findings of the book and the implications of the uptake of new media in electoral processes.

# 2

# Crafting Networked Politics

On March 5, 2003, presidential candidate Howard Dean and Joe Trippi pulled up to a campaign event at the Essex, a restaurant on Manhattan's Lower East Side. The event was part of the "National Dean-in-2004 Meetup Day." Over 4,500 supporters gathered at Meetups in over 80 cities across the country. In the weeks leading up to the day, campaign staffers watched in awe as the number of attendees for the Essex Meetup grew to over 300, and they decided to send Dean himself. The candidate and his campaign manager arrived to find nearly 600 supporters packed into the restaurant and huddled on the sidewalks outside. That evening, a commenter on the supporter-run Howard Dean 2004 blog challenged all Dean's Meetup supporters to donate $10 dollars to the campaign and reach out to 10 friends to do the same in order to raise a million dollars with FEC matching funds by the end of the first fund-raising quarter. The challenge spread across the netroots, with supporters then adding a penny to designate that the contribution came online. The result was over $750,000 in direct online contributions, $400,000 during the final week of the drive alone.[1]

For Dean, Trippi, and the campaign's Internet staffers, the events of March 5 and end-of-quarter fund-raising revealed the power of Internet tools such as Meetup, which enabled supporters to organize their own gatherings for the campaign. This story repeated throughout much of 2003 as Dean ascended to ever greater heights. Dean's meteoric rise—from being an outsider, insurgent candidate to becoming the consensus front-runner among the press corps—had much to do with the campaign's support at similar Meetup events and the rest of the campaign's Internet operations. Both fueled Dean's spectacular online fund-raising and captured the attention of journalists across the country. By the time of Dean's eight-city "Sleepless Summer Tour" in mid-August, supporters, campaign staffers, and journalists alike declared that the Internet was rewriting the rules of political campaigning. Trippi provided both a language and framework for understanding what was taking shape online, situating Dean's run as an extension of the "dot.com" boom that had seemingly refashioned much of social life.[2] Even more, on May 17, 2003, Trippi declared that the campaign's role was simply to "provide the tools and some of the direction . . . and get the hell out of the way when a big wave is building on its own" on the Howard Dean 2004 blog (later renamed Dean Nation).[3]

This chapter is about the behind-the-scenes work of the campaign that is left out of Trippi's account. Dean's Internet staffers provided not only many of the tools, but also much of the direction for supporters' involvement, guiding their activities toward the electoral priorities of the campaign. The development of goals, tactics, tools, and metrics of success for the mobilization of volunteers were hard-won organizational and technical achievements. The campaign's staffers translated Trippi's inchoate vision into a set of online organizing practices and tools, in the process creating a series of innovations that have subsequently become the foundation for online electoral campaigning. While previous campaigns used the Internet, the Dean campaign was the first to explicitly organize its operations around the communications and organizational tool. As such, these staffers could not draw on established online fund-raising and volunteer models; best practices for much of online campaigning did not exist in 2002. Even more, there was no standardized set of new media tools for use in political campaigning.

This chapter proceeds in three parts, which map chronologically onto the campaign from 2002 until the summer of 2003. I start with an overview of the political landscape at the start of the primary season and the early efforts of bloggers to promote Dean's candidacy in 2002. I then turn to how the campaign came together as an idea and organization in early 2003, paying particular attention to the role of Meetup in driving much of the campaign's volunteer operations. Finally, I follow the campaign through the late spring and summer, when Dean became the front-runner for the nomination, detailing the important role that staffers from MoveOn played in the work of the campaign and chronicling the ongoing development of the campaign's technical infrastructure.

## The Race for the Nomination

Throughout 2002, a number of potential Democratic candidates took their first steps toward running for president. The press's anointed "top tier" (most of whom did not formally enter the race until 2003) included: John Edwards, a first-term senator from North Carolina; Dick Gephardt, the former House majority leader; John Kerry, the longtime senator from Massachusetts; and Joe Lieberman, Al Gore's running mate and senator from Connecticut. There was also much speculation that Gore would run again, which would have instantly vaulted him to the top of the field. A host of lesser known public figures were also exploring their options. They included: Carol Moseley Braun, a former senator from Illinois; Wesley Clark, former commander of NATO in Bosnia; Howard Dean, governor of Vermont; Bob Graham, senator from Florida; Dennis Kucinich, House member from Ohio; and Al Sharpton, a longtime civil rights leader and African American advocate.

The party was at a crossroads. George W. Bush was a popular wartime president following the 9/11 attacks. Much of the party's leadership, including presidential candidates Edwards, Kerry, and Lieberman, voted for the Authorization for Use of Military Force Against Iraq Resolution of 2002 in October, the bill authorizing President Bush to use force against Iraq if he decided that the United Nations weapons inspections efforts had failed. The bill passed overwhelmingly. For many progressives in the Democratic party, incensed about the Bush tax cuts and the Patriot Act, both of which passed with significant Democratic support, this was the last straw for party elites capitulating to Republicans.

Campaigning throughout 2002 and 2003 unfolded with the war as its backdrop. The United States invaded Iraq on March 20, 2003. In less than a month, Baghdad fell and public support for the president soared. Bush appeared on the USS *Abraham Lincoln* on May 1, 2003, under a "Mission Accomplished" banner. As the summer wore on, however, U.S. and British forces faced a tenacious Iraq insurgency. While U.S. troops captured Saddam Hussein with much fanfare in December 2003, the insurgency continued throughout 2004 and remained a significant issue in the primaries and general election.

There was significant potential for an insurgent challenger, with the war providing much of the context for the election race and the top tier Democratic candidates adopting similar positions. Graham was the only presidential candidate among sitting senators to vote against the war authorization, and he enjoyed a national profile through his work on the Senate Select Committee on Intelligence in the wake of 9/11, but he failed to attract much in the way of donors and support. It was Dean's candidacy that many antiwar and progressive Democrats saw as a political opportunity.[4] Dean forcefully opposed the war with tough rhetoric, including his claim, borrowed from the late liberal icon Paul Wellstone, to represent the "Democratic wing of the Democratic Party" on a whole host of issues, including opposition to the Bush tax cuts and No Child Left Behind legislation. Among these disaffected Democrats was a new group of party activists who mobilized online.

## THE NETROOTS FINDS A CANDIDATE

During the 2002 debates around the Iraq War, a growing number of progressive Democrats began writing and commenting on blogs, many founded after the September 11th attacks. Frustrated by President Bush's policies and the complicity of the Democratic Party in the run-up to the Iraq War, progressives used blogs as spaces to gather, make themselves visible to one another, and formulate arguments. It was during this time that Daily Kos and MyDD became among the largest and most influential blogs in the progressive blogosphere. Helping fuel their growth was widespread opposition to the war in Iraq and a general assessment that the Democratic Party lacked values and stood adrift. Indeed, many progressives saw the failure of the party to stand for a clear set of values and policies as a significant factor in the Republicans winning a number of seats in the House and Senate during the midterm elections in 2002, a rarity for the president's party.

Blogs were also important sites for Democrats interested in the upcoming presidential election. As early as May 2002, the principals of sites such as MyDD and Daily Kos routinely aggregated and generated coverage of the Democratic candidates. Democratic activists used comment threads as forums to debate the party's future and the relative merits of the candidates. Blogs were often the only forum for this in-depth discussion of the race. Given that it was so early in the presidential campaign, newspaper and television reports on the upcoming elections were scarce. As in much of political reporting, coverage of lower tier candidates was even harder to find. At this stage, an article that mentioned a candidate such as Howard Dean might be published only once a month in a national publication.

During the summer of 2002, Jerome Armstrong's blog MyDD became a central gathering place for supporters of Dean's candidacy. Armstrong was a long-time environmental activist who had worked for a number of nonprofit organizations on a variety of issues. In September, with contributors to MyDD, Armstrong helped launch the supporter-created and managed Howard Dean 2004 blog as a dedicated site promoting Dean's candidacy. Howard Dean 2004 had among its writers many of the now-prominent voices in online progressive politics, including Armstrong, Matt Yglesias, and Ezra Klein.[5]

Throughout 2002 and even in early 2003, MyDD and Howard Dean 2004 not only provided supporters with ways to assist the campaign, they served as the candidate's de facto website. Howard Dean 2004 even became the top hit for the candidate on Google. This is not surprising, given the official campaign's small presence online at the time. Dean's presidential site was not launched until September. Similar to other candidates, including Edwards and Kerry, DeanforAmerica.com had limited functionality, providing citizens with ways to sign up for e-mails, contact the governor, read about the candidate in the press, and learn about the issues on which he was running. The link to contribute funds to Dean, now the most central component of any campaign website, only appeared in December 2002. The candidate's website offered very little in terms of discussion or organizing opportunities for supporters, save for the candidate's schedule, which bloggers publicized, urging people to go out and meet the candidate.

The traffic of MyDD and Howard Dean 2004 grew considerably over 2002, as did Dean's appeal in the progressive "blogosphere." Dean had hit on the right message at the right moment for mobilizing those upset with the direction of the Democratic Party. Meanwhile, disaffected Democrats gathering online were beginning to develop a sense of themselves as a coherent group of political actors. This online support translated into real resources for the campaign—not only money, volunteers, and press, but also expertise in the emerging practice of online campaigning.

The online mobilization around Dean's candidacy inspired Trippi, whose firm, Trippi, McMahon, and Squier, had handled Dean's media for all five of his gubernatorial campaigns. Eyeing the governor's future presidential bid while still a consultant in summer 2002, Trippi took notice of these independent efforts by supporters and recognized their potential utility to the campaign. Trippi reached out to Armstrong to talk about the campaign. Trippi was well positioned to see the possibilities of the Internet for electoral politics. A long-time political consultant, Trippi volunteered for a city council campaign for the first time in the mid-1970s and subsequently worked on the presidential campaigns of Ted Kennedy, Walter Mondale, Gary Hart, and Dick Gephardt, in addition to consulting for candidates at other levels of office. Trippi took a hiatus from politics during the late 1990s. During that time he worked for a number of Internet start-ups, including Wave Systems, Smartpaper Networks, and Progeny Linux Systems.[6]

Grasping the opportunity, Trippi reconnected with Armstrong in December 2002 and outlined his basic plan to use the Internet as a tool to counter the organizational capacity of the Kerry campaign. Trippi estimated that Kerry, with his elite support, already had the names of 20,000 supporters ready to help him with the campaign. It was a list that Kerry had built up in his two decades of holding national office. As the governor of a small New England state, Dean did not have access to the same resources. To win the nomination, Dean needed a list of an equal number of people around the nation, and he needed one that he could pull together virtually overnight.

Trippi and Armstrong began to speak more regularly, charting the strategy for Dean's run. Above all else, the Internet would become the "fund-raising backbone for the campaign as it emerged."[7] In the absence of institutional resources for the insurgent, outsider candidate, it was essentially innovation by necessity. Soon after their initial conversations, in January 2003, Trippi and Armstrong met to discuss strategy. Markos Moulitsas Zúniga, the founder of Daily Kos, joined them. Moulitsas was one of the first regular commenters on MyDD, and Armstrong and he had struck up a friendship, which led to a consulting partnership. The three talked about what tools the campaign needed to convene the independent efforts taking place on blogs for Dean. While they welcomed this participation, the three realized that they needed a better way to coordinate these efforts so that they were in line with electoral goals. As such, their goal was to fashion the Dean website into the central hub for supporters, helping to gather them together and make them visible to the campaign and one another.[8] In January, following these initial conversations with Trippi, Armstrong and Moulitsas put together a proposal that called for the campaign to launch an official blog and to make it the central vehicle for the campaign's communications. Armstrong and Moulitsas also proposed creating individual blogs for all 50 states to coordinate state fund-raising efforts, which ultimately never materialized.[9]

Soon after Trippi received Armstrong and Moulitsas proposal, Aziz Poonawalla, the administrator of the Howard Dean 2004 blog, brought Meetup.com to Armstrong's attention. William Finkel, a staffer at Meetup who was looking to expand the firm's business to the political sector, contacted the campaigns of all the Democratic primary candidates to offer them the formalized use of the service for a nominal fee. At the time, Meetup enabled event organizers to plan one offline gathering per month at a voted-upon venue of members' own choosing. Pug owners in Oakland, for instance, could create a monthly Meetup at a local bar for which they collectively voted. Finkel wrote to Poonawalla after mistaking the blog for the official campaign site. Poonawalla forwarded the message to Armstrong and added a link to Meetup on Howard Dean 2004. Armstrong quickly added a link on MyDD. Soon after, Dean had more Meetup supporters than Edwards, who had been the leader in supporters on the site. Armstrong then put Finkel in touch with Trippi. Throughout the month of January, Trippi called Armstrong almost every night to get updates on the number of supporters signing up on Meetup for Dean.

Together, Howard Dean 2004 and MyDD drove the initial use and growth of Meetups among the campaign's supporters. These blogs helped Dean become the only candidate that responded to the firm's initial inquiry. A Meetup link did not appear on the official campaign site until February, however, because there was little in the way of a campaign organization at that point. One year after these humble beginnings, the campaign would have over 160,000 Meetup supporters.

## Organizing the Dean Campaign

Howard Dean completed his sixth term as governor at the end of December 2002. At the time, much of the campaign consisted of meetings in which a dozen or so staffers sat in a circle and went around the room relating why they supported the governor for president, talking about their campaign activities, and counting off the days until the general election. During that winter, before he became campaign manager, Trippi occasionally visited headquarters in Vermont to encourage these staffers to do things online.

Throughout the early months of 2003, the campaign struggled to recruit staff and to create the technical systems that it needed. It took a host of organizational changes before the campaign was able to realize Trippi's strategy and maximize the resources of these online supporters. If the campaign organization and the technical systems and new media practices that it developed did not come together, much of this online support would have remained independently organized. As such, this online support would have been limited in its ability to deliver electoral resources to the campaign.

## STAFFING

During the period from January through April, the campaign made a number of new hires. Rick Ridder, a longtime Democratic political consultant who had worked for candidates including Gary Hart, Bill Clinton, Al Gore, and Bill Bradley served as the first campaign manager. Stephanie Schriock, a former staffer at the Democratic Senatorial Campaign Committee, joined Ridder soon after as national finance director.

During these early months, the campaign functioned as a small start-up, with staffers inhabiting multiple roles and sharing responsibilities for different aspects of the campaign's operations. There was little in the way of concerted hiring for the campaign outside of fund-raisers or a clear sense of structure. The fledgling nature of the campaign extended to the technical operations. Even if Trippi had the authority at the time to add a Meetup link to the homepage, the campaign lacked both the technical capacity and staff to do so. The website, which a Colorado company designed and hosted, could not be easily updated (see Figure 2.1). To make a change, the campaign in Burlington had to send over the new design, and it often took several days before it could be done. Even more, there were no dedicated staffers to manage the website. As in most other campaigns, Dean prioritized staffing his Finance Department to gain much-needed resources and had a moratorium on hiring nearly anyone but fund-raisers during much of the winter of 2003. As a result, the Finance Department had the most staffers and was the most formalized at the time. These staffers enjoyed their pride of place with a view of Lake Champlain from the campaign's old office above the Vermont Pub and Brewery.

The organizational and technical capacity of the campaign began to change, however, as staffers with experience in the technology industry joined the campaign. For example, Bobby Clark was an important early hire

*Figure 2.1*  Dean for America Screenshot, January 24, 2003

for the campaign. Clark had been working in marketing for a start-up in Colorado, and when it folded during the slowdown in the industry, he faced uncertain job prospects. To bide his time before returning to industry, Clark took a job as the state director for a ballot initiative. Soon after, he first heard Dean speak. Impressed with the candidate's opposition to the Iraq War, Clark got in touch with Ridder and subsequently joined the campaign. Clark was hired in the Finance Department; it was easier to justify the hire that way, but at that point, "Nobody really had titles. The only people that ever had titles officially were the senior staff and the more traditional departments like field. So we all just tried to call ourselves something that sounded descriptive of what we actually did. . . . There was no such thing as that is not my job, you do whatever you have to do. . . ."[10]

Although he worked for the finance team and had a marketing background, Clark did much that an information technology staffer would do, such as wiring computers, simply because there was no one else to do it. Indeed, when Clark joined the staff in January, he discovered that the campaign sent its mass e-mail to supporters through the receptionist's Microsoft Outlook program. This computer, meanwhile, also functioned as the office server. Given the rudimentary setup, donations were coming in, but staffers lacked the ability to collect the information they needed for the purposes of tracking supporter involvement. With his professional background, Clark recognized early on that the campaign needed the equivalent of a chief technology officer to coordinate the basic IT needs of the campaign. After getting approval from Ridder, Clark reached out to Dave Kochbeck, his former colleague at the startup in Colorado, and convinced him to volunteer for 30 days, at the end of which Ridder would consider hiring him if things worked out.

Things did work out, and Kochbeck joined the staff. Soon after, in early March, Trippi became the campaign director. In this position, Trippi ended up being a quasi-campaign manager. Dean formally tasked Trippi with focusing on strategy, while Ridder managed the campaign in key states. In practice, this arrangement created a confusing leadership situation, with multiple sources of authority required for any actions that staffers wanted to take. Staffers describe having morning meetings with Ridder, who laid out the campaign's priorities in areas such as finance and field. During an evening meeting with Trippi, staffers often heard something entirely different.

Further staff changes did not entirely resolve tensions around leadership and authority on the campaign. In April, Trippi assumed the role of campaign manager, replacing Ridder. Dean also hired Bob Rogan as the deputy campaign manager responsible for finance. Rogan had served as Dean's deputy chief of staff throughout the late 1990s. Staffers mentioned that there were still leadership conflicts, particularly on issues related to field and financial resources. With Trippi at the helm for the first time, however, the Internet became a central component of Dean's campaign strategy. The spatial layout of the campaign's new offices in Burlington, to which staffers moved in May, reveals this new organizational emphasis. Trippi placed the Internet team right outside his office.

## MEETUP

Alongside these organizational changes, Dean's staffers worked to create new modes of coordinating supporters' efforts online. In a technological context that supported new forms of autonomous collective action, Dean's staffers had to develop new practices to guide supporters and leverage the resources that their participation generated for the campaign. Dean's online supporters wanted to participate and be useful to the campaign, yet they were also independent, outside formal structures, and thus were not formally accountable to the campaign. Dean's supporters on Meetup, similar to the independent bloggers, made voluntary contributions of their time and efforts to the campaign. At the same time, the campaign had clear priorities that revolved around fund-raising and voter outreach. To balance the expectations of supporters with the needs of the campaign, Dean's staffers developed a host of tactics for working with supporters independently organizing around the campaign, from developing agendas for Meetups to signaling the campaign's priorities.

As the personnel changes detailed above took shape, the number of supporters organizing and attending Meetups continued to grow. On the first Monday of the month throughout the primaries, thousands of supporters gathered around the country at Meetups. This growth happened independently from any official campaign effort during much of the winter of 2003, but as time went on, the campaign developed practices of working with supporters to both encourage participation and to direct volunteer efforts toward the fund-raising and voter contact that the campaign needed.

Michael Silberman was the staffer responsible for figuring out how the campaign could effectively organize Meetup supporters who were both outside the formal organization and had little in-person contact with field offices. Silberman joined the campaign as a volunteer in February 2003, in the middle of his senior year at Middlebury College. For the first couple of weeks, Silberman answered phones and tackled a big challenge for the campaign: answering the hundreds of daily e-mails that came to an account hosted on the receptionist's old computer. The large March Meetup in New York City became the moment when startled staffers first recognized the potential of the service for the campaign. Shortly after the event, the campaign decided to devote a staffer to Meetup. Everyone pointed to Silberman, who between answering e-mails had been hanging around the field staffers, learning their jobs. As Silberman recalls, Trippi told him that he would be "kind of a virtual field staff. You are responsible for everything, not any state in particular, just the Internet. Figure out how to make it happen."[11]

Silberman became the national Meetup director. Although much attention has gone toward the power of Dean's supporters "self-organizing" on sites such as Meetup, after the March event there was a significant amount of behind-the-scenes planning that went into these gatherings so that they would be useful for the campaign. Silberman was tasked with developing a proactive approach toward using the service as a means of coordinating supporters and developing metrics for success. Silberman approached his work as a field staffer. While he reported to Trippi, he borrowed his model for online organizing from the field staffers, with whom he sat when the campaign moved its offices in May: "The Internet team was certainly more of the hot ticket where all the action was but some of what we were doing was building capacity and infrastructure and not really reactive stuff. . . . We were asking them [supporters] to do real stuff in their communities so the field team was where I landed."[12] In practice, this meant creating a matrix of goals and ways to track the progress of Meetups. Silberman created monthly Meetup agendas based on the electoral calendar to map out supporter activities and to have materials on hand to ship to people. These agendas passed along talking points to organizers and involved supporters in fund-raising and canvass events, as well as letter-writing campaigns to voters in early voting states. Silberman also recorded videos for these meetings and arranged conference calls with the organizers to plan Meetups in advance.

These practices helped Silberman take a proactive role in setting expectations for supporters and communicating the campaign's priorities according to its electoral agenda, while simultaneously honoring their independence. The campaign continually strove to balance its need for fund-raising and voter contact with the autonomy of supporters who were outside the boundaries of the campaign organization and often had more detailed knowledge of what was taking place on-the-ground. Indeed, it was more difficult to hold Meetup organizers accountable to the campaign's goals than traditional field volunteers, given their much wider distribution across the country and lack of in-person contact with field offices. And, while these local volunteer leaders wanted to further Dean's electoral bid, they had their own ideas of what worked in their communities, as well as their own plans. In this context, agendas and expectation-setting served as a soft way of coordinating volunteers in lieu of direct management.

While some supporters were experienced political veterans, others convening Meetups had basic questions about planning events and asked for a lot of help about activities such as organizing and collecting donations. Indeed, the campaign conducted an internal survey of Meetup organizers and attendees that found that this was the first political experience for many of these volunteers. Even further, organizers and attendees' experience with the Internet varied widely, meaning that there were varying levels of familiarity with even basic tasks, such as printing PDF files.[13] In sum, there were differing degrees of comfort and familiarity with volunteering for the campaign and the means of doing so. As such, Silberman often found himself in a supporting role: "Even though a lot of the campaign was described as self-organized, people wanted to check into the campaign and have this direct line, in some ways, to the few of us who were responding to their e-mails and phone calls as if they were sort of our VIPs."[14] Silberman often found himself playing the role of desk manager, supporting what was taking place on-the-ground, providing advice and materials for these volunteer efforts.

The campaign also closely tracked the candidate's numbers on Meetup, as well as those of Dean's rivals. By all accounts, Trippi "lived and breathed" these numbers. While staffers had no precedent for understanding what these numbers actually meant for the campaign, Trippi interpreted them as a measure of more active support than sign-ups for the e-mail list. As such, the campaign placed a premium on growing its Meetup numbers. One way that staffers did so was to look at data to optimize where and how the campaign promoted Meetups—an early example of the computational management practices that the Obama campaign expanded into all its new media operations four years later. Armstrong realized early on, for instance, that placement of the Meetup button on the homepage mattered a great deal in terms of the number of sign-ups. Zephyr Teachout, who started out within the Field Department of the campaign before becoming the director of internet organizing, describes: "The most important thing is that the growth is clearly correlated with how much it is featured. We could measure it . . . if it is above the fold we get X number, if it is below the fold we get Y number. Michael [Silberman] and I were constantly fighting to just get it above the fold, above the fold."[15] Following the numbers of their rivals, Dean's staffers also realized that the other primary campaigns did not know about the importance of placement in web design.

These early supporter efforts and optimization practices were not the whole story behind the uptake of Meetup, however. The candidate himself fueled the growth of the campaign throughout the spring, as his opposition to the war and confrontational rhetoric began to energize and mobilize even more of the progressive Democratic base.

## ORGANIZING INNOVATION

On March 15, soon after the New York City Meetup, Dean addressed the California State Democratic Convention. Dean's speech electrified the audience right from his forceful opening line that asked "What I want to know, is what in the world so many Democrats are doing supporting the President's unilateral intervention in Iraq?," as well as his claim to "represent the Democratic wing of the Democratic Party."[16] Transcripts passed virally through Democratic blogs. Dean's speech also received considerable press attention, which stressed both his enthusiastic reception in Sacramento and his growing popularity among the base of the party. Sensitive to the horse race, journalists, in turn, began to see Dean as a credible antiwar candidate (as opposed to Dennis Kucinich, whom the professional press did not take seriously). This is important because professional press attention was an asset that Kerry and Edwards commanded automatically as top tier candidates who performed well in national polls. For insurgent campaigns, press attention helps to legitimize candidates in the eyes of the elites, donors, and activists who pay close attention to primaries and shape their outcomes.[17]

The campaign also added new tools to its repertoire. The success of MyDD and Howard Dean 2004 in mobilizing supporters spurred the campaign to launch its own blog. The Howard Dean 2004 blog, in particular, was a central site for supporters to learn about Dean's speaking appearances, to post details and photos from events, and to discuss the race. Recognizing its utility, Trippi, Teachout, and Dean himself guest posted on the supporter-run site. The campaign did not have its own blog, however, until Matthew Gross showed up at the campaign unannounced. After hearing that Gross wrote for MyDD, Trippi hired him to launch the campaign blog. On the same day that Dean spoke to the California State Democratic Party, Gross created the Dean Call to Action blog, the first for a presidential candidate, on the free hosting service Blogger. Gross, who later became the director of Internet communications, Trippi, and Teachout wrote many of the initial posts on Dean Call to Action. The site quickly became a central messaging tool for the campaign. Staffers used the blog to drive the growth of Meetups and to mobilize supporters for fund-raising and voter outreach. Dean Call to Action did not, however, supplant the supporter-run Howard Dean 2004 blog as a platform, in large part because it did not support comments. As such, the blog served as a one-way messaging tool, albeit with the personal voice of the campaign's staffers.

The growing interest in Dean's candidacy and the expansion of online operations, in addition to the campaign's successful, more traditional Finance Department–led fund-raising program, led to a successful first quarter. In early April, the campaign announced that Dean had raised $2.6 million. While this did not match Kerry or Edwards's totals, both of whom raised a little over $7 million, the number was high for a lower tier candidate, as was the number of contributors to the campaign: over 12,000 supporters. Journalists took note of the online fund-raising and the campaign's use of Meetup, fueling growing speculation about the role that the Internet would play in the election.

As the campaign grew its online support during the spring, it expanded and reorganized much of its technical operations. Trippi hired Nicco Mele as webmaster in early May, the first dedicated technical hire for the campaign. Mele took over most of the day-to-day web operations, and much of his daily work involved the basic programming for the campaign's website—a role not previously filled. To help with this, Mele hired Jim Brayton as his deputy, with the title of web developer and systems administrator. Brayton was a former Unix systems administrator for Hewlett Packard, and had been maintaining the campaign's site as a volunteer. In practice, Brayton was responsible for everything from keeping the servers running, managing the blog, and teaching other staffers HTML to updating the homepage, sending bulk e-mails, and working with the field staffers to ensure that their events were publicized on the website. The two did much of the programming for the campaign. Brayton created a script that scraped the Meetup numbers for Dean and the other candidates every few hours (which, previously, Teachout had done manually) and e-mailed them directly to Teachout and Trippi. A large portion of Mele's time at the beginning of the campaign was dedicated to designing the website and creating buttons and icons, editing photos so that they were web friendly, creating HTML documents so that they read correctly online, and formatting and sending bulk mails. In this work, Mele took the aesthetic of the site's design seriously as a representation of the meaning of the campaign and supporters' stake in it. The goal was to use design as a tool to mobilize supporters. Mele strove to have a "grassroots" aesthetic for the campaign that had "a certain rough intensity, and avoid a corporate polished look."[18] One example was Mele's much-beloved little icon that said "hot" with a flame beside it to designate new content on the website, such as press releases.

As important as the technical hires for the campaign's uptake of digital media was the organizational structure that Trippi put in place. Trippi created a stand-alone Internet Department. Mele served as the webmaster and Gross as the blogger. Teachout, who felt marginalized overseeing the online organizing in a set of states that were not the top priority for field, reached out to Trippi. Teachout had always worked with the Internet within the Field Department. Much of Teachout's work when she first arrived entailed dealing with the flood of e-mail from supporters looking to get involved in the campaign. One creative way that she engaged these supporters was through crowd-sourcing opposition research, reaching out to supporters via e-mail to collect information about Dean's primary opponents. Teachout also worked with the "Dean Coordinators Council," an effort by three Ohio lawyers to create a local Yahoo! LISTSERV in every state to build a group of contacts for the campaign. Given this work, Trippi asked her to join the Internet Department, which was flexible and open to new projects. Teachout became the director of online organizing. In this capacity, Teachout used Yahoo! Groups to build state organizations. In a pattern of internal organizational fluidity, two other staffers who sat with different departments were de facto members of the Internet team and reported to Trippi. These staffers were Silberman, in charge of Meetups and working in field, and Bobby Clark, who met much of the early information technology needs of the campaign from within the Finance Department.

The decision to create a separate organizational department devoted to the Internet on the campaign was not novel (other campaigns had similar structures), but the role that the Internet Department played in the campaign was innovative. Trippi made the Internet operations central to the entire campaign, and devoted resources to its staffers accordingly. Under Trippi's tutelage, for example, the Internet Department hired programmers to perform design work and build new applications in-house. Trippi dedicated staffers to entirely new areas of campaign practice, such as Meetups and the blog. The Internet Department also had autonomy from the other powerful departments on the campaign, such as communications and finance, that had more formalized and established practices. This autonomy meant that Internet staffers were free to take up these new tools and to develop new ways of organizing and communicating that were qualitatively different from other areas of more established campaign practice.

In other words, the organizational structure, coupled with the fact that the Internet staffers had Trippi's support and patronage (given that they were at the "heart" of the campaign), shaped how staffers used networked tools. For example, a number of staffers describe how Trippi created an experimental culture within the department and protected this space from the larger campaign bureaucracy. In this sense Trippi served as a buffer between the department and the staffers in other parts of the campaign organization, which was particularly important before the campaign began generating large online fund-raising numbers. As

Teachout describes, in response to other staffers telling the Internet Department what they should not be doing, "Trippi would say 'oh you can ignore them' . . . that was really important that he had our back, even on stuff that he didn't believe in, to just be experimental."[19]

With the encouragement of the campaign manager and the freedom of their organizational position, staffers could experiment and pursue their work, often with only glancing regard for the metrics sought by the larger campaign organization. This experimentation, in turn, led to what ultimately were a series of innovations in practice and tools, such as staffers building custom event tools and social networking applications, as well as developing new ways of working with supporters online. As Teachout describes:

> The business plan which says "we are going to make more money"—that mode gets in the way of an experimental culture, which allowed us to try ten times as many things. Maybe only a few of them work. But if we had to have somebody who was giving weekly reports, and then say here is our 5 month plan and here is our 3 month plan then that would have made it impossible to experiment. I mean, we built a hell of a lot of stuff, and some of it looks crappy but we built a lot of stuff, and reporting would have made that impossible. Another big thing is that Trippi never checked any of my blog posts before they went up. I think that is a huge difference in the way that you think about writing. . . .[20]

This does not mean that Trippi was not concerned with metrics. Indeed, staffers describe his obsession with numbers, from fund-raising to the size of Meetups. Trippi's proximity helped ensure the Internet Department's focus and discipline regarding the pursuit of fund-raising. Staffers describe how Trippi would often jump out of his office to demand status reports on fund-raising and e-mail subscribers. There were large charts on the wall, constantly updated by staffers, that tracked the money raised and e-mail subscribers signed-up each hour. The veteran political campaigner knew that for Dean to have any chance, he needed the financial resources to match Kerry and Edwards. In this sense, innovation and participation still needed to come with an orientation towards the campaign's electoral goals. And, most of the work of Internet staffers focused on creating the tools and practices that would support the electoral needs of the campaign, chief among them being fund-raising. Indeed, the campaign did not develop new, highly participatory forms of policy development. Even though he gave them space to fail and try new things, Trippi still demanded that staffers make progress on the campaign organization's priorities.

Still, despite a focus on the financial and volunteer resources of the campaign, there was an experimental culture within the Internet Department, and it had the blessing of Trippi. For example, Teachout recalls that Trippi backed his staffers on projects even if they did not make sense to him from a political perspective. Initially, Trippi was skeptical of Get Local, the events tool described in greater detail below, because it would result in the campaign giving up too much control. It would enable supporters to host their own events outside the field campaign and independent from any planning or agendas created by staffers. As Teachout said, "He is a field guy, it didn't make any sense to him."[21] In the end, Trippi allowed his staffers to develop the tool and even approved considerable resources for the project, even though they could not actually articulate how these efforts would further the campaign.

Trippi endorsed this experimentation in part because there were really no clear models for Internet use in a presidential campaign. There were goals, such as around fund-raising or growing the e-mail list of supporters, but little in the way of best practices for organizing things such as Meetups. And, given that Dean's online operations continued to grow and supporters continually surpassed the fund-raising goals that the campaign had set, there was always a distinct sense of limitless possibility and the fear that not experimenting would result in an opportunity being lost. At the same time, there was also little in the way of a clear understanding of how this national online support would translate to the field goals of the campaign. As Teachout describes: "I think a lot of us didn't know; very few people win the presidential primary so it is not like it is an area where a lot of people have expertise."[22]

Much of this experimentation also took place under a cloud of legal uncertainty. The campaign was ultimately unsure if its use of volunteers was legal under federal elections rules about volunteer and other in-kind contributions. Teachout describes how she spoke with the campaign's counsel, Eric Kleinfeld, nearly every day for three months at the beginning of the campaign, as they struggled to figure out legal obligations and reporting requirements. The questions were new, given the new opportunities that supporters had to participate. As Teachout describes: "The lawyer plays a massive role in a lot of the decisions that we make. . . . The fear was a legal fear. . . . It was just a constant question of whether what we were doing was legal. And he is making it up as he goes along too, because nobody has really delved into this area."[23] For example, was a supporter who organized a Meetup and provided refreshments making an in-kind donation that needed to be reported? Could volunteer programmers create technologies such as Internet applications for the campaign for free? How should the campaign treat the thousands of supporters designing websites for the campaign using their own time and resources? Could the campaign trade e-mail lists with organizations such as MoveOn?

The legal uncertainty surrounding the online operations shaped staffers' work. Staffers describe how supporters clamored for access to the campaign's e-mail list so that they could find and organize other supporters in their area. The legal team believed that giving supporters' information away, however, would violate the privacy of these individuals. The campaign also had to redesign the original version of DeanLink, the campaign's social networking application modeled after Friendster, because the volunteer who originally coded it was a foreign national and the legal team was worried that this would be an illegal contribution.[24]

With a campaign manager who endorsed and protected a space for experimentation on the campaign, staffers voraciously consumed books about the Internet's effects on social life, such as *The ClueTrain Manifesto*, and looked far afield from politics for potential models for their practice. As new entrants to politics, these staffers seldom described their work as the continuation of previous campaigns such as those of McCain or Gore (aside from Mele, who had a background in this work). Indeed, many staffers recalled rarely even looking at what Dean's rivals were doing, other than tracking numbers on sites such as Meetup. Instead, Teachout recalls going regularly to Alexa, an Internet traffic service, and looking at the most highly-trafficked sites to see what they were doing and to determine whether the campaign could imitate it. Staffers even went through the spam e-mails they received to find ideas for types of content that would elicit higher response rates, and looked at pornographic and file-sharing sites for ways of approaching online community building.

Dean's Internet staffers knew about these sites—or looked beyond the political for models—in part because they themselves came to the campaign with experience in many of these new online communities. The department's leadership deliberately hired staffers who lacked experience in electoral politics and were drawn to the technological and social vision that the campaign embodied. As Mele describes his hiring:

> When I was looking through people's resumes to come work here I always wanted to know what communities were they a part of, if they could use ebay, if they could post Amazon reviews—what communities online were they a part of? I was looking for people who understood intuitively the online communities and the online interaction. That was the job, that's what we were after.[25]

Many other staffers just showed up at the campaign drawn to the candidate and the technological vision of a more participatory polity. As Clark describes, "We were often lucky, one of the things that seemed true to the campaign is that people just showed up when you most needed them, sometimes miracles are miracles. . . . they just appear."[26] The campaign also utilized its volunteer networks to find staffers. Even more, Internet staffers often sought to cultivate members of technical communities on the Internet, such as SlashDot, to recruit volunteers or even staffers. Staffers, for instance, developed an explicit candidate policy position that a Dean administration would use open source technologies to appeal to this community.[27]

## THE INTERNET DEPARTMENT AND THE WIDER CAMPAIGN

Given that they were housed in a department organized around a communications medium, Internet staffers inevitably crossed organizational boundaries in their work. This was not a frictionless process. The Internet Department had a deeply ambiguous role and set of responsibilities on the campaign. Its staffers assumed tasks that spanned the domains of finance, communications, and field; in essence, there was a series of shadow departments housed under the rubric of the "Internet." The domain-spanning roles of Internet staffers are readily apparent in their titles. For example, Teachout served as the director of online organizing and Matthew Gross was the director of Internet communications. The department as a whole constantly engaged in fund-raising efforts. As the national Meetup coordinator, Silberman sat with the field staffers, but at the end of the day, even though he felt that he was not always sure who his supervisor was, he reported to Trippi.

These domain and departmental boundary-spanning activities and the lack of clarity about reporting provided Trippi with the opportunity to implement strategy without coordinating with other senior aides or consulting department heads. The other departments on the campaign, such as field, policy, finance, and communications, had their own directors, with considerable degrees of autonomy to do their jobs. A number of staffers describe how Trippi served as the defacto head of the Internet Department, sometimes to the neglect of the wider campaign organization. Even more, Teachout characterizes the Internet Department as being "at the bleeding edge of all kinds of things."[28] For example, Trippi could make "communication decisions through his very willing foot soldiers on the Internet team, as opposed to through a communications person who is expressing any kind of judgments about the nature of messaging."[29] In other words, Trippi used the Internet team to make communications and finance decisions without going through established decision-making channels. This happened to such an extent that other senior staffers tried, ultimately unsuccessfully, to place intermediaries between Trippi and the Internet Department. There was a sense that Trippi was unaccountable for his actions, and could simply implement his own decisions through his Internet charges. In the words of one staffer, the campaign's senior leadership "wanted somebody at senior staff meetings that could say [to Trippi] 'what is your plan,' 'what are you going to do tomorrow,' 'what is your long term vision?'"[30]

The Internet Department helped Trippi contend with other staffers over strategy, resources, the candidate's ear, and Dean's public image. While Trippi was Dean's campaign manager, and thus formally responsible for all of the campaign's operations, advisors who had long relationships with the candidate from his time as governor and who held his trust made competing claims on organizational power. The campaign was divided among the governor's top advisors, with senior leadership such as Trippi, Bob Rogan, and Kate O'Connor, Dean's longtime aide, often working at cross-purposes. There were a lot of overlapping responsibilities among senior staffers, not only early on when there were essentially two campaign managers, but throughout the campaign. A number of staffers described how internal decision-making processes, management, and structure tended to be chaotic, with staffers getting contradictory marching orders from Trippi and the other senior Burlington staff in the same day.

This is not to say that there was no collaboration between departments on the campaign. The Internet operations were enmeshed with those of field. Silberman and Teachout coordinated their efforts with Tamara Pogue, the national field director for the campaign. Teachout and Matthew Gross worked closely with communications. Brayton worked with Garrett Graff, who was in communications and wrote most of the press releases and worked with visiting journalists. Mele and Brayton worked closely with Trippi and the Finance Department.

The Internet and Finance Departments, in particular, collaborated often. Brayton also spoke with Stephanie Schriock, national finance director, and Larry Biddle, the deputy national finance director, about the campaign's databases. Biddle, who saw himself as part of the Internet team although he reported to Schriock, went to the department's meetings, which helped the finance team leverage the Internet and data in its operations. For Finance, the ability to gather and record data on supporters was crucial. Biddle, for example, captured data about the actions of supporters, such as if they hosted an event or attended a party, by asking them to sign up for events online. Biddle then followed up with the most active people and asked them to up their involvement and to make a financial contribution—what campaigns call creating a "ladder of involvement." Biddle also represented the finance team when the Internet Department developed or implemented new tools in-house, such as Get Local. As a result, many of these tools enabled finance staffers to track supporter activities and events and ultimately craft tailored, instantaneous messages to supporters. Biddle, for instance, created a menu of different tiers of support and then specified what the funding would go to, well established practices of direct mail marketing that he brought to online appeals. The campaign urged supporters to make small donations, and then followed up with them asking for additional support, such as amounts of $5.00 to ensure that volunteers had water.

Meetups were a particularly vexing new aspect of campaigning, given that these self-organized supporter meetings cut across so many domains of campaign practice and organizational activity. For example, in April 2003, the campaign held a series of fund-raisers around the anniversary of Vermont's first-in-the-nation law allowing same sex couples to join in civil unions, which Dean signed as governor in 2000. As Clark recalls, these fund-raisers brought the Internet Department's small donor emphasis into conflict with the high donor, special events of the Finance Department:

> And then one day it was our first big big fundraiser, the anniversary of civil unions. There was going to be three events; one in San Francisco, one in Los Angeles, and one in New York. Dean went to the one in San Francisco. The Meetup people had heard he was going to be there so they naturally assumed that if Dean was coming to San Francisco, they'd get to see him. So they showed up at the event and it was not an event that had a small dollar component so the finance team was kind of livid that there were all these people crashing their event.[31]

Given these differing expectations among staffers, supporters, and donors, Trippi and Schriock worked together to add a small-donor component to all of the candidate's future fund-raising events. This helped ensure that supporters who could not support the candidate at the same level as the high-donor fund-raisers would have the ability to meet Dean, even as the campaign still created special events to preserve the access of high-level donors to the campaign. In this, the small donors to the campaign, giving online and through Meetups, changed the way in which the finance team worked, even as staffers held the same objectives (fund-raising).

Campaign manager Trippi expected every department to embrace the new medium, just as he called upon the Internet staffers to further the goals of finance, field, and communications. When staffers in other departments did embrace the Internet, they often appropriated the medium in ways that accorded with and amplified their own professional practices.[32] How staffers used networked tools varied across departments, according to their professional backgrounds and skill sets, the goals of these departments, and the norms for working with supporters outside the campaign organization. For example, within the Finance Department, many of the over two dozen staffers under the direction of Schriock were veteran fund-raising professionals long active in party politics. For these professionals, the Internet vastly extended their well-codified work, as in using e-mail as an extension of direct mail and donor events solicitations (as detailed below).

# Standing on Top of the World

In June, the campaign launched Blog for America on Movable Type, at the time a more sophisticated blog software than Blogger.[33] With commenting functionality, Blog for America quickly became the central gathering place for supporters and the primary conduit for communications between them and staffers. Blog for America enabled the campaign to convene a community around the candidate in which supporters motivated each other, formed social ties, and reaffirmed their commitment to the candidate in the face of press or other candidate attacks. Comments on the blog, in turn, enabled Internet staffers to take the measure of supporters. As Joe Rospars, who joined the campaign during the summer after blogging at the site Not Geniuses, describes: "The blog was used as the lifeline to the supporters. Trippi spent a lot of time reading blog comments. . . . the center of gravity was the campaign blog."[34]

Blog for America was central to the massive fund-raising push before the close of the second quarter on June 30. The campaign also created an online graphic of a baseball player wielding a red bat to show donors their progress toward the campaign's financial goal, much like the fund-raising thermometers used by nonprofit

*Figure 2.2* Howard Dean's Fund-raising Bat

organizations. (See figure 2.2 for an image of the bat from the 3rd quarter of the campaign.) The "bat," as it was affectionately known, became a wildly successful donations tool and icon for supporters and staffers alike. Shortly after the close of the second quarter, on July 2, the campaign launched a massive volunteer effort called "Adopt-an-Iowan." At that point, the campaign had over 50,000 supporters signed up for Meetups, and more than 230 groups around the country wrote over 30,000 letters about why they were supporting Dean to Iowa voters identified through the voter file.[35]

The end of quarter fund-raising push and Adopt-an-Iowan campaign were impressive feats of organization that received a significant amount of press coverage, with many journalists focusing on the campaign's use of the Internet.[36] They were just warm-ups, however, for the crush of media attention on July 15, when the campaign announced that Dean netted $7.6 million in the second quarter. Dean had not only come out at the top of the primary field in fund-raising, he broke the record for donations in a single quarter, surprising most political observers. Dean instantly catapulted into the top tier of candidates. Dean's fund-raising haul also mattered internally. Staffers from the campaign's other organizational departments no longer looked skeptically at the Internet Department and its new style of campaigning. The fledgling department's staffers essentially had proven their work.

## MOVEON AND THE DEAN CAMPAIGN

Shortly after Dean's formal announcement speech in Burlington on June 23, Joe Trippi turned his attention to the "MoveOn primary" to demonstrate the campaign's organizing capacity.[37] With over 750,000 members in 2003, MoveOn was the largest and most influential online progressive organization. On June 24 and 25, the organization held what it referred to as "the first online primary of the modern age. . . . to determine if there was consensus among MoveOn members for a candidate endorsement for the 2004 presidential contest." As Nicco Mele, the campaign's webmaster, explained: "Trippi was very focused, MoveOn became a critical focal point for Trippi and consequently for the whole campaign. . . . the focus was to impress MoveOn, and attract MoveOn's attention, and to win the MoveOn primary. It really just gave focus to the campaign."[38] Trippi not only saw the volunteer and fund-raising potential of the 317,647 members who voted, he anticipated that the primary would serve as an early metric for political journalists to judge the strength of the party's online activist base's support of the primary campaigns. Dean ended up winning with 43.87% of the vote in a field of nine. While this was short of the 50% threshold necessary to win the official endorsement of the organization, the primary received wide coverage. This included a *New York Times* editorial that noted the sheer scale of the online primary: "the virtual tally . . . would top the combined turnouts in Iowa, New Hampshire and South Carolina in 2000."[39]

The online primary was not the most important connection between the social movement organization and the Dean campaign. There was considerable and direct knowledge and technology transfer from MoveOn to the campaign. This connection served as the vehicle through which key innovations in online organizing and technology diffused to electoral politics.[40] MoveOn got its start as a viral online petition articulating popular resentment against the Republican attempt to impeach Clinton. In the ensuing years, MoveOn's staffers drew on the organizational resources that this petition provided to promote progressive causes and candidates. To help in this effort, MoveOn created a powerful technical infrastructure and e-mail organizing practices that both sustained and grew MoveOn's membership and enabled its members to take action online.

MoveOn staffers subsequently carried many of these tools and practices to the Dean campaign. In 2003, Zack Exley became the organizing director of MoveOn. Exley was a former programmer and union organizer who had worked for the 1199 local of the Service Employees International Union. For Exley, MoveOn offered a new and interesting organizing model. MoveOn's staffers identified and mobilized people across the country around particular action items. A quintessential MoveOn action, for instance, are lobby days. MoveOn provided the rationale and occasion, some content around policy, and urged its members to organize their own meetings with their congressional members. The MoveOn lobby day in advance of the Iraq War, for instance, encompassed over 400 different districts around the country.

In early 2003, Exley reached out to all of the Democratic presidential campaigns and offered to help them with their Internet organizing. Only the Dean campaign responded. Exley and Eli Pariser, then the campaigns director of MoveOn, first visited Dean's Vermont headquarters in April 2003. Teachout describes the importance of their trip to the campaign: "That visit, more than any other single day, transformed the way we thought about much of the Internet campaign. In that day we moved from chaotic creativity to creativity driven by the need for e-mail list growth."[41]

This "chaotic creativity" was readily apparent to staffers. There was a minimal amount of strategy in staffers' online organizing work, given the rapid scaling of the campaign, which made planning and developing routines difficult during the early months of 2003. The campaign was understaffed through much of this period and often relied on volunteers, as resources did not really come in until the summer. There was very little planning for what an Internet Department should look like, what staff roles needed to be filled, and the priorities that the campaign had for its growth. Staffers described struggling to find their own way and to figure out what needed to be done. Meanwhile, it was difficult to create and implement online tools while using them, and the campaign suffered from technical capacity issues throughout the primaries. The campaign did not roll out a customer relations management (CRM) platform, provided by Convio and described in greater detail in the next chapter, until May. Meanwhile, Internet staffers had little in the way of best practices or defined metrics for their work. In this context, MoveOn itself was the closest thing to a successful online organization at that point.

There was also a defined ethos in the Internet Department around both valuing and preserving a less structured online campaign. Staffers were acutely conscious of the fact that supporters had largely come together on their own around Dean and were driving the campaign's success. For many, the New York City Meetup demonstrated the revolutionary power of online communities. As such, staffers had really high hopes for what supporters would be able to achieve on their own. Many staffers defined their role in terms of simply creating tools for supporters to self-organize. As a consequence of this ethos, one staffer describes how leadership "was always half hearted because it really wasn't part of their vision about how the organization should work."[42] This was by no means the way in which all of Dean's Internet staffers conceived of their work and the campaign more generally. Indeed, a number of former staffers cited friendly, yet engaging, debates over beers that stretched late into the night about the Internet and politics and new modes of collaboratively producing free and open source software.[43] These debates centered on the nature and value of leadership, hierarchy, and organization, and were often attempts by staffers to reconcile their own paid roles with a deeply felt political valuation of "participatory democracy," a concept that in practice was interpretively flexible enough to mean everything from a "decentralized," self-organized campaign to a campaign that invited meaningful participation.

Drawing on his organizing background in labor and with MoveOn, Exley urged the campaign to create more structure in the online organizing efforts and to provide clear instructions to supporters. For Exley, staffers needed to plan their work with supporters more proactively to maximize the resources they could offer the campaign. Foremost among Exley's advice was for the campaign to place new emphasis on the content and timing of e-mails. To this end, Exley (who also returned to the campaign in the summer on a two-week leave of absence from MoveOn) and Pariser helped Dean's Internet staffers develop more stable goals and routines relating to e-mail list growth and organizing. This entailed staffers adopting MoveOn's mobilization-oriented narrative e-mail style, as well as the tested format of writing e-mails in short text blocks, with embedded links to donation or action pages. As Mele explains:

He [Exley] was really indispensable in helping us realize what we were doing right, realize what we were doing wrong, and really helping us to imagine where we might go . . . he broadened our horizons and ability to think about it, he validated the approach. Until Zack showed up a lot of our Web stuff was really just reactionary. . . . After Zack we thought much more proactively about what we could do to build momentum and energy. . . . Two things we took a lot more seriously post Zack's visit. One was writing e-mails, and the tone and structure of the e-mails. Trippi was actually already really focused on e-mails, but our focus became even more intense, we thought very carefully about each individual message, how they related to all the other messages, the whole narrative arc. The other thing was his direct role in helping us get serious about events organizing. . . .[44]

As Mele suggests, Exley also worked with Dean's staffers on an events organizing tool called Get Local, which MoveOn had developed. Exley used it to organize candlelight vigils in protest of the Iraq War. The tool had a number of advantages over Meetup and Yahoo! Groups. At the time, Meetups were very restrictive for the purposes of campaign organizing. Supporter organizers could plan only one event per month, and the data available to the campaign on the activities of supporters were limited. While the campaign had an agreement with Meetup that enabled it to access some data, this generally only entailed the names of attendees and locations of Meetups. The campaign also lacked data on supporters' activities at Meetups, since they were not planned on the site.

Yahoo! Groups also posed a number of organizational challenges for the campaign. Yahoo! Groups was a critical tool that supported independent, local organizing among supporters and provided important opportunities for the campaign to identify talent and hire staffers. Supporters organized these groups around locality or affinity, such as New York City for Dean or Dog Lovers for Dean. From the perspective of both group organizers and the campaign, however, the functionality of Yahoo! Groups was severely limited. On one level, the challenge was that all of these supporters were using Yahoo! Groups, but the groups were not connected to each other in any meaningful way. As such, supporters could not coordinate their efforts, share information about challenges that they were facing on-the-ground, or find one another, even if they were only blocks away. On another, the Dean campaign did not have data on the activities, or even the existence, of these groups, which meant staffers could do little to organize them. The campaign also had no way of receiving the e-mail addresses of group participants, which meant that staffers could not systematically reach out to local leaders or supporters.

Given the limitations of Yahoo Groups!, the campaign came up with a number of work-arounds, such as Teachout setting up a "Dean Leader's Group" and encouraging all of the local organizers to join so that the campaign could at least communicate with them. The campaign also appointed a young volunteer, Gray Brooks, to manage what Dean's staffers simply referred to as "the spreadsheet." The spreadsheet was an Excel document with a list of all the active Yahoo! Groups the campaign knew about across the 50 states. The task of identifying these groups was challenging enough; Brooks also attempted to find a contact person and the e-mail addresses of members so that the campaign could organize these supporters. The spreadsheet gradually grew to encompass contact information on the individuals behind other independent efforts for Dean, such as on blogs and other websites. The result was a massive document that staffers collectively referred to as Brooks's "baby" for the duration of campaign.

In contrast to Meetup, Get Local, which the campaign hired a MoveOn developer to adapt and implement, offered the flexibility for supporters to organize their own events whenever they wanted. Meanwhile, unlike Meetups and Yahoo! Groups, the data from Get Local went back to the campaign so that staffers could gauge the success of events and plan accordingly. Keeping the data within the campaign meant that staffers could better track and coordinate supporter efforts. This included tracking the locations and attendance of events in order to recruit new hosts or deploy field staffers in places that lagged in activity. Staffers also followed up with the most committed supporters to encourage them to increase their involvement. In addition to maintaining the spreadsheet, Brooks became the campaign's liaison to the Get Local groups and urged those supporters organizing on outside sites to adopt the campaign's tools. The campaign also used the tool to provide supporters with resources, such as a customizable Dean flier template, to publicize their events.

In the end, Get Local ended up supplementing, not replacing, Meetup and Yahoo! Groups on the campaign. While Get Local offered supporters greater flexibility and staffers more data, Trippi did not want to lose the independently verifiable metric of supporter participation that Meetup provided journalists. A number of supporters persisted in using Yahoo! Groups for varied reasons, not least of which was the time and learning curve involved with moving to a new system. In the end, supporters used Get Local to plan tens of thousands of events. Dean's New Hampshire field campaign, discussed in greater detail in Chapter 3, used Get Local to help supporters plan house meetings and track attendance in organizing efforts.

## Conclusion

With Meetups booming, new tools in development, and a robust e-mail program, the campaign staged a high profile fund-raiser on July 29 that not only received widespread press coverage, it became canonic for staffers, supporters, and many others as a demonstration of the power of the Internet and its potential to revolu-tionize the political process. During a $2,000-a-plate fund-raiser hosted by Vice President Dick Cheney, the campaign posted a picture of Dean eating a turkey sandwich on DeanforAmerica.com. Small donations poured in, and Dean out-raised Cheney by nearly $200,000—raising more than $400,000. Dean's feat grabbed headlines throughout the country as many awestruck journalists watched, and wrote excitedly about, the campaign's stunning success in online fund-raising.

One week later, Dean landed on the covers of both *Time* and *Newsweek*. At this point, through robust fund-raising, rising poll numbers, and the press attention they brought, Dean had become the front-runner in the race for the nomination. The campaign sought to capitalize on its newfound strength, organizing an eight-city "Sleepless Summer Tour" that cemented his status at the head of the primary field. Aaron Myers, who in addition to working for Gore served as the director of Internet operations for Edwards's primary bid in 2004, describes this period as one when "it was obviously tough to be an online guy for a campaign other than Howard Dean's."[45]

# 3

# Dean's Demise and Taking on Bush

On a warm August night, Howard Dean, unlikely front-runner for the Democratic presidential nomination, bounded onto a stage with a graffiti backdrop in Bryant Park in New York. The candidate carried a red inflatable baseball bat. In the midst of a drive to raise one million dollars before the governor's appearance, a comment on the campaign's blog suggested that, in recognition of their achievement, Dean carry the bat, a reference to the online graphic that showed donors the progress toward the fund-raising goal. For Trippi, the campaign's Internet staffers, and supporters around the country, the bat was a symbol of Dean's extraordinary rise through the collaborative efforts of thousands of supporters. Ten thousand people turned out in Bryant Park, the last stop on Dean's Sleepless Summer Tour. The whirlwind four-day trip was a great success for the campaign, resulting in over one million dollars in donations, lots of press attention during a slow time of year, and impressive crowds a half a year before any voting took place. The candidate drew 900 in Spokane, Washington, 4,000 in Chicago, Illinois, and 4,000 in Falls Church, Virginia—over 40,000 people in all. Outside these rallies, volunteers and staffers sat huddled over laptops, taking down the e-mail addresses of supporters and uncommitted alike, building an e-mail list that grew to 650,000 by the end of the campaign.

This chapter focuses on Dean's evolving organization and technical systems from this high point of the campaign to the disaster of the Iowa caucuses. Dean's networked tools continued to power the new front-runner's campaign, albeit through much hard work by staffers who kept their patchwork of systems up and running. While much scholarship tends to provide accounts of technologies being ready-to-hand for campaigns, in the process suggesting that technical systems are far more stable, comprehensive, and planned than they are, this chapter reveals a markedly different picture. Dean's staffers developed and implemented much of the campaign's technical and data systems quickly and without formal planning, given the unanticipated scale of a campaign that quickly broke fund-raising records. As a result, early choices—made within severe resource and time constraints—affected later ones, but not in a deterministic way. Modifications, work-arounds, redesigns, and even the scrapping of entire technical systems took place. The process of technical development was messy, filled with stops and starts, constrained by a lack of financial and human resources and time, and deeply contingent. Meanwhile, the desperate search for resources and embrace of the Internet at the most senior levels of the campaign led to the medium being at the center of strategy, even to the exclusion of other areas of campaign practice, such as the field effort in Iowa.

This chapter proceeds in three parts, which tell the history of Dean's downfall and reveal how the staffers on the Kerry campaign crafted their own technical practice and grappled with similar capacity issues. I first detail the campaign's evolving technical infrastructure that supported practices such as the effective use of e-mail as well as development of new tools that were innovative not only in the political field, but also in the commercial sector, such as DeanSpace, the open source content management system, and DeanLink, a social networking platform. In the process, I show how staffers faced ongoing data and capacity issues throughout the summer until the caucuses, as the massive flow of data and demand on servers placed serious constraints on what the campaign could do with the Internet. I then look at the Dean campaign's Iowa field operation from the perspective of the technology staffers who were deployed there. Finally, I turn to the Internet operations of Kerry's general election campaign.

## The Technical Infrastructure of the Campaign

As detailed above, when Bobby Clark joined the campaign in January, staffers sent mass e-mail through a Microsoft Outlook program hosted on the receptionist's computer, which doubled as the office server. Thinking about a much-needed upgrade, Clark found that a number of nonprofit organizations used CRM software provided by the firm Convio. At the time, Convio was the largest firm providing back-end content management and editing tools, mass and targeted e-mail services, online fund-raising applications, and supporter and contribution databases to the nonprofit sector. In early 2003, there were no dedicated tools for political campaigns, save for the FEC contribution reporting tools provided by the Democratic firm NGP Software (which the campaign found prohibitively expensive). As a result, the Dean campaign had to cobble together solutions to problems such as sending mass e-mails, tracking donations, and providing supporters with tools to organize.

Clark found Convio's "software as a service" model attractive in its flexibility.[1] Nonprofits leased the use of specific application modules depending on their needs, which meant that the campaign could start with a basic platform and expand as needed. Meanwhile, the firm's clients shared the servers and applications, making it cheaper for all these organizations. In other words, the Dean campaign would not be paying for multiple e-mail servers, it would pay for using only part of them, depending on its needs. Once he decided to go with Convio, Clark then worked to convince Ridder, then the campaign manager, of the platform's necessity for the campaign and to justify it, given its expense.

Clark ultimately got approval in the spring and in May began implementing Convio with Nicco Mele. Convio provided the campaign with one system to manage all of its content, communications, fund-raising, and data. Early on, Jim Brayton, the longtime volunteer whom Mele hired as his deputy, took on much of the organizational work of managing the Convio system and helping other staffers use it. Brayton now could more easily update the homepage through Convio. Once trained, staffers across the campaign could update their sections of the site without going through Brayton. He also worked with the Finance Department to ensure that the new Convio software was reporting contributions correctly for the purposes of the FEC.

Convio also changed the data practices of the campaign. Dean's staffers now had the ability to generate multiple streams of data and query across them. Staffers writing e-mails, for instance, had the newfound capacity to segment their lists of subscribers and more narrowly direct communication based on supporter attributes such as prior engagement with the campaign and geographic location. Staffers could do so because every supporter interaction with the campaign now went through the Convio platform and was logged in one centralized database. For example, the campaign could send targeted, directed e-mails to all the people living in Iowa who donated twice and signed a petition, but who were not active in the last month. The system also provided staffers with the capacity to send e-mail much more quickly than before. This meant that the campaign could move beyond general fund-raising requests and could make specific appeals around the daily events occurring during the race.

## THE GROWTH OF E-MAIL

With a better technical infrastructure in place, and with the lessons they learned from MoveOn, staffers fashioned the e-mail program into the central fund-raising and messaging tool of the campaign. In doing so, these staffers helped develop and extend the genre and practice of e-mail communications in ways that are now widely used by campaigns and advocacy organizations. While campaigns prior to Dean maintained lists of supporters' e-mail addresses, there was little in the way of developed strategy for using e-mail. Messages were often adapted from extant communications and fund-raising content and lacked a standard, optimized format. The Dean campaign, however, approached e-mail much more systematically. Staffers oriented much of their practice toward e-mail list growth, and surpassed what was then the largest campaign e-mail list at the time, that of

John McCain. Staffers helped develop e-mail as a distinct genre of campaign communications, separate and apart from the appeals of fund-raising professionals, with a highly personal voice and calls for action.[2] Meanwhile, used as a broadcast medium, Dean's Internet staffers were the first to deploy e-mail to reliably garner financial and other resources, which helped provide stability to the campaign.

For example, staffers began to craft e-mails with narrative in mind, telling the story of the campaign and constructing the meaning of Dean's candidacy. Following MoveOn, the campaign's e-mails focused on mobilizing Dean's supporters, providing specific action items such as a fund-raising appeal or an opportunity to volunteer. To do so, staffers created a time line of quarterly finance deadlines and major political events so that e-mails leading up to them sustained interest and gradually mobilized supporters to build toward these fund-raising or volunteering requests. At the same time, the campaign sent "rapid response" e-mails to fund-raise off of daily campaign events, such as charges from Dean's rivals or hostile questions from the press. Meanwhile, the style of e-mails differed from that of other campaign communications. As Kelly Nuxoll, the e-mail manager hired by the campaign in the summer of 2003, describes, staffers strove to create e-mail narratives that were lively, written from a personal point of view, and authentic in order to inspire collective action, even though they were mass-mediated communications. Internet staffers wrote messages using their "own voice" and worked to instill in supporters a sense of their ownership of the campaign. As Nuxoll details, staffers learned to: "avoid [phrases such as] 'we need your help,' 'help us,' or phrases that suggest the campaign is divided between any kind of 'us' and 'them.' Dean for America is always 'your campaign.'"[3]

At the back-end, Convio enabled the campaign to do the format, content, and design testing that improved response rates. From MoveOn, the campaign learned the basic, optimized format for e-mails and the best times for them to arrive in inboxes. This format entailed providing a paragraph, a link to an action item, another paragraph, and another link. By August, the campaign was routinely testing its content and design, and was able to make a science out of this method of fund-raising, achieving a 50% response rate. Importantly, this enabled staffers to better predict how much each e-mail pitch for funding would garner and therefore better control resource flows. Based on MoveOn's and Dean's success, this approach has subsequently become the "industry standard" format of e-mails widely adopted as a best practice.[4]

The approach that Internet staffers took to e-mail was not standard across the campaign, however. With Convio staffers in departments across the campaign had access to the internal e-mail list, and numerous departments used e-mail in their work. Given this, Clark describes how managing the flow of communications to supporters and ensuring that there was consistent messaging became a "new problem on the campaign."[5] E-mail was central to the entire campaign, with a number of different departments using this "mundane mobilization tool" routinely in the course of their work.[6] Finance Department staffers generally incorporated proven text from direct mail letters into their e-mail requests, writing lengthy, formal messages in the style of nonprofit fund-raising appeals. These missives were generally impersonal and were directed toward high-dollar supporters. For instance, Larry Biddle, the deputy national finance director, argues that he brought his 30 years of experience as a nonprofit and political fund-raising professional to bear on his approach to e-mail, wherein he took previously successful direct mail packages, turned them into e-mails, and sent them out.[7] Field staffers, meanwhile, sought to mobilize supporters, using emotional language in appeals for volunteer organizers and publicizing campaign events at the state level.

With all these departments using this mundane tool, the campaign's e-mail operations were extensive, so much so that there were jokes in newspapers about Dean's spam and capacity issues with the Convio platform, as detailed below. As the primaries went on, staffers also wanted new functionality and tools beyond those to which they had access on the Convio platform. To this end, staffers modified the Convio tools and built entirely new ones. As they did so, staffers created a number of work-arounds for the technical limitations they faced and encountered enormous integration issues with the in-house applications they developed.

## NEW TOOLS: TEAMRAISER, DEANSPACE, DEANLINK, AND PROJECT COMMONS

One example of how staffers modified the Convio platform to better meet their needs as a political campaign is TeamRaiser, an online application that the firm developed for nonprofit fund-raising activities such as walkathons. Given its design for the nonprofit sector, TeamRaiser had many complicated layers of administrative access that enabled organizations to manage teams of volunteers. This was not ideal for the campaign, however; staffers wanted supporters to easily be able to work independently and set up personal fund-raising pages to solicit small donor funds from their networks of friends and family.

To get around this problem, the campaign made a number of modifications to TeamRaiser, including setting up a way for individuals to create personalized fund-raising pages hosted at a dedicated URL: www.deanforamerica.com/FIRSTANDLASTNAME.[8] Once a supporter created a page, she received an e-mail from Bobby Clark with a simple link to forward to her friends. Clark also created a script that enabled supporters to upload their e-mail address book into the application to send out fund-raising solicitations. The campaign launched its revamped TeamRaiser pages in July and then did a big push for donations near the end of the quarter. Clark also worked closely with David Salie, who ran the "house party" fund-raising program, which involved supporters in organizing and hosting fund-raisers in their homes for Dean. Salie spent hours cultivating organizers and hosting conference calls, and the house party program used TeamRaiser as its fund-raising platform.

In the years after the campaign, Convio created a new version of TeamRaiser that afforded the personal fund-raising that campaigns wanted. It was but one example of an innovation in campaign technology that came out of the Dean campaign. The campaign also went beyond the tools offered on the Convio platform, developing a host of new tools that grew out of Dean's staffers and technically skilled volunteers' ideas about what would further the electoral effort. DeanSpace, an open source content management tool kit that enabled supporters to set up their own websites and plan events for Dean, was one of these innovations. DeanSpace is remarkable, both for its innovation in the political space and the fact that its creation was the result of a collaboration between the campaign's paid staffers and technically skilled volunteers.

The development of DeanSpace illustrates how supporters leveraged the affordances of networked technologies to participate in the campaign, even in the domain of technical development. Zack Rosen led the effort to create DeanSpace. Rosen was a sophomore at the University of Illinois Urbana-Champaign in 2003. The 20-year-old computer science major spent many of his days reading about the implications of the Internet in books that ranged from David Weinberger's *Small Pieces Loosely Joined* and Albert-Laszlo Barabási's *Linked: The New Science of Networks* to Lawrence Lessig's *Code* and *The Future of Ideas*. Intrigued by these authors' arguments regarding the transformative effects of the Internet on social life, and in the early stages of a presidential election, Rosen began "looking for an avenue to get involved in politics." What he found surprised him:

> I started doing political research and I heard about this candidate named Dean who was doing all this creative stuff on the Internet. . . . It was kind of a perfect match. I realized that all the stuff I was reading about in these books was coming to life in a campaign. And it coalesced with a lot of things I was passionate about. . . .[9]

Soon after this discovery, Rosen reached out to volunteers creating online tools for Dean's effort and launched a mailing list called "Hack4Dean" to coordinate the programming efforts happening outside the campaign by volunteers. Working independently from the campaign, the members of the Hack4Dean LISTSERV first debated the group's role—whether to serve as a resource for the campaign when staffers needed technical help or to work on an actual, independent project for the campaign. Eventually, a number of the group's principals, including Rosen, decided to build a tool for the supporter groups active around Dean's candidacy.

They noticed that a number of independent mailing lists and other sites existed for Dean, such as Hack4Dean and Doctors for Dean. They were not linked together, however, and relied on promotion on the official Dean website for their growth. To help supporters better coordinate their efforts, the Hack4Dean group wanted to build a platform that linked the numerous websites and groups that supporters had set up independently.

A couple of members of Hack4Dean drew up a list of things that these groups needed in terms of functionality for organizing. The list included basic website and content management tools and applications for supporters to send e-mail updates to their memberships. With these basic needs in mind, the Hack4Dean group then turned to trying to figure out how to build a platform that included this functionality. The group made the decision to use open source technologies early on for a mix of practical and cultural reasons. Participants in Hack4Dean cite how open source technical production fit their own mode of collaborative work. Even as it accorded with their programming practices, these volunteers believed that this technical decision would enable the group of developers working on the project to expand as the campaign went on and the Hack4Dean membership grew and changed.

On a cultural level, using open source technologies reflected what these volunteers saw as the openness of the campaign. Indeed, even though other campaigns could adopt what they decided to call "DeanSpace" given the underlying public source code, these volunteers believed that the campaigns of Dean's rivals did not have the same open culture and therefore would be unable to take full advantage of this organizing tool. As volunteer developer Aldon Hynes, a member of Hack4Dean, explains:

> It was important that it [DeanSpace] reflect the openness of the campaign. We argued that the Bush campaign could not use what we were working on because their culture could not produce the openness. Unlike Dean, Bush was not willing to be open to other people. It's all about the openness, the underlying deep structure to the technology.[10]

After evaluating a number of potential approaches, the Hack4Dean group decided to build their tool using the open source content management platform Drupal. Rosen believed that Drupal was well suited to their needs. As a platform, it had flexibility in that it that could sustain a variety of applications. As Rosen details:

> Drupal was the most robust CMS system out there that was built really as a web application platform as well. . . . We didn't want to build it ourselves because the chances of us building a successful open source CMS

system in addition to adding all of these organizing features would have been pretty minimal we thought. . . .[11]

By July, Rosen had dropped out of college and, with the help of his fellow hackers, was working on the prototype of DeanSpace. Zephyr Teachout both encouraged and embraced this effort. It took these volunteers about a month to develop the platform with the functionality they needed. DeanSpace provided the means for supporters to launch sites and mailing lists for Dean, to find other groups, and to share news and information. In the months following the launch of DeanSpace, more than 100 activist sites bloomed, including "Music for America," "Seniors for Dean," and "Catholics for Dean." For example, Hynes used DeanSpace to create a Connecticut supporters site. DeanSpace also enabled these sites to easily share and replicate content. Supporter sites could also incorporate Really Simple Syndication (RSS) feeds from headquarters, which staffers used to disseminate news and calls to action. At the back-end, staffers at the Burlington headquarters had access to usage data on supporters and content.

Teachout subsequently hired Rosen in the fall of 2004 as the web developer and technical volunteer coordinator. As paid staff, Rosen gained an intimate sense of how the campaign was "building a plane while trying to fly it." [12] Rosen describes 100-hour work weeks for many of the Internet staffers, with 20 people doing the work of 50. Even more, to Rosen there seemed to be little formal organization, with staffers having little in the way of defined roles and responsibilities and pursuing projects as they arose and needed to get done. It was in this context that volunteer-led development projects such as DeanSpace were so crucial.

These hours were necessary to maintain the campaign's unprecedented level of in-house technical development. Many of these projects were coordinated by young staffers, for whom this work was their first experience in politics. For example, Rosen shared a cubicle with Gray Brooks, the staffer handling the spreadsheet and Get Local, and Clay Johnson.[13] Johnson was the first programmer to join the campaign when he was hired in June and moved to Burlington a couple of weeks later in July. Johnson was one of those field crossers who found his way to the Dean campaign from the technology sector. Having recently resigned from Ask Jeeves and working on a startup around the MP3 precursor to podcasting in Atlanta, Johnson attended a Dean Meetup. At the time, the 24-year-old's mother had cancer, and he watched as her health care bills soared from $300 to $3,000 a month. For Johnson, who had heard Dean speak, the candidate offered a chance to solve the health care problem.

Like many others who found their way to the Dean campaign from careers in the technology sector, Johnson applied his deep knowledge and skills to electoral politics. In the days before Get Local, Johnson noticed that the organizers of the Meetup in Atlanta had few ways to track who actually attended these events and what electoral activities they said they would engage in. Johnson approached this problem by writing some software in May 2003 that helped organizers capture data from Meetups. Soon after, Johnson founded Georgia for Dean. Johnson met Teachout through his participation on the Georgia Yahoo! Group, and she subsequently brought him onboard.

Predictably, as the first dedicated programmer for the campaign, Johnson was inundated with requests for tools, even before he drove to Staples to buy his computer and desk. It was unusual for a campaign to have a dedicated, in-house programmer to write software, a job that most other campaigns outsourced to third party firms. Johnson found himself alone and with little in the way of an environment that was conducive to programming. In large part, this was because the leadership often called upon Johnson to work on projects that made little sense from a strategic or technical perspective. As Johnson describes: "We went and made this stuff and it didn't make any sense and also you sort of came to the realization that campaigns just weren't a place for a programmer because programmers needed to be managed differently and really needed to be insulated from people like Joe Trippi."[14]

For example, the first thing that Johnson worked on at the behest of Trippi was "Pledge for America," an application that enabled supporters to commit their vote to Dean on state websites. Johnson worked on the project with Joe Rospars. Rospars worked for the campaign as a writer, a job that encompassed everything from speeches and policy statements to blogging and e-mail.[15] Pledge for America was a learning experience for the two young staffers, and subsequently informed their approach to their firm, Blue State Digital. Johnson built the Pledge for America application, while Rospars handled the content. The process took up an inordinate amount of time, and there were no clear goals for the application. There was no plan for reaching out to people who pledged to vote, for instance, no clear theory of why it mattered that they pledged, and no argument for why it mattered to the campaign. In short, there was questionable (or nonexistent) strategic value to this application, and yet the campaign dedicated two full-time staffers to it.

Even more, the campaign's new tools such as Pledge for America could not be integrated at the data back-end with the Convio platform, which was a significant limitation for the online and field organizers. Convio was a closed system at the time; with no published "applications programming interface" (API), the campaign could not develop applications that would write to the Convio database. As a proprietary system, staffers were frustrated by being "forced to play in somebody's else's [Convio's] sandbox and not able to just change the code so that it does something slightly different."[16] All of which meant that the databases for tools such as DeanSpace, Get Local, and Pledge for America were not integrated with the campaign's e-mail and donation data.[17] Meanwhile, as detailed above,

Meetup data resided with the company, and the Yahoo! Groups data only existed within a large spreadsheet compiled and maintained by Gray Brooks—all of which limited the utility of these tools for staff and supporters alike. Separate databases meant that staffers necessarily had incomplete data on the activities of supporters and were constrained in their ability to organize those mobilized for the Dean campaign or to allocate their resources effectively. For supporters, there was both the inconvenience of having multiple logins and the fact that they had to move across a number of applications to do what they wanted. As Rospars describes:

> If you were an active Dean volunteer you could have had six different user names and passwords for the different tools and things that you were required and expected to use to accomplish your mission. . . . Which is insane.[18]

The technology staffers made some attempts at integration, most notably "Project Commons." Johnson created DeanLink, the campaign's proto-social networking platform, modeled after Friendster, in September 2003. For the campaign, the utility of DeanLink lay in the nearly 20,000 supporters who profiled themselves. Even more, DeanLink helped to increase the number of Dean events, as supporters began reaching out to one another based on geographic location. The problem is that supporters then had to use a separate system—Get Local—to plan their events. The need to integrate DeanLink and Get Local was the impetus behind Project Commons, which launched in December (see figure 3.1) with the goal of enabling supporters "to sign up for grassroots events and communicate easily and effectively with other Dean folks."[19] For Project Commons, Johnson rewrote Get Local and DeanLink into one system, and then wrote a new application, "Victory Days," on top of it. Victory Days was an application that enabled supporters to create letter writing events hosted on the 18th of each month for Iowa and the 22nd of each month for New Hampshire. Organizers could access lists of voters in these states for supporters to write letters to. Johnson also added phone banking and "Instant Messenger" applications to DeanLink, the latter of which field staffers and interns in Iowa used to contact voters on the day of the caucuses. This integrated platform ultimately became the kernel for the Blue State Digital platform.

While Project Commons integrated a number of the disparate applications used on the campaign and enabled supporters to use just one ID and password to access these tools, at the back-end the campaign still had numerous data and capacity issues. Project Commons captured data from three applications, but there were still entirely different data streams, including the voter file and contribution system. This meant that the campaign was "missing out on a lot of opportunities to

*Figure 3.1* Screenshot of DeanLink a Month after Its Debut, October 31, 2003

motivate people by culling together the complete picture of what it is that they are doing."[20] Meanwhile, as the campaign grew, the Convio platform faced severe strains on its capacity.

## DATABASE AND CAPACITY ISSUES

The campaign's rapid, unprecedented online growth and the often under-resourced and informally organized technology operations resulted in suboptimal technical systems. A lot of basic technological needs were met by accident in a highly reactive campaign environment. The campaign lacked resources throughout the early months of 2003 and staffers were only able to hire for some key technical positions well into the summer. As the campaign progressed, it developed all sorts of discrete systems in response to pressing needs that were disconnected from each other. Over time, the problem of the initial lack of planning for growth and technical development simply compounded. As Jascha Franklin-Hodge, who joined the campaign in the summer of 2003 as the national systems administrator, details: "There was very little thought given to long term—in terms of the technical realm—and had Dean actually won in the primaries there would have been a whole other set of challenges in their systems."[21]

In particular, as the campaign moved through the fall and winter, the need for better data management became urgent. Project Commons enabled supporters to have only one password to access DeanLink, Get Local, and Victory Days. The data generated by Project Commons was not, however, integrated with the supporter data hosted on Convio or the campaign's voter file. In November 2003, the campaign hired Ben Self to help solve this problem. Self succeeded Ken Herman, the original database manager. Prior to joining the campaign, Self was an IT consultant for commercial firms and the federal government. In the Bluegrass State, Self was volunteering for the Dean campaign when he saw that the campaign was seeking someone to help manage its large-scale databases. Self got the job and soon after moved to Burlington.

When he arrived, Self, who had never worked on a campaign before, discovered that the campaign was collecting a lot of aggregate data but had little capacity to analyze or process it in any meaningful way. There was a ton of data being generated and collected by the campaign, but it was being stored in what were essentially a "bunch of different filing systems" at the back-end of the web applications.[22] For example, there was no single place to access a complete supporter file.

The challenge for Self was to pull all of this supporter data together in one place and integrate it with the campaign's voter file. This project was made even more difficult by the fact that Self came on during the height of the campaign, with the caucuses three months away. Self supplemented the Convio supporter database and contribution system with the open source database MySQL. It was not a complete fix, however, and staffers describe their work with data in terms of doing their best to make a bunch of database patches work during the fall and winter.

Meanwhile, there were capacity issues with the Convio platform. During the late summer and early fall, when the campaign sent out fund-raising solicitations Convio's servers ran at near capacity, slowing all of the campaign's applications and those of the firm's other clients, given the shared server space. As Rospars describes:

> It took 12 hours for the mass mailer to send out our e-mail to our 500,000 people—so we would have to hit send at 1 o'clock in the morning and then it would finish up sending at noon and so you missed the optimal times for people to be receiving your e-mail. We would hit send on e-mail and the contribution pages would go down and so we would have to segment the e-mail by different contribution systems and point some at one processing system, some at the other, which created a big mess for tracking how much money we were even raising and updating the [fund-raising] bat.[23]

The campaign not only struggled to keep its e-mail systems working, staffers also needed the ability to better segment lists of voters and supporters. Staffers describe how targeting individuals based on geographic location or whether they were previous donors was essential, but there was no easy way to do segmentation in Convio at the time. The campaign struggled to automate this segmentation, attempting to figure out how to make it so that staffers did not need to manually create lists for targeted e-mails. To solve this problem, Franklin-Hodge created an alternate system that allowed the segmentation of e-mails coming from Burlington, while state directors and the Finance Department continued to use Convio. This meant that, by winter, the campaign was actively using two different e-mail systems. As a consequence, the campaign faced many new problems at the back-end. The campaign had to make sure that all of the people in the Convio database were transferred to the new system so that there was one complete list. The campaign also had to make sure that individuals seeking to unsubscribe from the e-mail list were removed from both of these databases.

To work around the challenge of integrating these various databases, during the winter the campaign created a catchall database known to staffers as "the candle." Staffers designed "the candle" to collect the data that came in from all of the different applications. This integrated data was not very user friendly, however, and much of the finance team lacked the ability to query the data directly for FEC reporting purposes—all of which meant that the finance staffers could not look at the data themselves, but had to go through the systems administrator (who essentially wrote scripts on an as-needed basis). Managing the flow of data was such an enormous challenge that by the end of the campaign four people were dedicated to recording and integrating the online data coming into the campaign.

The campaign also placed demands on the Convio system at a scale far beyond that of the typical nonprofit. On the contribution end, the campaign estimated it was using over 70% of the total capacity of Convio's servers when there was a large burst of fund-raising, typically at the end of the reporting cycle. Knowing that this would only get worse as the year went on, in the summer of 2003, Patrick Michael Kane, who developed the technical infrastructure for MoveOn, and Franklin-Hodge built a backup contributions system in case Convio could not handle the scale of transactions at any point. The campaign had to use this back up transaction system only once during the third quarter because Convio made the extraordinary decision to put the campaign in a dedicated environment. The firm took this step because it did not want to lose its high-profile client in the midst of national attention to Dean's innovative use of the Internet and staggering online fund-raising operation.

## The End of a Dream

Dean held his front-runner status up until the caucuses. The campaign's Internet fund-raising continued to grow, the candidate's national numbers remained robust, and a number of party elites lined up behind Dean. There was trouble beneath the surface, however. Shortly after Bryant Park, the dynamics of the race changed. The retired general Wesley Clark entered the race two weeks after the Sleepless Summer tour, which changed the mood in Burlington. Throughout the fall and winter, Clark and other candidates trained their attacks on the front-runner. And, Dean made their job easier. A series of gaffes in the fall exposed him to intense criticism. In December, only days after receiving Gore's endorsement, Dean argued that "the capture of Saddam has not made America safer." While the statement itself was true, the other Democratic candidates roundly condemned it. Meanwhile, far more devastatingly, NBC found and aired excerpts of Dean's appearance on a Canadian talk show four years earlier where he described the Iowa caucuses as a platform for "extremists." Meanwhile, there was general disarray in the campaign's Iowa effort, a state that was crucial for the candidate to win.[24]

## THE FIELD CAMPAIGN

In January 2003, Trippi and Mark Squier, media consultants for Dean, asked Tamara Pogue to volunteer for the campaign and drive out to Iowa. Pogue served as the campaign manager and deputy transition director for former Maine Governor John Baldacci, for whom Trippi and Squier also consulted. Once Baldacci took office, Pogue heeded Trippi and Squier and went to help Jeani Murray, former executive director of the Iowa Democratic Party, set up Dean's campaign in the state. A month later, Pogue made her way back to Burlington. With Rick Ridder as campaign manager, Pogue filled in where the fledgling campaign needed help. By the summer, Pogue had become the acting field director of the campaign, and ascended to become the national field director in the fall. In a revealing moment, Pogue describes how Trippi had tried to hire a more qualified field director interested in the Internet effort: "I know the campaign had tried to find someone with more experience, but as Trippi couldn't find anyone who was interested in a 'new way' of presidential campaign organizing I think I just became the 'de facto' director."[25]

The crux of this "new way" of field operations, as envisioned by Trippi, lay in moving much voter contact traditionally conducted through the state field offices to the Internet. This included such activities as providing online volunteers with names from the voter file to call from their homes instead of making supporters show up at local campaign offices. Trippi also created an "online precinct captain" operation that enabled online volunteers to assume responsibility for organizing a subset of voters in Iowa and New Hampshire. An online precinct captain program, implemented to a limited extent on the Dean campaign, was also used by Bush during the general election under the rubric of "virtual precincts" (and by Obama four years later as "virtual precinct captains").[26]

As field director, Pogue was responsible for setting up state organizations, overseeing the delegate strategy, and "interacting" with the staffers who strad-dled the Internet and Field Departments.[27] The national field campaign in Bur-lington was small. At its height, Pogue had three or four staffers under her direction, in addition to several state directors reporting to her in places such as North Carolina and Washington. Trippi was very involved in overseeing field operations, in particular working through his Internet staffers to try to integrate the two domains of campaign activity. Pogue reported to Trippi and Mike Ford, a veteran of presidential politics and former organizer at the American Federa-tion of State, County, and Municipal Employees, who served as a senior adviser to the campaign and mentor to a number of staff. The field and Internet efforts were largely kept separate from a managerial standpoint—even though the staffers of these departments spoke often on informal terms. Pogue recalls that Trippi was very clear that she was not "managing" Silberman and Teachout; the Internet field staffers "couldn't be told what to do . . . they were simply given the tools to do what they thought needed to be done and given ideas about what needed to be done."[28]

Following Trippi's instructions, much of Pogue's work focused on using the Internet to build the campaign's field operations. The campaign used Convio to run the online precinct captain program, providing supporters with access to the campaign's voter file. Pogue and her staff also used e-mail, Meetups, chat rooms, and the blog to recruit, mobilize, and coordinate supporters. In states such as Texas, for instance, the entire field operation was Meetup-based. This reliance on finding supporters online and having them use new media tools to set up their own field operations had its advantages and disadvantages. While the Internet provided tools that enabled supporters to independently create field operations in places where the campaign would not have had the resources to, at the same time Pogue notes that staffers could not:

> control Meetup. We could suggest to our Meetup captains that they do certain things, but we couldn't always count on a specific captain doing a specific thing. . . . Figuring out how to get the on-line support off line was a constant struggle. I think the Dean campaign began the process of doing this, but didn't completely succeed. Sometimes we would defi-nitely get the on-line support off-line but it wouldn't always be in way we needed it.[29]

These "specific things" were the nuts and bolts of a traditional field operation. The activities in which the campaign wanted supporters to engage included making phone calls and canvassing neighborhoods to identify voters and recruit volunteers, as well as hosting house parties to organize support. Staffers also wanted supporters to follow the campaign's priorities in terms of focusing their efforts on particular precincts and districts, which volunteers often ignored.

In a central problem for the campaign, the degree to which Meetups and online operations were integrated with the on-the-ground field operations varied state by state. For example, state field staffers in New Hampshire managed Meetups themselves and communicated with the volunteer organizers, providing them with information on field activities and receiving data on supporter activities. This helped to ensure that the activities of supporters were coordinated with the priorities of the field campaign.

In Iowa, however, there were few Meetups. And, there was little coordination between the national field and online effort and the field offices in the state. Indeed, Pogue's responsibilities pointedly *did not* include overseeing the field efforts in Iowa and New Hampshire, the directors of which reported directly to Tom McMahon, the deputy campaign manager. Thus there was a fragmented field campaign and little integration between online and field in the critical caucus state. As one Burlington Internet Department staffer describes:

> We were told to leave Iowa alone. We were told that the ancient rights of Iowa would be handled by the professionals and there was nothing for us to do there except to get as many people to show up and volunteer as possible . . . not to worry about the training of them, not to worry about the filtering of who we would expect to come, not to worry about anything like that—just get them to show up. We were told to make 5,000 people show up there. That was the only thing that we were told to do for Iowa.[30]

## THE PERFECT STORM

"The Perfect Storm" was the banner under which these out-of-state volunteers recruited by the national Internet campaign convened upon Iowa in the days before the caucuses. Named for a Joe Trippi blog post about the volunteer energy around Dean's candidacy, Perfect Storm volunteers donned orange hats and knocked on the doors of voters to try and persuade them to vote for Dean. In the end, the number was closer to 3,500, a disappointment for the campaign.

Even 5,000 volunteers could not have made up for the larger lack of strategy and planning around the Iowa field operations, a failure that dated from the very beginning of the campaign. Even more, the campaign's senior staffers realized too late how far behind Dean's rivals the field effort was. While the timing and extent to which the campaign's leadership in Burlington was aware of what was happening on-the-ground in Iowa is unclear, staffers describe a general concern with field operations in the state beginning in the fall. In response, Dean's senior leadership more than doubled the staff in Iowa, including hiring many volunteer leaders from around the country and deploying them to assist with the field effort in Iowa. The campaign tasked these newly minted staffers with recruiting volunteers and precinct captains. When not doing that, staffers took on the task of calling through lists of voters directly. By the time the Perfect Storm volunteers arrived, it was a last ditch, and fundamentally misguided, attempt to salvage a Dean victory. And yet, their effectiveness was further limited by the fact that the Iowa campaign had few tools in place to contact voters. As Adam Mordecai, who ran the Iowa Internet team, describes, the field operations were "a total disaster on the technology front."[31]

Mordecai ended up on the Dean campaign just before the Sleepless Summer tour. An out-of-work actor living in New York during the summer of 2003, Mordecai read a Deborah Soloman "Questions for Howard Dean" piece in the *New York Times Sunday Magazine*. Mordecai liked Dean's candor and message, and began getting involved on Dean message boards. Soon after, he saw a volunteer listing for a night assistant to the manager of the New York State Dean campaign organization posted on the New York Dean news group. Mordecai sent in an application and got the position. Mordecai subsequently helped to coordinate the Sleepless Summer rally in Bryant Park, and sat behind huge tables with laptops alongside other staff and volunteers capturing the e-mails of attendees. In Bryant Park, Mordecai met Tim Connolly, a videographer who went on to run Iowa's field operation in the fall. Connolly asked Mordecai to train his staff in Iowa on Convio, and Mordecai ended up moving permanently to run the Iowa Internet team in November, a position that involved maintaining the state web page and the Convio supporter database for the state.

Mordecai also embarked on a large project to create a volunteer database for the field effort in Iowa, which the campaign lacked. Mordecai reached out to Zach Rosen for help, and Rosen suggested that he get in touch with Aaron Welch, a volunteer developer for the campaign working with Drupal, based in Seattle. Welch flew to Iowa to join the state staff as a web developer.[32] Together, the two built a robust volunteer management system called "StormCenter" that the campaign used for the Perfect Storm operation. Staffers on-the-ground used the volunteer management system to coordinate the logistics of the event, including deploying volunteers, tracking their activities, and finding them housing with local Dean supporters.

The relative smoothness of the logistics around the volunteer effort could not overcome the problems with voter data and the strategic error that was the Perfect Storm. Reflecting the state of the Democratic Party's voter file at the time (detailed extensively in Chapter 4), the campaign's data was in complete disarray. The campaign used voter database technology provided by a Wisconsin firm. The database lacked the capacity to handle the needs of the ground campaign; the servers repeatedly crashed when field staffers went to upload their data, and data would update so slowly that reporting took hours. Without reliable and timely data uploads, Dean field staffers and volunteers contacted the same Iowa voters numerous times.[33] Meanwhile, field staffers had to work all night just to generate walk lists. For example, staffers used the commercial application MapQuest to identify the streets to which they wanted to send volunteers. They then looked through the campaign's databases to find the names and addresses of individuals on these streets, and then plotted maps for volunteers. Meanwhile, despite the national campaign's Internet operations, field staffers on-the-ground in Iowa lacked very basic tools (with the exception of staff at state headquarters in Des Moines). Former staffers describe, for instance, having to use their own software to send bulk e-mails to local supporters and lacking access to the tools and databases that enabled staffers to personalize their communications.

The Perfect Storm was also a strategic misstep. The campaign sent hordes of Californians and New Yorkers, who had signed up to volunteer online, to Iowa. A number of veteran political organizers with experience in Iowa, along with journalists and Dean field staffers, described how this effort fell flat, given that Iowans expected local volunteers to contact them, not people coming from out of state. There was also a widespread perception that Dean's volunteers were culturally very different from Iowans and plenty of anecdotes about young Dean staffers with piercings and pink hair talking to conservative caucus goers. While there is no way to verify the demographics of Dean's volunteers, at the very least Kerry field staffers took a different approach, organizing veterans to descend upon the state in the final days before the caucuses. Even more, Dean's staffers spent so much time managing and deploying these orange-hatted volunteers that it took time away from the activities they could have been doing to further the ground efforts.

In many ways, however, the Dean campaign had little choice but to send these out-of-state volunteers to Iowa. The campaign lacked precinct captains and had only an outdated list of Iowa volunteers who had signed up online to support the campaign. To organize Iowa, the campaign needed local precinct captains to do the hard work of contacting their neighbors on behalf of the campaign and organizing the candidate's support on the night of the caucuses. By all accounts, Kerry and Edwards had better field operations in Iowa, being more successful at recruiting seasoned, veteran precinct captains beginning in early 2003. In contrast, a Dean staffer recalls that upon arriving in Cedar Rapids in December (the second-largest city in the state and a Democratic stronghold), he discovered that they had no captains in half the precincts. Furthermore, while the campaign had significant national support on college campuses, in urban areas, and on the coasts, it lacked a support base and volunteers within Iowa. Staffers had lists of people who had signed up online, but when they called them, many were burned out or no longer supported Dean. In more general terms, the overall campaign's strength correlated with larger patterns of Internet use in 2004. A former staffer at Democracy for America, Chris Warshaw, describes this phenomenon:

> When I actually saw the national numbers of people we had signed up on the e-mail lists in various states ... the number of people proportionally that we had in the Great Plains kind of states was just lower, even proportional to the population. We had two problems in these kinds of states, the population was lower and ... people didn't seem to sign up online at the same rates ... that might have been because lack of Internet use, it might have been because of lower income.[34]

In the end, senior staffers realized that the issues on-the-ground were too much to overcome. With few other options, to supplement the ground effort the campaign launched television advertisements produced by Trippi's firm Trippi, McMahon, and Squier in the final week of the caucuses. The ads, which featured the candidate appealing for political participation against a white background, nearly bankrupted the campaign.

## KERRY EMERGES AS THE NOMINEE

Dean placed third in the caucuses. There was no contingency plan in place for a campaign that had everything riding on winning Iowa. Indeed, much of the campaign's leadership itself appeared to have imagined Dean eking out a victory in Iowa. According to staffers, the campaign spent over a million dollars providing its field staffers with cell phones in December, signing *yearly* contracts with AT&T. The staffers and volunteers who traveled the country to come to Iowa were devastated by a campaign whose fortunes, for those who were not aware of the problems on-the-ground, had seemingly reversed overnight. Dean lacked a concession speech, which resulted in his infamous "scream" in an attempt to rally supporters, which played endlessly on cable news.

The nearly bankrupt campaign limped to New Hampshire. Give the Iowa debacle, Dean may have finished last were it not for the impressive field operation in the state. A number of young staffers who later played key roles in the Obama field campaign orchestrated Dean's New Hampshire effort.[35] Karen Hicks, the New Hampshire state director, adopted the field model from the United Farm Workers with the help of the famed organizer and social movement scholar Marshall Ganz. Field organizers identified and recruited volunteer leaders and then helped them to develop skills to gather other volunteers themselves. These trained volunteers then identified new leaders within that group, and so on from there, so the groups would scale rapidly. As Ganz describes the approach:

> You have to recruit, you have to build an organization in order to be able to get enough people to come to the house parties to launch something. . . . Your mission as an organizer is to find the people that will agree to host meetings. You start with a one on one meeting. . . . In the one on one meeting you tell your story, you establish a relationship with a person and then ask if they will commit to inviting their friends over to talk about the campaign. When they do, you say "ok make a list of 50 people that you know." It turns out everybody can make a list of 50 names and say "ok now let's start down the list." And you get them started phoning right then and there. It really is through attention to detail that this stuff actually works. So right then and there the person makes the first calls, they get coaching on the call, and then the organizer is doing follow-up with the person to make sure they actually make the calls. And then when you do all of this stuff the meeting actually happens. When the meeting actually happens, then the organizer goes and does this same sort of thing and recruits every person there to have their own meeting and then it starts growing. . . .[36]

This ever expanding cadre of volunteer leaders hosted meetings across New Hampshire. During the four months before the primaries, staffers and volunteer organizers hosted approximately 1,000 meetings that had over 10,000 attendees, a proportionally large number for a small population state. Their efforts helped the campaign stave off a complete collapse. Dean placed second in New Hampshire behind Kerry. Soon after, Trippi resigned after being demoted in favor of Roy Neel, the longtime Al Gore aide who became Dean's campaign manager. With Dean's poorer-than-expected showings in Iowa and New Hampshire, the candidate's poll numbers in states such as Michigan and Wisconsin dropped precipitously in the span of a week. There was little his staffers could do, except soldier on through the other primary contests until Dean dropped out of the race following the Wisconsin primary on February 17. One journalist captured the consensus of political insiders: Dean's "performance since people started voting—not winning a single state, blowing through $40 million, exploding like an unattended pressure cooker on primary night in Iowa—has not been stellar."[37]

And yet, Dean's staffers, and the candidate himself, would have an outsized impact on Democratic politics in years ahead. First, however, a number of Dean's former charges made their way to the campaign of the presumptive nominee.

# The 2004 General Election

The Kerry campaign had a very different approach to using the Internet than the Dean campaign from the outset of the primaries. There was a very small Internet team on the campaign throughout the first half of 2003. It was not until the fall that JohnKerry.com changed from a relatively static Senate site to a presidential campaign site. A team of Internet staffers hired during the late summer and early fall implemented these changes on the Kerry site. Similar to Dean's staffers, a number of these individuals were new to electoral politics and came from the private sector. This included the campaign's chief technology officer, Sanford Dickert, who was the former director of marketing for the predecessor of Yahoo! Groups and worked as the chief technology officer for an online recruitment site in the United Kingdom. Dickert was joined by Morra Aarons, who was responsible for the campaign's online fund-raising and communications, after having worked for an online travel firm and a women's portal site in the United Kingdom. After these staffers arrived, the Kerry campaign launched its blog, and prominently placed calls for supporters to sign up for the campaign's e-mail list, donate, and attend a Meetup for the candidate on its website—all of which the Dean campaign had done months prior.

In the fall, Josh Ross, the former chief operating officer of the V2 Group, a Silicon Valley product strategy and development firm, began consulting for the campaign. In December, Ross became the campaign's director of Internet strategy. It was, at this point, still a small Internet team with a small budget, although under Ross's leadership the campaign launched a number of new features on the website. They included an "Online Action Headquarters" encouraging supporters to attend a Meetup and to tell their friends about the campaign through e-mail and Friendster.

It was only after Kerry won Iowa that staffers describe how the "Internet really got on the map" on the campaign.[38] It was for a simple reason: the campaign began to raise money online. The massive amount of online fund-raising in the wake of the caucus win helped legitimate the Internet operations, given that these staffers generally had the least amount of electoral experience and were low in the organizational hierarchy.

## ORGANIZING ONLINE CAMPAIGNING

In the wake of the Iowa win, Kerry's Internet staffers received more resources and as a result began thinking about the general election in a much more systematic way. During the spring and summer, the campaign made a number of key hires. Aaron Myers became the director of Internet development, responsible for website production. Two staffers who played a significant role on the Dean campaign joined Kerry as well. Amanda Michel, who had coordinated Dean's youth outreach operation called Generation Dean, became an online organizer responsible for Kerry's "Media Corps" program that organized supporters online to write letters to the editor and collected supporters' stories for use in promotional materials.[39] Zack Exley became Kerry's director of online communications and organizing, working under Josh Ross. In that capacity, Exley ran the e-mail lists, online organizing, and online fund-raising up until the summer of 2004, when he recruited Tom Matzzie—the former online mobilization director for the AFL-CIO—to assume the role of director of online organizing.

Despite much talent, former staffers describe Kerry's Internet operations as being "one tier down from the heartbeat of the campaign."[40] Ross was a senior staffer, and the Internet Department had a representative in the campaign's important "war room" with the rest of the communications staffers. Despite these positions, former staffers describe being removed from the inner circle around the candidate. This organizational position, in turn, had consequences for how the campaign used the Internet. For one, it meant smaller budgets and fewer staffers than other departments, although during the general election the Kerry campaign had what was then the largest allocated budget in an electoral effort to date for online operations, about $3 million. The Internet Department also lacked the status of other organizational departments and had little in the way of autonomy on the campaign. Other departments had domain over what on the Dean campaign was the provenance of Internet staffers. The Communications Department, for example, vetted Kerry's blog.

One of the first projects carried out by the Kerry team during the general election was developing the back-end systems to handle what staffers anticipated would be the unprecedented scale of the nominee's online fund-raising and volunteerism. Dean's run mobilized activists, and his prodigious online fund-raising had helped to create a larger pool of party voters who were now familiar with donating money online and using networked media to volunteer. The party also united behind Kerry to defeat Bush. All of this translated into the enormous scale of the online campaign when Kerry was the nominee, far outstripping anything Dean had achieved. Millions of individuals came to the Kerry website every day to sign up for e-mails, to volunteer online, to watch videos of the candidate, and to receive news about the campaign. As a comparison, Dean's e-mail list was about 650,000 at its height, while Kerry's list had over 3 million names.

Planning for this inevitable growth, the campaign hired a Silicon Valley firm called SolutionSet, run by Josh Ross's business partner Alex Kaplinsky, to build a custom platform. This platform later became the technical core of Hillary Clinton's 2008 presidential campaign site, with the design by Ross's firm Mayfield Strategies, which he co-founded in 2005. At the time of Kerry's run, the SolutionSet platform was the most advanced in politics, supporting online fund-raising, an events tool, and digital video. The campaign also built a number of new applications on top of the platform. As the manager of software development, Josh Hendler headed up a team of in-house programmers developing new tools, such as an online calling system for volunteers to contact supporters in battleground states, detailed below. Hendler came from the Clark campaign and subsequently became the director of technology for the DNC during Dean's tenure. All these tools were integrated at the back-end, a marvel for Dean's former staffers, who were used to multiple login IDs and passwords, as well as data that was siloed across a number of different applications.

Staffers used these tools for fund-raising and communications. For example, the campaign's e-mail fund-raising requests centered on small-dollar amounts of $25 and $50 and were often tied to calls to defeat "King George." The campaign also used e-mail for communications purposes. After each debate the campaign e-mailed supporters claiming a Kerry victory. Although both used e-mail extensively, there were significant organizational and strategic differences between the Dean and Kerry campaigns that shaped digital practice. For example, as the de facto head of the Internet Department, Trippi wrote, and asked his staffers to write, fund-raising requests in response to campaign events. This meant that the campaign's Internet staffers continually monitored the daily charges of rivals and coverage in the press, and had the authority to rapidly respond. On the other hand, former Kerry staffers describe a very different communications strategy directed by the leadership of the campaign "which translated into online strategy."[41] Kerry, his former Internet staffers argued, did not respond immediately or, to quote an oft-used phrase, "fight back" when criticized by Bush. The Internet staffers, in turn, had to follow the communications strategy of the campaign, which, they argued, meant that they could not capitalize on the moment.

The campaign also worked to have online operations complement field efforts. To assist in this effort, Matzzie hired Judith Freeman, who was working at the time for the political consulting firm M + R on online campaigning. As on the Dean campaign, the challenges of integrating the online and field operations were numerous. One issue was technical. As a result of the rudimentary nature of the party's voter files at that time, the Internet Department of the Kerry campaign received data from field staffers in Excel files, which were nearly impossible to work with. Another issue was cultural. Field staffers were skeptical of how new media could further their work. As Freeman describes: "It was like pulling teeth because the field people were like 'your Internet stuff is not going to help me. . . .' It seemed like there was almost nobody in the field that actually thought that any of the Internet stuff was going to help."[42] At a time well before the Internet was an established campaign tool staffers had to prove the medium's utility for field operations. This was made more difficult given that field staffers were long accustomed to recruiting volunteers face to face, an established community- and union-organizing tactic. Internet staffers describe the inertia of these well-established practices as contributing to some of the hesitancy among field staffers to take up the Internet as a complementary tool for their own work. Beyond that, Internet staffers describe how there were prevalent misperceptions among field staffers that only computer geeks signed up online.

This disconnect between field and Internet translated into a host of concrete organizing challenges. For example, Internet staffers had the names of thousands of supporters who indicated that they wanted to volunteer, but without buy-in from the field staffers there were few ways to plug supporters into extant on-the-ground efforts. This meant that e-mail sign-ups were underutilized. Field organizers preferred to call old county lists of Democratic Party volunteers, instead of using lists of supporters who had self-identified themselves online as potential volunteers for the campaign.

An episode on the campaign highlights this problem. By the end of the summer, the campaign's senior staff realized that the field operation was not meeting its target voter contact numbers because there were too few volunteers. To make up for this, the Internet staffers set up a system to generate lists of self-identified potential local volunteers culled from online sign-ups to the campaign's e-mail list of 3 million. Internet staffers then forwarded these lists to the state and regional field directors. The Internet staffers heard in conference calls that these individuals actually did not want to volunteer. After some investigating, Internet staffers found out that few of these potential volunteers were actually being called because the state and regional directors were not forwarding these lists to local organizers. Internet staffers conducted their own research on the supporters who signed up online, documenting whether they had been contacted and had actually turned out in several battleground states, to convince field staffers that these lists were indeed valuable.

In the end, the Internet staffers worked to accommodate the Field Department's routines. Field staffers were busy, with well-defined routines and developed understandings of how on-the-ground campaigns should be organized to help them manage their work. Asking them to change their approach, particularly in the middle of a general election campaign, was not realistic. Therefore the Internet team decided to e-mail volunteers based on zip code, urging them to turn out at their local field offices. Internet staffers also set up online campaign event systems in a few battleground states such as New Mexico. Internet staffers managed the updating of these state pages themselves, uploading the details on volunteer canvass events that they received from local field staffers so supporters could learn about them online and attend. These proved markedly successful, turning out as many as 300 volunteers at some events.

The campaign also developed new tools to assist in this effort, including an application built by Hendler that enabled online volunteers to call and e-mail other Kerry supporters. After Kerry's speech accepting the nomination, over a million new volunteers signed up on the campaign website looking for a way to get involved. Unfortunately for the campaign, many of these volunteers were in non-battleground states. To capitalize on this resource, the campaign developed an online calling tool in-house that enabled volunteers to call individuals whom the campaign had identified as supporters in battleground states to urge them to get involved. In other words, volunteers in non-battleground states called into battleground states such as Missouri and Ohio to urge Kerry supporters to turn out at the local office and volunteer. This Internet-based calling tool was an innovation in online campaigning and served as the predecessor of later systems such as the Neighbor-to-Neighbor tool developed by Blue State Digital for the Democratic Party described in subsequent chapters.

## Conclusion: Coming up Short

In the end, the Kerry campaign's Internet staffers created a number of innovative tools and practices. In addition to the calling tool and work integrating Internet and field operations, the campaign urged supporters to join the e-mail list in order to learn who the vice presidential nominee would be, a tactic for identifying supporters and building the e-mail list that the Obama campaign used in 2008 with text messages. The campaign was also innovative in online advertising and was the first to use a "splash" or landing page to encourage visitors to give their e-mail address or make a donation to the campaign, another tactic that the Obama campaign used (see figure 3.2).[43] Kerry's staffers also tested different design and content on the website to increase sign-ups for the e-mail list and donations—early practices of optimization and computational management used to such effect on the Obama campaign. In the process, staffers were able to increase their e-mail signups by over 10%.

The Kerry campaign also extended Dean's innovations in the use of its e-mail list for volunteerism and especially for fund-raising. Most of the campaign's online fund-raising was driven by e-mail, and it was by far the most successful online effort at the time. Kerry raised approximately $125 million online—a large number, especially given that his fund-raising stopped after the Democratic National Convention, when the candidate accepted public financing.

MoveOn was another key driver of technical innovation during the cycle. MoveOn used its array of networked media tools to develop and decentralize the execution of its national online and offline political actions, from fund-raising to volunteering.[44] For example, the organization used its vast online fund-raising capacity to support the production and airing of pro-Kerry television advertisements and to support allied organizations such as America Coming Together, a voter mobilization effort.[45] MoveOn also ran an independent shadow field

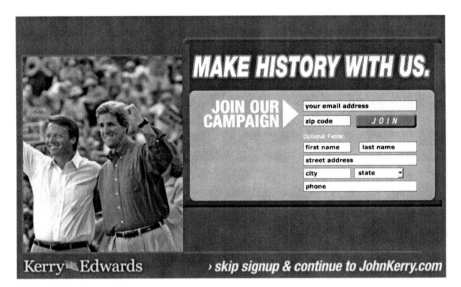

*Figure 3.2* Screen shot of Kerry-Edwards Splash Page, August 13, 2004

operation to identify and encourage Kerry supporters to vote. The organization's staffers recruited precinct leaders from their membership and had these individuals in turn find and organize volunteers for door to door canvassing. These activities resulted in more than a half million volunteer-conducted voter contacts in 13 swing states.[46]

Despite the efforts of the campaign and allies, Kerry's bid came up short. New media alone are not enough to determine the outcome of an electoral race; the War on Terrorism, the advantages of incumbency, and a turnout operation that exceeded the expectations of Democrats contributed to Bush's victory.[47] The Bush campaign also developed its own robust set of online campaign practices.[48] The Bush campaign focused its new media efforts on complementing its extensive field operations. For example, the campaign urged supporters to circulate e-mails to their social networks to recruit volunteers and join online canvassing teams to contact voters. The campaign recruited supporters to be stewards of "virtual precincts" and to turn Republicans out to vote.[49] The campaign developed its own house party program that enabled supporters to plan events online. By any measure, these were highly successful. For instance, new media were instrumental in mobilizing the more than 350,000 participants that rallied for the president at events across the country on a single day during the summer of 2004.[50]

Even as the nominee went down in defeat, however, Dean's former staffers (and after the election many of Kerry's) launched new firms and ventures that carried their innovations in online campaigning across Democratic politics. Together, they provided many Democratic campaigns in 2006 and 2008 with new tools and practice for their candidates' runs.

# 4

# Wiring the Party

After a bleak January 2004, Dean's staffers had little left in the nomination calendar to look forward to. Staffers at Dean headquarters in Burlington felt sadness and exhaustion after the campaign's fortunes dramatically reversed in a short period of time. Some just drifted away, heading back home to make up for missed classes and neglected families. Others took up last stands against the presumptive nominee in states such as Michigan and Wisconsin. And yet, during that harsh winter of 2004, as comments on Blog for America tapered off, fund-raising fell to a trickle, and their guru Joe Trippi headed for sunnier climes, the phones of Dean's Internet staffers were ringing off the hook. Michael Silberman, national Meetup director, recalls that in the midst of a wreck of a campaign the future was unexpectedly bright, as everyone in the political world wanted to hire him and his colleagues: "We all received calls from people trying to poach us. . . . We were all pretty well marketable at the time, probably more so than we knew."[1]

With their extraordinary validation as the arbiters of a new kind of politics and an acute sense of the technological needs of campaigns, these staffers found a number of employment opportunities and potential clients at hand. As such, even as Democrats across the country began to focus on electing John Kerry (or defeating George W. Bush), many of Dean's former staffers were hard at work creating new political ventures. The result was an impressive array of political organizations, such as the New Organizing Institute (NOI), and consultancies, such as Blue State Digital and EchoDitto, which together helped disseminate, formalize, and extend many of the Dean campaign's innovations in online campaigning. This new generation of political intermediaries helped create an infrastructure for Democratic online campaigning. While there was little carryover in personnel working with new media between the presidential cycles of 2000 and 2004, these intermediaries provided staffers who got their political start during the 2004 elections with opportunities to stay in politics. In turn, drawing on what they learned in 2004, Dean's former staffers built dedicated electoral tools and developed best practices for engaging supporters online. These intermediaries also helped to create a stable pool of political staffers with specialized skills and tools who worked on a number of Democratic electoral and advocacy campaigns.

These organizations were not alone in providing digital campaign services. Incumbent firms such as Convio and Kintera that provided many of the tools for the 2004 campaigns both remained active and sought to expand their businesses after the cycle. Blue State Digital and EchoDitto did, however, become among the most prominent in the field by landing many high-profile political clients in the years between presidential elections, in effect taking business from these more established companies. Even more, these organizations brought about qualitative changes in online organizing practices and tools. Unlike the large, nonprofit-oriented firms, these start-ups were explicitly partisan, working only with Democratic campaigns and causes.[2] These firms also created dedicated campaign tools that had increased capacity and functionality, being developed explicitly to overcome the numerous limitations of the various technical systems and applications used on the Dean campaign. Finally, through strategy consulting, staffing, and training, these firms and nonprofit organizations such as NOI extended many of the organizing practices of the Dean campaign in terms of engaging and coordinating supporters in electoral tasks such as fund-raising, messaging, and volunteering.

To illustrate these changes in digital campaigning, this chapter focuses on the history of Blue State Digital, a firm whose four founders played a leading role in the elections of 2006 and 2008 in providing tools and strategy for the Democratic Party and campaigns such as Obama's. This chapter proceeds in four parts. It begins by detailing the creation of Blue State Digital, the work of its founders in helping Dean get elected chair, and the development of the firm's proprietary platform through work with a number of high-profile clients such as MoveOn Student Action and ProgressNow. The chapter then follows the work of Ben Self and Joe Rospars, two of BSD's founders, for Chairman Dean at the party. I chronicle Self's effort to build a new national voter file and the technological systems to support it, which resulted in the database and interface system VoteBuilder. Finally, I detail Rospars's online organizing work at the party, then conclude with a discussion of early efforts to integrate the data back-ends of VoteBuilder and PartyBuilder, the electoral platform that BSD developed for the party.

## Blue State Digital

During the waning days of the primaries, three Dean staffers—Jascha Franklin-Hodge, national systems administrator; Clay Johnson, lead programmer; and Ben Self, data architect—found themselves in a bar near the campaign's offices in Burlington talking about their future careers. With Franklin-Hodge's programming and system administration skills, Johnson's programming skills, and Self's database administration experience and consulting background, the three were well positioned to start their own firm. The trio reached out to Joe Rospars, a writer for the campaign, and he subsequently became the fourth partner for their fledgling company.

The four grasped both the need for better election tools and the opportunities within Democratic political consulting. One of the key motivations of the founders, especially programmers Franklin-Hodge and Johnson, was their experience developing tools on the Dean campaign. Both knew how challenging it was to work during the campaign, and wanted to create a stable, long-term, and well-managed development environment that enabled programmers committed to Democratic causes to be active in politics. Meanwhile, with their business backgrounds, BSD's founders grasped the needs of Democratic campaigns and advocacy organizations and saw the market opportunity. As Franklin-Hodge explains:

> We had recognized very early on, myself and some of the other co-founders, that there was a lot of opportunity in this space. . . . myself, Joe Rospars, Clay Johnson, and Ben Self. And everyone except Joe had come out of a high tech business environment. Clay and I had both worked either for venture firms or a number of venture-backed companies. All of us recognized that there was a business need that was going on. And all of us recognized in a very intuitive way that the process by which the Dean campaign came to its technology innovation was less than optimal from a technical standpoint and from a best practices standpoint.[3]

Shortly after establishing their partnership, Franklin-Hodge came up with the name "Blue State." This was well before the "blue state"/"red state" meme of post-2004 election analysis; "Digital" was added later because a lighting company owned Bluestate.com. From this start, BSD grew into one of the most powerful digital strategy and technology firms in Democratic politics. Well before the business model for the start-up firm was ironed out, however, Rospars worked with an influential early client, Democracy for America (DFA), and assisted in the effort to get Dean elected chair of the party.

## DEMOCRACY FOR AMERICA AND THE RACE FOR CHAIR

After their initial conversations, Johnson went back to Atlanta, Self to Lexington, Kentucky, and Franklin-Hodge to Boston to work virtually on their fledgling business. Rospars stayed behind in Burlington a little while before moving to Washington, D.C. BSD's first client came through Johnson, who approached Georgia U.S. Senate candidate Gary Leshaw at a Meetup of former Dean supporters in Atlanta. Leshaw was looking for the backing of Dean's former sup-porters in his run for Senate, and Johnson basically "sold him a bunch of software that we didn't have yet."[4] While Franklin-Hodge was working on building this software as the chief technology officer, Rospars helped land what was to become the new firm's most important early client: Democracy for America.

In March 2004, Dean launched DFA, an organization intended to serve as a mobilization vehicle for the former candidate's supporters. Incorporated as a political action committee, DFA had control over the Dean e-mail list and technol-ogies used on the campaign. In the early days of DFA, there was little in the way of formal management or a developed strategy for engaging with Dean's supporters. There were also few staffers, as many who worked on the campaign scattered soon after Dean withdrew from the race. Given all of this, the new organization had some initial missteps that diluted the numbers and good will of Dean's supporter community. A fund-raising solicitation for Jesse Jackson Jr.'s congressional cam-paign went out over Dean's e-mail list, netting less than $5,000 dollars. In response, thousands unsubscribed from the e-mail list. Meanwhile, the paltry fund-raising sum provided fodder for pundits who argued that Dean's influence within the party had all but disappeared with the collapse of his campaign.

It was in this context that Rospars traveled back to Burlington and negotiated a deal with Dean to have BSD provide the technologies and online strategy for DFA. As part of this agreement, DFA transferred the intellectual property in many of the tools used by the campaign to the firm in exchange for their ongoing maintenance and extension. The transfer of intellectual property enabled BSD to retain clear control over what the campaign had put together, and to invest in rebuilding these tools for DFA and its other clients. This formalization of legal ownership was important for the new firm because a number of former staffers and vendors attempted to lay claim to the Dean tools and data, including an effort by former staffers to make the tools an open source project. This arrange-ment proved highly consequential for the firm in the years ahead. Although these tools evolved, subsequent generations of BSD's platform were "still based on some of the technology that we built on the Dean campaign."[5] As such, the transfer of the intellectual property in the campaign's tools to the firm provided the "legal protection just in case anything did happen. . . . some intellectual prop-erty clearance."[6]

Meanwhile, Dean had not yet made a decision as to what he would do next. The immediate goal was to use DFA to position the former candidate as a leading voice in the Democratic Party and to pull candidates toward his policy stances, especially opposition to the war in Iraq. To do so, staffers sought to keep Dean's name in the news through engaging in press outreach and arranging interviews for the former candidate. Dean also endorsed a number of 2004 candidates under an effort branded as the "Dean Dozen" (although there were a number of installments of endorsed candidates during the cycle, which totaled far more than a dozen). These candidates were progressives who were not incumbents and were running in races ranging from state representative to U.S. senator, including Barack Obama, then running to be the junior senator from Illinois.[7] Strategists intended the Dean Dozen to provide the former candidate's supporters with an outlet for the energy that the primaries had generated. These candidates also provided an opportunity for supporters residing in states outside of the contested battlegrounds of the general election to become involved in electoral activity. In other words, DFA attempted to make local races newly relevant for those drawn to national politics, and was often the only game in town for progressives in a presidential election where vast swaths of the country were effectively ignored.

Rospars stayed in Burlington to help with the new media side of this effort. The former writer for the campaign took control of the e-mail list, launching a couple of initiatives designed to build the list back to where it was during the campaign, renew the engagement of supporters, and bring new people into the fold. These initiatives included generating e-mail petitions and action items focused on progressive issues. Through these efforts, the DFA e-mail list grew to be larger on Election Day than it was during the primaries. Meanwhile, the day after Kerry's defeat, Rospars crafted an e-mail from Dean that declared his defiance in the wake of a sweeping Republican victory, cited DFA's victories at the local level, and laid out a plan to reinvigorate the party. As Kevin Thurman, BSD's "employee number 3," describes: "It was sent out to thousands but it was read by twice as many people as it was sent out to is what our stats showed. It was one of the best performing e-mails that we have ever had. . . . Right after that Joe is in DC and Dean starts running for DNC chair."[8]

The reconstituted e-mail list proved valuable in the months that followed the 2004 general election as Dean ran for party chair. With the party in deep disarray and a vacuum in leadership, Dean announced on Blog For America and in an e-mail to supporters in January that he was running to become the chairman of the Democratic National Committee.[9] The announcement echoed much of the rhetoric from the campaign, as Dean staked out a confrontational position toward the "right-wing fringe" and criticized Democrats for abandoning their "true values."[10] More generally, Dean's argument for the chairmanship was premised upon the former candidate having a vision of a more participatory and grassroots Democratic Party that would revitalize the state parties, compete across the country, and not be afraid of taking strong, principled stands. Dean also promised not to run for president in 2008.

Rospars worked half-time on the race, and BSD continued to provide technology services for DFA. While the chairman's race and Dean's strategy of appealing to state party members of the Democratic National Committee has been extensively covered by *Nation* writer Ari Berman in *Herding Donkeys*, it is worth noting that Rospars's work with new media during this unconventional election prefigured his work with the Obama campaign to secure superdelegate support three years later. The chair's race is unlike primary or general elections in that Dean had to appeal to the 447 members of the Democratic National Committee who selected the next chair, not the wider electorate. The effort to elect Dean as chair was the antithesis of the Perfect Storm, where masses of unorganized yet mobilized and committed volunteers swept across Iowa to knock on doors haphazardly in a last ditch attempt at electoral victory. Approaching the members of the DNC was a targeted, meticulous process. For staffers, the task was to demonstrate that Dean actually commanded the local, grassroots support that he claimed and that would be central to revitalizing state parties. Even more, demonstrating this local support would help reassure party leaders who were skeptical that Dean could appeal beyond the liberal base.

Rospars furthered these goals by using new media to conduct a geographically targeted mobilization effort. The centerpiece of the strategy was to have DFA members appeal to DNC members at the state level who were dissatisfied with the national party. Through targeted e-mails to DFA's list, Rospars encouraged supporters to reach out and directly contact their local DNC representatives through telephone, mail, and in-person office appearances. Importantly, the bulk of this mobilization work occurred at a local level, removed from the wider, more nationally oriented netroots that received much media, party elite, and academic attention in the wake of the 2004 elections.[11]

Through successful appeals to rank-and-file state party members, Dean was elected chair in February 2005.[12] Under his tutelage, the national Democratic Party worked to reorient itself to the states and its supporters in fundamentally new ways. Dean's 50-state strategy drove these changes, adding new priorities to the agenda of the party's staffers: the rebuilding of the state parties; the implementation of online and on-the-ground organizing; and the encouragement of supporter participation. To carry out these changes the national party restructured its organization and embarked upon a number of infrastructure-building projects that increased its capacity to contest elections and to organize supporters.

## TRANSFORMING THE TOOLS FOR CAMPAIGNING

While Rospars helped DFA rebuild its e-mail list, his colleagues at BSD worked on their first big project: improving the tools used on the Dean campaign and redesigning DFA's website. BSD rebuilt and extended the bundle of Project Commons applications for DFA. For example, BSD built e-mail and fund-raising applications onto the Project Commons social networking and events tools. The firm also integrated the back-ends of all these applications. This meant that DFA staffers could use one platform to target, send, and track response rates on e-mail communications, to process contributions, and to access information on supporters. For their part, supporters could use one integrated tool set to take actions such as independently fund-raising and planning events for DFA. BSD also created a more user-friendly and polished interface for the organization (see figures 4.1 and 4.2).

Around the time of the Democratic National Convention in July 2004, BSD opened an office in Washington, D.C., and Johnson left Atlanta to staff it. Johnson found himself in high demand in D.C., given the star status of Dean's Internet campaigners and a wide open market for political technologies. Johnson recalls that campaigns and advocacy organizations saw his firm as "the Dean team, so people were calling us up and wanting to meet with us."[13]

Johnson recalls that his primary competitors at sales meetings were the new firms founded by his colleagues on the Dean campaign, especially EchoDitto.[14] Soon after Dean dropped out of the race, Nicco Mele and Michael Silberman launched EchoDitto with six of their colleagues, including Harish Rao, who worked in information technology on the campaign, Garrett Graff, the deputy national press secretary for the campaign, and Justin Pinder, a web developer for Dean. EchoDitto had a very robust digital strategy and custom tools business, and Johnson often found himself pitching against Nicco Mele. EchoDitto got the better of those sales calls throughout much of 2004 and 2005, growing faster than BSD in terms of staffers and revenue. Reflecting the extraordinary national attention to Dean's Internet operations, EchoDitto landed a few prominent early clients in 2004, including the Service Employees International Union and Democratic Congressional Campaign Committee, as well as Barack Obama's Senate campaign. Meanwhile, with DFA providing the core operating revenue for the

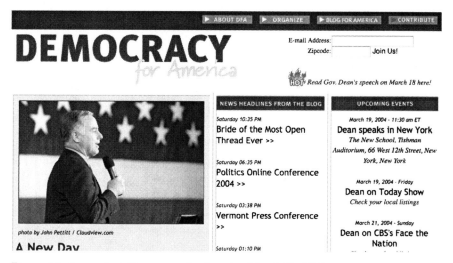

*Figure 4.1* Screenshot, Democracy for America, March 21, 2004

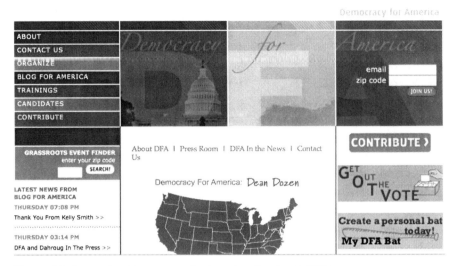

*Figure 4.2* Screenshot, Democracy for America, October 1, 2004

firm, BSD worked for the campaign of John Lynch, who was elected governor of New Hampshire in 2004. During this period, Johnson describes that he and his colleagues still "didn't realize what kind of business that we were, even though we had all of these tools, and we had these technologies, and we were developing new tools and technologies."[15]

Over time, through work with a couple of large clients, BSD's business model crystallized, and its strategy services and technology platform grew more sophisticated.[16] One early important client for the digital strategy side of the business was Senator Ted Kennedy's 2006 reelection campaign. For BSD's staffers, Kennedy posed a novel challenge: How could the firm build an online program for someone whose brand was primarily established offline? BSD first worked with the senator's staffers to create the basic components of an online campaign, such as building an e-mail list and website from scratch. As Kevin Thurman, the early BSD staffer, explains, at the time the firm often had to walk clients through very basic technological planning:

> A lot of what Internet strategy was in 2005 was explaining to everyone else what needed to be happening so we could raise the money and build the list and accomplish all the other goals that they [the clients] wanted to accomplish depending on who they were. It also just kind of involved the mundane work of going through a website design process with people who hadn't really done that kind of thing before. Now most of those kind of staffers have done it a half dozen times and have opinions about what that was, but at the time it was difficult.[17]

Rospars and Thurman worked on developing the Kennedy campaign's e-mail program. Rospars found himself having to write for an entirely new candidate for the first time. To develop Kennedy's online voice, Rospars and Thurman studied the candidate's major and most recent speeches and immersed themselves in his biography, including buying memorabilia from previous campaigns on Ebay. Thurman describes the importance of this process for the young digital consultants: "Learning how to do that and create that voice was a really important piece of the puzzle and it's not anything new, it's not inventive . . . but the difference was the kind of quality that was created through the process."[18]

On the technology side of BSD, MoveOn Student Action was an important early client. Ben Brandzel founded MoveOn Student Action in August 2004 to register youth and turn them out for the general election. Brandzel was a Dean field staffer in New Hampshire who later became the advocacy director for MoveOn and worked for Edwards in 2008 and Organizing for America. Clay Johnson and Brandzel talked for months before coming to a deal. Ultimately, Brandzel hired BSD to build new tools for MoveOn Student Action, in large part on the strength of the appeal that the organization would be funding developments in a platform that could benefit the entire progressive community. Through its work with MoveOn Student Action, BSD made a number of improvements to its contribution and mass e-mail systems. The firm also developed new tools, including a team fund-raising application.

In addition to MoveOn, two other large clients made significant contributions to the platform: ProgressNow and the Democratic Party. In its work for these clients, BSD developed its platform as a modular structure. Clients such as ProgressNow and the party funded new modules for the platform, and could opt into the different functionalities of the system on an as-needed basis.

## MYPROGRESS

A couple of months before the campaign ended, when Dean still looked likely to win the nomination, Clay Johnson and Bobby Clark, director of Internet fund-raising, began talking about what, in an ideal world, they wanted for the general election in terms of technology. The two took stock of what they had learned and what they wished they had at the beginning of the campaign, as well as imagined what the possibilities were "to go big."[19] They had just started that conversation when the campaign began to fall apart. Clark and Johnson both ended up staying on until the bitter end, when the remaining staffers had a big picnic and snowball fight on the day that Dean announced he was withdrawing from the race.

While Johnson was launching BSD soon after the primaries, Clark consulted for a couple of campaigns and ballot initiatives in Florida and Utah, mostly setting up Convio systems to handle donations and e-mail. After subsequently working on some local political issues in Colorado, in January 2005 Clark became the deputy director of ProgressNow, then a Colorado-based progressive advocacy organization.[20] ProgressNow was one of a number of initiatives founded in the wake of Kerry's defeat. And, like many other organizations at this time, donors wanted ProgressNow to "really actively and aggressively engage people online."[21]

ProgressNow provided Clark and Johnson with the opportunity to extend their conversations and to rethink the tools the two had used on the Dean campaign. While brainstorming ideas for ProgressNow with Johnson, Clark called Zephyr Teachout and asked her what the most useful technology during the campaign was. Teachout's answer was Yahoo! Groups. From Teachout's perspective, Yahoo! Groups were a key part of the campaign as a tool for local supporter organizing and a means for staffers to identify talent. Yet, as detailed above, the tool's utility was limited by the fact that campaign staffers could not systematically gather data on group members or activities and lacked the ability to communicate with volunteer organizers. Local groups, meanwhile, had no way of identifying the existence of other groups in their geographic region, and supporters had no easy way of finding or joining a group.

In early 2005, Clark and Johnson wrote a proposal to ProgressNow outlining a "MyProgress" campaign platform. The core of their proposal was to build new group-building functions on top of the platform that BSD was providing to DFA and MoveOn Student Action. This proposed group functionality would enable individuals to launch their own local organizing efforts. ProgressNow staffers, in turn, could capture information such as e-mail addresses and track the activities of groups through the platform. Clark and Johnson worked out a licensing and pricing deal, with ProgressNow funding significant components of the BSD platform's development.

After months of development, in September 2005, BSD rolled out MyProgress in Colorado, with testing continuing throughout the year. Blue State Digital then launched the platform for ProgressNow's Ohio affiliate in 2006, and subsequently for its affiliates across the country, 12 in all by the 2008 election. While staffers describe MyProgress as a success, as Clark puts it, "having a platform available doesn't mean that anybody is going to use it."[22] While the e-mail and database functions of these platforms received a lot of use, the social networking suite of tools and group applications were underutilized. Unlike the Obama campaign, which used the same BSD toolset, ProgressNow struggled to draw its supporters to the platform for organizing purposes. Clark explains this discrepancy in terms of the difference between the extraordinary attention to presidential politics and singular goal of the Obama campaign and the more complex, multi-issue advocacy of ProgressNow: "We think part of the difference [is that] there is (A) a charismatic candidate; (B) a very clear purposeful organization where everybody clearly shared the same objective and we are just not like that. We are multiple organizations, we work on lots of things, we aren't like a campaign for president."[23]

## Restructuring the Democratic Party

While Johnson worked with ProgressNow, his business partners Joe Rospars and Ben Self followed Dean to the party. Soon after his election, Dean asked Rospars and Self to take 30 days to assess the party's technical and organizational infrastructure. In addition to the widespread problems with voter data documented extensively below, Rospars and Self found that the party lacked an online presence and effective organizational infrastructure for leveraging technology in its operations. A sprawling, 30-member Technology Department worked out of the basement of the party's headquarters. There was little in the way of role specialization for this department, with these staffers in charge of everything from the party's servers, software, and making sure everyone had a computer, to managing e-mail fund-raising, blogging, and content on the website. There were, for instance, a number of teams responsible for information technology, Demzilla (the party's Federal Election Commission donations reporting tool), Datamart (the original party voter file), technical systems, and the Internet. Some staffers even served on multiple teams. Confusingly, a separate small Internet team existed in the Finance Department and engaged in e-mail fund-raising. Meanwhile, across all of its departments, the party relied on systems that rarely worked well and lacked much of the functionality that Rospars and Self anticipated needing for an effective electoral effort during the next presidential cycle.

### ORGANIZATIONAL STRUCTURE

To remedy this, a report by Rospars and Self outlined a four-year strategic plan to implement new online outreach efforts and to rebuild the party's voter file. It also proposed a new organizational structure to facilitate these technical projects. Dean and Tom McMahon, the party's new executive director and veteran political staffer who had served as the deputy director of the Dean campaign and head of Democracy for America, embraced this plan. Rospars and Self took a leave from BSD to head up these efforts. With the two at the DNC, Clay Johnson took over management of the firm in D.C., with Franklin-Hodge leading the newly launched Boston office.

At the party, Self became the technology director, flying to Washington, D.C., on Mondays and returning home to Kentucky on Friday nights for four years. In this capacity, Self was initially responsible for the Technology Department. Under the tight time line that Dean had set out, Self quickly got a website and online system up and running that were similar to what BSD had implemented for Democracy for America. This enabled the party to engage in online fund-raising and organizing as well as send mass and targeted e-mails to supporters. Johnson helped integrate the party's content management system with its online applications. Rospars, meanwhile, immediately took on the task of building the party's e-mail list, signing up over 400,000 supporters in 2005, all without having access to Kerry's e-mail list.

As they sought to meet these immediate needs, Rospars and Self worked to restructure the party's technical operations. They recognized, even as they helped usher in, the increasing specialization of technology staffers and development of distinct genres of online communications that occurred in the wake of the 2004 elections. Rospars and Self created a stand-alone Internet Department, responsible for all online organizing, communications, and fund-raising, staffed by a number of individuals from the Technology Department. Reorganization meant that staffers could develop and utilize distinct skill sets, whether that entailed fixing hardware, maintaining a financial database, or fund-raising over e-mail, which was now distinct from the direct mail efforts of the finance staffers.

The newly reconstituted Internet Department, meanwhile, took on increased prominence within the party as part of the 50-state strategy. The party made the head of the Internet Department a member of the senior staff, and moved staffers' offices to the third floor of headquarters, right outside the chairman's office. Rospars became the first head of this department, assuming leadership over the online organizing efforts, a position he held for more than 15 months. In this role, as detailed below, Rospars guided the party's online electoral work through the 2006 midterm elections.

Under Dean's leadership, the party also embarked on other large infrastructural projects: rebuilding the party's voter file and implementing a new online platform for electoral campaigning. Both made substantial contributions to Democratic electoral victories in 2006 and 2008, as well as provided the Obama campaign with better data and more powerful platforms for its new media and field operations.

## The Democratic Party and Voter Activation Network

After helping to reorganize the technical operations, Self turned to building a truly national voter file and interface system to support the field efforts of the party's candidates and national and state organizations. This was a priority for Dean, given his vow to contest elections in all 50 states and to rebuild the state parties. Rospars and Self's findings made it clear that the national party's voter file was in complete disarray. The data was of extremely low quality and, despite the considerable investment of former chairman Terry McAuliffe in a national voter database, the party's basic technology was lacking. The national party had few means of compiling and storing data on the electorate or even its supporters.

The state parties' voter files were not much better. State parties often relied on a host of questionable outside vendors for their data, the voter files they did maintain were outdated, and many state databases crashed during the 2004 elections. Meanwhile, staffers at the national and state parties had antagonistic relationships, and there was little buy-in among the states for McAuliffe's initiatives. In lieu of any national and centralized voter file and database system, which the Republicans had developed in the mid-1990s, data was incompatible across state lines and presidential campaigns had to rely on many separate systems for their field operations.[24] Indeed, data was such a problem that during the 2004 general election the Democrats' moneyed elite developed independent voter file efforts and turnout operations.

As the former data architect for the Dean campaign, Self knew well the patchwork nature and varying quality of the national and state voter files and the challenges that this posed for candidates. Even more, Self knew that there was no standardized set of tools for working with the national and state parties' voter data, which meant that candidates mostly had access to raw data sets. Self decided to commission an audit of the entire voter file, focusing on what went right and wrong in 2004 and what the party would need to accomplish to run an effective field operation in 2008. To do so, he hired Zack Exley, the Kerry campaign staffer who consulted for the Dean campaign while at MoveOn, and Josh Hendler, the manager of software development for the Kerry campaign who got his start in politics as a programmer for Clark for President. Hendler subsequently became the party's director of political data and analytics and later the director of technology, after Self stepped down.

This report became the blueprint for the party's effort to rebuild its entire data infrastructure from the ground up. Understanding the difficulty of this task requires a close look at the history of Democratic Party data over the last decade.

## PARTY VOTER DATA AT THE TURN OF THE CENTURY

Candidates often repeat the aphorism that "all politics is local." For much of the twentieth century and well into the first decade of the twenty-first, the saying was true for the Democratic Party's voter data.[25] Unlike the Republican Party, which had a strong centralized party organization and corresponding national voter file that grew out of pioneering direct mail efforts, the Democratic Party had a more decentralized structure, with strong state party organizations. The voter files of the state parties reflected this. Each state maintained its own record of its electorate, chose the information it collected and the systems it used to house data, set its own rules of access, and determined the data's format. Across states, there was little in the way of standard categories of information collected or practices for updating voter records. The Iowa Democratic Party, for instance, kept detailed caucus records dating back over a decade, while other states lacked anything more than a list of registered voters.

Meanwhile, many of these state party voter files were of lower quality than those provided by commercial vendors, which meant that candidates often had to rely on third parties for their field operations. For example, the most reliable way for Democratic presidential candidates to access voter data in a state such as New Hampshire was to hire one of the commercial vendors that dominated the market for political data up through the 2004 election cycle. One such vendor is Aristotle, one of the largest voter data firms that provides both Democrats and Republicans with a host of demographic (race, ethnicity, gender, etc.), public (addresses, party registration, turnout records, real estate purchases, etc.), and commercial marketing (credit card purchases and magazine subscriptions, etc.) data on the electorate, grouped by congressional district.[26] The firm stores this voter data in-house. Before these files were widely available online after 2004, candidates would pay Aristotle for particular types of data, which would then be sent to campaigns on index cards six weeks before the election. Campaigns then organized these cards into "walk lists," which volunteers took with them into the field. As they made in-person contact with voters, volunteers scribbled notes about their conversations all over the walk lists. Volunteers then returned their lists with the information from these voter contacts to the campaign offices. All too frequently, these walk lists would just sit in big boxes and the information would never be entered into any sort of filing system or database.

In other words, for most of the first half of the decade, the value of voter contact for Democratic campaigns lay in the moment of interaction. Without developed practices and attendant technologies for gathering and storing data, as well as transferring and sharing it across campaigns and election cycles, candidates lacked the capacity to know much about their potential supporters and the electorate more generally. Data often just disappeared between election cycles or was otherwise on a proprietary platform that rendered it unusable.

## THE ROOTS OF VOTER ACTIVATION NETWORK

The same structure that resulted in a highly fragmented voter file system ironically also fostered the local innovation and competition that enabled the Democratic Party's data efforts and field operations to surpass those of the Republicans by the 2008 presidential campaign. A mounting frustration with the lack of quality data for field campaigns led to a number of state-level party, candidate, and commercial efforts to improve the situation. As they matured over the years, Self was in a position to consider the best of these initiatives during the process of planning the national voter database. In contrast, the Republicans had nationalized their voter file much earlier and had built modifications to their database system on an older technology base. Given that they had superior voter files, databases, and turnout operations, in addition to enjoying the presidency for much of the 2000s, there was little incentive to develop new systems.[27] As a result, the Republican Party had fallen behind the Democrats in its knowledge of the electorate by the 2008 presidential campaign.

Voter Activation Network (VAN) began as one of these state-level efforts to improve the party's voter data. The firm had modest origins in the electorally important state of Iowa. In 2002, Iowa Governor Tom Vilsack and Senator Tom Harkin were both facing reelection campaigns. The two campaigns were collaborating with each other on a shared campaign finance database, an effort that was led by Mark Sullivan. Sullivan had been working in Iowa politics for over a decade, having gotten his start as a delegate tracker for Harkin's presidential campaign in 1992. During Harkin's 1996 Senate reelection race, Sullivan built a database that catalogued every vote the senator had made and every bill he sponsored. As the data consultant to both Vilsack and Harkin's campaigns in 2002, Sullivan was asked to solicit and vet proposals from companies to build an Internet-based voter file that the two campaigns could share so that they were not replicating their canvass efforts. The idea was ultimately to make this voter file accessible online to all other Democratic campaigns in Iowa so they could upload and share the results of their field operations, making the voter file more comprehensive, accurate, and powerful.

In 2002, using the Internet to build a distributed voter file was not a new idea, and campaign consultants widely discussed the potential advantages of doing so. In addition, many thought about the potential of using mobile technologies for the purposes of canvassing and storing data. There were, for instance, attempts in a number of states soon after the 2000 elections to build Internet-based systems so that organizers could download voter records, update them on their Palm Pilots as they went door to door, and later synchronize them with voter files. This was inspired in part by the Gore campaign's innovative and successful push for supporters to vote absentee in select states during the 2000 presidential election, an effort that required field coordination and reliable data. Meanwhile, campaigns believed that Palm Pilots would help solve the problem of generating quality data. Creating technologically enforced pre-determined data categories on personal devices would not only make it easier to enter and store data, it would preclude the entry of information that campaigns generally deem irrelevant (information other than party affiliation, vote preference, likelihood to vote, and issue concerns). For state campaigns, an Internet-accessible database would allow headquarters to track the progress of field efforts in different locales, allocate resources more effectively, and monitor the mood of the electorate. Meanwhile, even rival primary campaigns would be able to benefit from each others' field efforts, as would nominees, and ultimately the databases of the state parties would be improved. While the advantages of an Internet-based and shared voter database were clear, efforts to create one failed in the face of a large technical challenge relating to access. There was simply no easy way to build a shared system with multiple users accessing, downloading, and uploading information simultaneously.

While the Harkin and Vilsack campaigns began soliciting bids in 2002, they ultimately asked Sullivan to build a cheaper system in-house. Steve Adler, a programmer and consultant to the Massachusetts AFL-CIO who was also working on voter databases, joined Sullivan. When working out the details of an arrangement with the Harkin and Vilsack campaigns, Sullivan and Adler broke with the contractual norm of the industry. As noted above, historically a host of commercial firms controlled most of the quality voter data and sold their services to individual campaigns. This created a situation in which state parties and candidates not only were beholden to firms such as Aristotle for their basic field operations, but there was no way to share data across Democratic campaigns and electoral cycles. To remedy this problem, Sullivan explicitly set out to "break the vendor hold on data" in the hopes that the system they built would not just benefit Harkin and Vilsack but also the state and perhaps national Democratic Party.[28] To this end, Sullivan and Adler intentionally wrote their contract so that the Iowa Democratic Party owned the data after the election and had the ability to control access to it.

Sullivan and Adler completed their prototype in 2002. Calling their firm "Voter Activation Network" followed soon after, when a designer needed a quick decision on a name. The decision about the ownership of data influenced Sullivan and Adler's design for their prototype voter file interface. Since their company would not own any data, its database and interface system was designed to be entirely data and vendor neutral. In other words, it would not matter where the data originated, it would become formatted for the interface as it flowed through the system. One consequence of this design decision is that later on the interface could easily incorporate other state voter files, even though the data varied in terms of the types of information stored and its format. It also meant that commercial data could easily be added to these state voter files. It is worth quoting Mike Sager, a current VAN staffer, at length as to how this model works:

> Think about it [VAN] as Excel. Excel doesn't care whether you are
> working on an accounting spreadsheet or a whatever. You've got your
> columns, you've got your rows. VAN is the same thing, whatever the

data is you got your columns and your rows and then depending on the types of data you have . . . there are new sections that can be turned on and off for it. The data is not uniform between states. Each state's voter file is different so the data that will come from individual states is completely different in format and layout and how they record things. One state might have one column with voting history separated by commas, another state might have it where they have a column for each piece of voting history. All of that stuff is different state to state and some states have party registration and some states don't have party registration, states carry different things on the file, some states have age, some have the birth date. The VAN system . . . once the data is processed, whatever the data is, whatever form it comes in, . . . standardizes the user interface so that a user who sees data in Virginia, uses it in Virginia, will be instantly familiar if they jump into Colorado.[29]

This prototype developed for the 2002 electoral cycle in Iowa was, by all accounts, a considerable improvement over what was available in voter file interface and database technology at the time. The Iowa state party provided campaigns across the state with online access to the VAN, which enabled them to generate walk lists and to upload the results of their canvasses. The VAN also featured a Palm Pilot application, which facilitated the ability of campaigns to collect and store data at voters' doorsteps. The VAN was also widely used. Unlike other systems, Sullivan and Adler expressly designed the interface of the VAN with field staffers in mind. Given Sullivan's extensive work on-the-ground, he knew the cultural hurdles to getting field staffers to adopt new technologies, given well-developed and long-established work practices. All of which made for a successful debut. Harkin's campaign, for instance, used the VAN to expand upon Gore's absentee voting field push. As a result, Harkin was able to amass a lead of 60,000 votes going into election day in 2002.

## THE 2004 ELECTION CYCLE

Soon after VAN's debut, the Missouri Democratic Party sought to have the firm build a similar system for their voter file. A number of states followed suit; heading into the 2004 elections, VAN was active in 11 states. The firm's work in Iowa provided the basic template for the VAN model. First, VAN helped clean the voter files of its state party clients so that they could enter the firm's system. The core of these voter files is the basic list of all registered voters, their addresses, gender, party affiliations, and congressional districts, and a host of other information that varies by state (such as phone numbers), all of which state governments periodically update. VAN then combines this public voter roll with the data files maintained by the state parties. These party voter files contain supplementary information, such as the information gleaned during canvasses when volunteers go door to door to find out whether individuals are registered to vote, what candidate they support and the degree to which they support them, and what issues matter to them. These canvasses are also key to updating voter information, such as changes of address. Under proprietary systems, this canvass data was often lost because candidates and parties did not have direct access to voter databases. In contrast, under the VAN model, state parties retain ownership and control over their data in exchange for payment for use of the system, so the file is continually updated.

Second, state party clients set access policies for their voter files. States decide whether to sell or provide their voter files for free and determine which candidates can access the VAN. The standard model is for state parties to sell all primary candidates on the ballot access to the voter file. The Iowa Democratic Party, for instance, charged presidential candidates $50,000 to access its data in 2004 (in 2008 this fee was $100,000). Then, when a nominee emerges, the winner takes control of all the data generated during the primaries by her opponents for the purposes of the general election and the losing candidates are locked out of the system. The advantage of this system is that it facilitates data sharing across electoral cycles and campaigns. For one, VAN's approach helps keep the addresses and contact information of voters who change residences over the years up to date, and creates an evolving record of voter contact. Meanwhile, during an election cycle, all the Democratic candidates in a particular state, from U.S. senator to state representative, simultaneously upload their canvass data into the same voter file. This practice amplifies the reach of all Democratic ground efforts, enabling candidates for different offices to benefit from each others' field programs. These data-sharing practices are not always rosy in practice. Indeed, conflicts over access to data and candidates seeking strategic advantage over competitors means that data is not always perfectly shared. Over time, VAN built a more nuanced system that enables state parties to close parts of the voter file database off, depending on internal party negotiations. The firm also built a number of modifications to its interface that refined its tiers of access. Campaigns can provide senior field staffers with access to greater functionality than low-level volunteers, such as the ability to define canvass queries, to set universes of targets, and to generate reports on field operations.

In addition to the 11 state parties that worked with VAN in 2004, America Coming Together (ACT), a privately funded mobilization and turnout venture founded by party financiers such as George Soros, Democratic advocacy organizations, and unions, hired VAN to provide voter file services in 11 swing states. Changes in election law with the passage of the Bipartisan Campaign Reform Act (otherwise known as the McCain-Feingold Act) made organizations like ACT (organized under section "527" of the federal tax code) an important new site of election activity in 2004. ACT became the primary vehicle for Democratic allies to spend "soft money" (money not given directly to federal candidates or used to promote specific candidacies) on voter registration, turnout, and issue advocacy. Importantly, ACT could not formally coordinate its efforts with the Kerry campaign or the national and state Democratic parties. ACT was part of a larger coalition called America Votes, another 527 founded at the same time by the heads of a number of influential organizations, such as EMILY's List and the Service Employees International Union. Whereas ACT attempted to be a large field operation, America Votes served to promote issues, coordinate activities, and share infrastructure and data among the disparate groups active during the 2004 elections and the progressive community more generally.

Under the direction of Steve Rosenthal, the former political director of the AFL-CIO, ACT staffers vetted the market for voter file service providers in the run up to the 2004 presidential election. ACT hired VAN for a pilot project to build a system for the Philadelphia mayoral race in 2003. In the process, VAN rebuilt its Palm Pilot application with increased capacity to handle what would be a much more extensive presidential field effort. During the general election, ACT parceled out its states to VAN and two other firms.

With 11 ACT states and 11 state parties using its data infrastructure, VAN was at the center of ground efforts in 2004. Given that ACT could not coordinate its efforts with the state parties under the restrictions of the 527 tax code under which it operated, VAN set up two parallel multistate systems. The data that ACT deployed for its field efforts, however, was much more extensive than that of VAN's state party clients and the campaigns using these voter files. In 2004, most campaigns started from standard precinct-level modeling and supplemented it with the state party voter files. For example, campaigns receive precinct-level data furnished by the National Committee for an Effective Congress (NCEC), a political organization cofounded by Eleanor Roosevelt in 1948, which provides a host of campaign services to Democratic candidates. The NCEC analyzes precincts based on historical voting trends, turnout rates, registered voters, and partisan identification, and scores them for their likelihood to vote Democratic. Facing resource constraints, campaigns would generally spend only in places where they have the strongest likelihood of turning out their voters. Campaigns, for instance, wanted to focus on precincts where they would have high impact, such as places with high percentages of Democrats but low voter turnout. They wanted to avoid precincts where they might have low impact, such as places with few Democratic voters. In 2004, given the low quality of much state-level data, campaigns would often just focus on the entire priority precinct, knocking on everyone's door. This was highly inefficient. In-person contact is not only resource intensive, but blanketing a precinct netted many contacts with Republican voters. For those campaigns with access to better data, such as in states with more developed voter files, field operations would target particular voters within high priority precincts. In other words, rather than knocking on every door, campaigns used voter files to target independents or, in cases where more information was known from canvassing, voters who have crossed party lines to support Democrats in the past.

These precinct-level operations are ultimately about the efficiency of deploying volunteers in geographic space. Better data on the electorate enables campaigns to route around the inherent inefficiencies of targeting whole precincts. One advantage that Republicans had in 2004 was a much more sophisticated individual voter identification and turnout operation, which enabled field staffers to "cherry pick" the electorate. Operatives identified and selectively targeted Republican voters to turn out in heavily Democratic precincts.

Seeking the same ability to target individuals, but lacking the party voter file data that Republicans had, ACT purchased a trove of credit card data. Groups such as ACT found the possibility of exactly knowing the electorate so intriguing that they invested millions of dollars in acquiring these databases, generated complicated statistical models of the electorate based on hundreds of variables, and targeted their field operations around what the data supposedly foretold. In practice, this meant that ACT relied on factoids about market behavior to create micro-niches of voters that had limited utility. For example, ACT generated these niches by analyzing data about what kinds of cars people purchased, magazines they read, what they bought at the grocery store, and demographic information such as ethnicity and geographic location. In the end, however, the profusion of data simply posed a new problem: there was no effective way of making it meaningful. As Mark Sullivan notes:

> They [America Coming Together] were trying to be more forward with data. At this point everyone was enthralled by consumer marketing data, and we all felt clever that we could now tell you who buys cat food at the grocery store and who buys dog food—or who reads this magazine and that magazine. But nobody knew what to do with that information.[30]

In the end, these long strings of variables and complex formulas offered little predictive insight over basic party identification and turnout data. As detailed below, the practices of predictive voter modeling that more effectively made this data on the electorate meaningful developed through much trial and error and only really came to fruition for the Democrats during the 2008 election cycle.

In the end, ACT's use of this commercial data both strained extant database systems and left the organization spending scarce resources creating voter models that had only tentative connections to vote choice. Despite ACT deploying over 10,000 canvassers—3,000 in Ohio alone—the organization could not counter a strong Republican voter contact effort and the larger dynamics of a race decided by national security concerns.[31] Meanwhile, while ACT and the Kerry campaign purchased data from each other as a way to maximize resources as much as was legally permissible, the fragmentation of field efforts hurt the nominee. The state voter file systems did not perform much better. A month before the election, the voter file databases in Ohio, Florida, and Pennsylvania all collapsed under the demands of the field operations, and organizers were left cobbling together data from a host of third-party firms. Even more important, given the fact that many states relied on different vendors to manage their voter file, the staffers on the Kerry campaign had to spend a lot of resources learning different systems and negotiating and coordinating with state parties and local candidates. In the end, Democratic field and data efforts came up short. Amanda Michel, who ran Kerry's Ohio Internet operations with Zack Exley, describes the field effort in 2004:

> The Kerry campaign was basically a parachute operation, or more like a traveling circus. A bunch of well-intentioned earnest college graduates were dropped-in mid summer. It took them a month to figure out who actually knew what in town and what they were doing and by then we were already in the end phase of get-out-the-vote. It seemed like a totally ass backwards strategy to me. And then, at the end of the campaign I watched everyone walk out of the Kerry office with boxes of contact information. All of the people we had worked with, they had the sense of like "oh not only did we lose the election, we just kind of lost the whole infrastructure."[32]

## REBUILDING THE PARTY'S DATA INFRASTRUCTURE BETWEEN THE PRESIDENTIAL ELECTIONS

Kerry's defeat found much of the party and its allied groups wandering in the political wilderness. A number of Democratic Party allies underwent significant changes. Perceived as ineffective by many in the party, America Coming Together disbanded. The consensus among progressive leaders was that America Votes would be able to replace and improve upon ACT's field efforts and coordinate voter registration, identification, and mobilization. One positive result of the 2004 presidential election for Democrats was that the VAN system captured the data that thousands of ACT canvassers had generated going door to door during the campaign and made it available to the other members of the America Votes coalition. Indeed, VAN was one of the few organizations that had its reputation bolstered during the general wreckage of the 2004 campaign cycle, given that its systems proved to be the most reliable of the providers on the market. After the election, the firm immediately invested in its hardware and software. In addition to VAN, other actors set out to rebuild the data infrastructure of the party from the ground up, very much with an eye on 2008. For example, the long-time Democratic political consultant and advisor Harold Ickes launched the firm Catalist in 2005 to provide data and analytics services to campaigns and political organizations.[33] Ickes started Catalist with ACT data from the 2004 election, and many former Democratic Party staffers from Terry McAuliffe's tenure took on leadership roles in the organization.

As these organizations sorted out the field of Democratic allies after the election, Ben Self and his team set out to completely rebuild the data infrastructure of the party for the 2006 midterm elections. To do so, the national party had to forge a new relationship with the state parties. This was a significant challenge. There were years of distrust between the national party and the states. Many of the state parties complained that the only time they heard from the national party was during important federal races, when staffers demanded that the states run their electoral operations in particular ways. As chairman, Dean started to change this dynamic. For example, to implement the 50-state strategy, the national party started asking states what their priorities were in terms of resources. Meanwhile, Self remembers that he was tasked early on with reaching out to the state parties. Self attended his first meeting with a state party two weeks after he started and his "instructions were just get in front of the room and let them yell at you for an hour or so and hopefully that will end the yelling and then you will be able to start repairing."

Repairing this relationship was crucial, given Self's need to negotiate data "swap agreements" between the national and state parties. These swap agreements were an integral part of Dean's 50-state strategy, as they would build the infrastructure of the state parties even as they would help the party's presidential candidate in 2008.[34] As such, the national party offered to clean and supplement the data of the state parties, as well as provide the databases to house and fund an online interface to access this data. This came to be an approximately $6 million undertaking, requiring both technological development and hiring staff and outside vendors. The national party proposed funding all of this in exchange for the state parties sharing their data. While state parties would still retain formal ownership, they had to provide their data to the national party. The state parties, meanwhile, would set their own rules to determine which candidates could use the voter files and what functionality and types of data they would have access to. States would also be able to charge campaigns for access to their voter files, provided that it was a fixed price. These voter files, meanwhile, would be continually updated through canvassing conducted by campaigns during election cycles.

Negotiations between the Association of State Democratic Chairs, state party heads, and Self's team took over six months. In the end, the national party signed up 45 states during this time period. During the 2008 cycle, 48 of 50 states used the national party's database.[35] These agreements between the national and state parties created the basic institutional arrangement and contractual obligations that underpinned the construction of the party's first truly national voter database. With the swap agreements in place, Self and his team rebuilt the data infrastructure of the national party from the ground up. This included buying new servers and creating a new database for these voter files, which was designed by the Boston firm Intelligent Integration Systems. The database created voter file silos for each state that kept their data separate. At the same time, the national party's staffers and presidential candidates could access all of these silos and query across them. The party also came up with guidelines for data quality, type, and format, creating a set of standards for how the state parties needed to maintain their data.

In building their national voter database in 2006, the Democrats had a technical advantage over the Republicans.[36] Party staffers utilized a new generation of database systems and Internet applications for their effort, as well as leveraged dramatic improvements in storage capacity and processing speeds. In addition to having more sophisticated tools at their disposal, the Democrats built their database and, later, interface in a much more integrated fashion than what was possible when the Republicans launched VoterVault in 1995. As such, the narrative of a game of technological "catch-up" often reported in the political press is not quite accurate. Different systems have different paths of development. The Democrats were able to surpass the Republicans in 2008 in terms of their database infrastructure because their technical efforts occurred in a markedly different context with different underlying technologies.

The party also engaged in a massive data-cleaning effort to make its information on the electorate as accurate as possible, hiring firms to provide such things as correct phone numbers. Staffers also hired vendors to provide better data on voters, particularly in states that the national party and presidential candidates had long ignored but that were newly relevant under Dean's 50-state approach. The party also purchased commercial data on the electorate and hired analytic firms to create better voter models and micro-targeting programs.

The 2006 election cycle was also the source of much learning about the effective use of these various data streams. As detailed above, in 2004, Democratic campaigns mostly used precinct-level data to develop their field plans. Depending on the quality of state-level data, campaigns would either knock on every door or identify targets within priority precincts. Meanwhile, during that cycle, organizations such as ACT used extensive commercial data to create micro-niches of supporters based on their lifestyle and demographic characteristics, which often proved counterproductive in practice.

In 2006, data consultants began using these thousands of individual data points to construct mega "clusters" (12 in all) of the electorate along the lines of "suburban values" voters and "latte-drinking young urbanites." Essentially, this was the attempt to develop composite categories (clusters) out of the mess of micro-level factoids used in 2004. The problem, however, was both that field organizers were still swimming in data and these lifestyle clusters were not tied in any real way to voter attitudes or behavior. Junior-level staffers, for instance, often had the ability to access consumer marketing data, and could engage in such activities as searching for people of a certain income or looking to see how many kids they had, in addition to seeing what lifestyle clusters their universe of contacts belonged to. The lifestyle clusters, meanwhile, were not helpful in terms of the information most useful to field campaigners. As Sullivan describes:

> In 2006 all the rage was these clusters. . . . There are all of these people buying these things, these life cycle models that described voters as within these 12 groups, such as "angry catholic manufacturers". . . . And all that stuff was the rage, and everybody talked about it. And after the 2006 elections they just all disappear off the face of the earth. I am sure that there must have been a lot of analysis done saying this is not really where it was at. And, in 2008 you got down to the really standard scores over and over: turnout, persuasion, candidate support.[37]

The data challenges of 2006 were part of a necessary process of trial and error that helped improve practices of data modeling and management for the 2008 elections. After the midterm elections, data consultants began to much more systematically use data to create models of voter attitudes and behavior. What proved effective was distilling hundreds of data points into even simpler categories of voters: likely supporters, those who can be persuaded, and those supporting the other candidate. As detailed in Chapter 6, these voter models were key to the turnout and persuasion operations of the Obama field campaign. Alongside the refinement of modeling techniques, VAN and campaigns also came up with more sophisticated ways of *managing* data flows around field efforts. After assessing its work during the 2006 midterm elections, VAN staffers created more refined tiers of data access, enabling campaigns to restrict the ability of all but the highest level staffers to see the raw data. The VAN actually became more effective by the decision of many subsequent campaigns to limit the ability of field organizers to access data.

Meanwhile, right after the 2006 midterm elections, Self and his team issued a request for proposals to build an interface for the new national Democratic Party voter file. As detailed above, state parties had existing relationships with their own vendors, and there was a wide range of providers and very large variation in the quality of database and interface technologies when Self issued this RFP. The databases of the state parties in Ohio and Pennsylvania, for instance, both crashed in the months leading up to the midterm elections. VAN's reputation, however, was enhanced through its work during the 2006 midterm elections. VAN worked with 25 state parties, making it the largest vendor to the states. In addition, the firm was active in two dozen states through the work of America Votes, which coordinated independent field efforts for Democrats in races across the country for governor, U.S. House, and U.S. Senate. America Votes hired VAN to provide the interface to the Catalist data, which was fashioned from the multiple and fragmentary data sources used in ACT's field operations during the 2004 presidential campaign. America Votes subsequently became one of VAN's largest clients, and the primary way in which the firm's technology spread among Democratic-allied organizations.

The party hired VAN in February 2007 to build the interface for the new national voter file, partly on the strength of its work with the state parties and America Votes. The choice was fraught with difficulties, given that states had existing relationships with different data vendors. In addition to its reliability, VAN also had the advantage of having already worked with multiple state parties. This meant that many state-level organizers and political operatives would be familiar with the new system. In essence, there was a:

> sub generation of field organizers who had used the data . . . They had already used it for a cycle, many on state-level races. . . . So, suddenly you could drop the field organizer into a brand new state and not have to train them on a completely new tool set with totally different capabilities.[38]

This system became "VoteBuilder," the branded name that refers to the Democratic party's data (the state voter files as well as commercial data) and the VAN interface system around it. For states already using VAN, the national party took over their extant contracts. VoteBuilder offered field organizers and campaign staffers a range of tools. Like earlier incarnations of the VAN interface, campaign staffers could run queries on the electorate, target particular voters, and then easily plot them on a map to create walk lists for volunteers (see figure 4.3). These organizers and staffers could upload data, ensuring that canvassing information was routinely captured. The VAN tool also continued to offer campaigns a well-designed, user-friendly interface. The VAN interface also included some new features developed during the 2006 election cycle. The firm's staffers noticed that its state party and organizational clients were creating spreadsheets and files outside the VAN to track and manage the work of volunteers. At the time, there was nothing in the VAN that helped campaigns manage their volunteers. In response to this need, VAN built "MyCampaign," a volunteer management

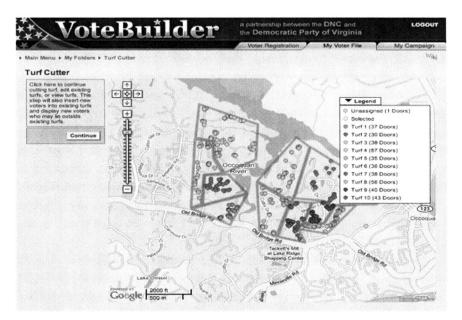

*Figure 4.3* Screenshot of VoteBuilder

database that enabled field staffers to input the names of supporters, track their activities, interests, and history, and schedule people for events.

Meanwhile, the national voter database and interface furthered the party's efforts to strengthen its nominee in 2008, a key reason that Dean invested in the effort. For one, the party's general election candidate would have access to a national voter database that contained the best of what each state had to offer, in addition to all the improvements in data that the national party made and the data generated during the primary campaign. This meant that the nominee would have much better knowledge of the electorate during the election. In addition, the system was far more reliable than those of the patchwork of vendors active during the 2004 and 2006 elections, which would enable the nominee's campaign to conduct field efforts in critical battleground states without fear of losing its data infrastructure. Campaign staffers would also have the ease of needing to know only one system (which proved important for Clinton's and Obama's staffers during the extensive primary campaign). At the same time, given the data-sharing model, the massive volunteer mobilization and field efforts behind the presidential primary campaigns would benefit state-level candidates, even as their canvass efforts improved and extended the data available to the nominee. As Mike Sager, the VAN staffer and the former national VoteBuilder administrator for the Democratic Party, describes:

> From the data perspective, the beauty of VoteBuilder and the whole DNC contract is that someone running for state senate or mayor has

access to the same exact data as someone running for president. There is no tier there and no matter what you are running for you have access to the same information and the same tools and as a result you are enriching the file just as much as the presidential campaign.[39]

By the end of 2007, the party had created the institutional arrangements necessary to build a national voter file, had rebuilt much of its core database infrastructure, had commissioned VAN to build the interface for the database, and had enrolled the state parties in the new VoteBuilder system. Together, this work built the core of the data infrastructure for Democratic candidates during the 2008 cycle. However, this is only half of the story of the effort to wire the party and its affiliated organizations between election cycles. As Self was putting VoteBuilder into place, in the newly formed and independent Internet Department, Joe Rospars was implementing both new practices for online organizing and a powerful new online electoral platform that the party deployed in 2006 under the name "PartyBuilder."

## PartyBuilder: Online Organizing at the Democratic Party

In early 2005, Rospars's team first turned their attention to creating a culture and practice of volunteer participation at the party to further Dean's 50-state strategy. Indeed, as much as placing organizers in all 50 states, the party's leadership wanted to use the Internet to convey that a new era of participatory Democratic politics had arrived. One of the Internet Department's first actions, for instance, was hiring a designer to rebrand the website from the "Democratic National Committee" to the more user friendly "Democratic Party," a message that Rospars echoed time and again in e-mails to supporters. This messaging was only one aspect of a complete overhaul of the party's web presence that encoded a new relationship with supporters. The party's leadership saw the new package of online event-planning and fund-raising tools that BSD launched for the party in 2005 as the very instantiation of a style of politics that had moved beyond professional consultants, air wars, and narrowly defined battleground states. Meanwhile, the Internet Department's practice reflected this new emphasis on supporter participation. Through its new tools for supporter engagement, the Internet team actively invited participation in building the party. For example, a National Organizing Kickoff on November 15, 2005, became the roll-out event for the new Internet team that helped staffers mobilize and define supporter participation. To demonstrate the 50-state strategy, Internet staffers encouraged supporters to plan events using the web tools (see figure 4.4). Supporters who did so received literature from the party and calls from the nationally funded

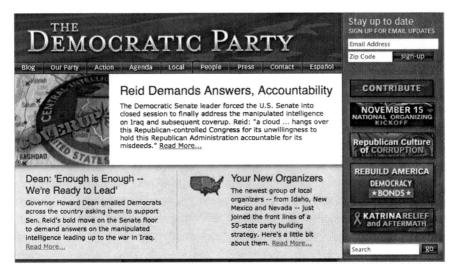

*Figure 4.4* Democratic Party website, November 5, 2005

organizers that Dean deployed to all the states. In the end, volunteers organized over 1,000 events across all 50 states.

The party extended this work during the run-up to the midterm elections in 2006. BSD launched its full platform, which it had been developing for Progress-Now, for the party under the name "PartyBuilder" early that year (see figure 4.5).[40] The platform did not feature much in the way of new functionality beyond what the firm created for MyProgress, with integrated fund-raising, groups, social networking, event planning, and organizing applications accessible through one interface. Supporters also had the ability to create personal contribution pages to fund-raise for the party, write blogs, set up and circulate petitions, and send letters to newspapers with party-provided talking points and the e-mail addresses of editors. Party administrators also had comprehensive access to data on the site's use across the contributions, groups, organizing, and fund-raising applications. This enabled administrators to track individual efforts and reach out to highly active users to encourage them to increase their involvement. This data also enabled the party's Internet staffers to tailor messages to supporters, segmenting out particular demographic, affiliation, or geographic groups to mobilize them around particular issues and for specific electoral purposes. The party also commissioned some modifications to the platform, in effect investing in the technical infrastructure that its candidates (and allied organizations) used during the elections in 2006 and 2008. For example, BSD developed its "Grassroots Match" application for the party, which paired first-time donors with long-time supporters in order to inspire the pair to up their commitment and contributions to Democrats. Tens of thousands of individuals used this application on the first day of its launch.

*Figure 4.5* Democratic Party website, November 1, 2006

Much of Rospars's work during the midterm elections in 2006 informed his approach to the Obama campaign. Rospars and another early BSD staffer, Macon Phillips, served as senior staff members on Rod Smith's campaign for the Democratic nomination in the governor's race in Florida in 2006. While Smith lost the primary to Jim Davis (who subsequently lost to Republican Charlie Crist), the two had a lot of responsibility and learned much from the experience, from overseeing ad shoots to using e-mail to mobilize the activist base of the party. For the party, Rospars piloted many of the new media messaging and organizing practices that he later carried with him to Obama's bid. The Internet Department of the party framed PartyBuilder in terms of facilitating offline electoral action. The landing page for PartyBuilder declared that: "Through technology, we're moving people from e-mail and websites to canvasses and rallies." Staffers' new media practice attempted to realize this offline supporter mobilization. For example, on April 28, 2006, the Internet team organized a national canvass called the "Neighbor-to-Neighbor Organizing Day" to demonstrate the party's capacity to run a national field effort (see figure 4.6). The event resulted in over 1,000 organizing events and a highly touted over one million conversations between party supporters and voters.

Behind the scenes of the Neighbor-to-Neighbor Organizing Day, Rospars and his team worked to integrate online organizing with the party's field efforts. While the Dean campaign had very little strategy behind its Internet operations and there was a pervasive disconnect between the campaign's online organizing and on-the-ground field efforts, for Organizing Day and the midterms Rospars worked with the party's field staffers and state party representatives to leverage

*Figure 4.6* Neighbor-to-Neighbor National Organizing Day, April 7, 2006

the online tools to serve electoral goals. This integration came about through work practices that Internet Department staffers crafted to complement field operations. For example, staffers targeted e-mails by state and district to recruit volunteers for local campaign and party offices. Meanwhile, the Internet staffers passed the names and contact information of people creating volunteer events online to the party's field offices. Staffers also made all the materials that field staffers and volunteers used as they went door to door, such as door hangers and literature, available online for supporters to print out and take with them as they canvassed their own neighborhoods. Through these efforts, supporters signing up online were better integrated into general field operations, and their independent local canvassing was incorporated into the party's professional communications.

The Democrats achieved resounding success at the ballot box in 2006, taking control of both houses of Congress and the majority of governorships and state legislatures. While PartyBuilder performed well, the midterm elections lacked the long primary season, concentrated national attention, and prominent candidates of a presidential cycle that would truly leverage the value of—and test—the platform. Within a matter of months, however, BSD's platform would be called into service to coordinate the extraordinary mobilization around the Obama campaign.

## NEIGHBOR-TO-NEIGHBOR

During this time, the party launched a major effort that subsequently became a key component of the technical work of Obama's staffers: the integration of Vote-Builder and PartyBuilder. In other words, the party took the first steps toward integrating the applications and data of its voter file and electoral organizing platform. This was a key aspiration for party staffers, given its tremendous electoral implications. Party staffers imagined that this integration would facilitate an unprecedented distributed field operation, enabling supporters to engage in online electoral projects such as canvassing voters and updating the core voter file. This was a challenging technical project and a key area of innovation. While the work practices of field staffers on the Obama campaign ultimately limited Neighbor-to-Neighbor's utility, as detailed below, during the general election of 2008 volunteers used the system to access the voter file through the Internet and to make canvass calls to priority voters.

The Democratic Party was in a unique position to bring the VAN and BSD systems together, having commissioned the voter file interface of VAN and modifications to the online electoral platform of BSD. As the client organization of both firms, the party provided the financial incentive for this integration. Without the capacity of these two systems to work together, there were limits on the utility of supporter participation. The online volunteers using PartyBuilder, for instance, could not pull walk lists directly from the voter file or upload canvass data directly back into the system. Meanwhile, field staffers using VAN's volunteer database could not access the groups using PartyBuilder.

The first project to integrate these two systems was Neighbor-to-Neighbor (N2N). Dave Boundy, the party's political director at the time and partner in Grassroots.com, conceived of Neighbor-to-Neighbor in 2007 as a tool for the presidential election. While it ultimately went through a number of iterations, the core idea was integrating VoteBuilder and PartyBuilder so that the party and its eventual presidential nominee could distribute the ability to make voter contacts, in the process rendering intermediary field offices unnecessary. The idea grew out of Kerry's experience in 2004, when after the candidate's appearance at the Democratic National Convention over a million new volunteers signed up online. Most of these potential volunteers in the battleground states never received a follow-up contact from a field or Internet staffer. To get around the need for this staff contact, the initial idea was that Neighbor-to-Neighbor would enable supporters to access the voter file online so that they could print out walk sheets and customizable fliers, organize door to door canvass efforts in their own neighborhoods, and upload data directly back into the system.

This proposed system was a departure from extant field practices and means of accessing voter data. Traditionally, field operations are very much an embodied activity, with volunteers showing up in person at field offices, receiving tutorials in voter contact and data gathering, and then being dispatched to go door to door. After returning their marked-up walk lists, office volunteers or field staffers would upload this information into the voter file. These practices enabled field staffers to provide on-the-ground instruction, coordination, and motivation to volunteers in lieu of any formal managerial relationship. It also provided campaigns with a degree of verification that those conducting field efforts were, at the very least, somewhat competent. The proposed Neighbor-to-Neighbor tool, in contrast, would distribute the authority to access the voter file and enable volunteers to generate walk sheets online. In other words, the implication was that the party website would become a radically open field office. The danger was that a simple login ID would be enough to access the party's prized possession, and staffers had few ways of knowing if people logging on were abusing the system.

From this concept, Blue State Digital built a demonstration version. BSD piloted the system in two Virginia state Senate campaigns during the fall of 2007, with the goal to make Neighbor-to-Neighbor available on PartyBuilder and then to provide it to the general election nominee. It was only by coincidence that the Obama campaign was BSD's client, given that Neighbor-to-Neighbor was a party-funded initiative being developed for the nominee. The first version of N2N enabled volunteers to use PartyBuilder to pull down geographically targeted names from the voter file to use for door to door contacts. While volunteers could upload the data from the canvass into PartyBuilder, it did not immediately synchronize back to the voter file because of technical challenges. While Neighbor-to-Neighbor opened a small hole that allowed data to pass back and forth between the two systems, the system segregated the voter records available on PartyBuilder so that online volunteers were not updating records simultaneously with field staffers. After a volunteer entered the data, the field organizer responsible for that "turf" was supposed to briefly vet the data. This meant that there was accountability built into the system. In reality, however, this extra step was impractical, and no one really vetted the data from these volunteer canvasses.[41]

As such, as a project it was a very narrow integration of the systems of these two firms, VAN and BSD. While the party's staffers considered this pilot to be a success, the challenges that staffers faced in building this first version of Neighbor-to-Neighbor proved simply to be the first in the long struggle to integrate VAN and BSD's tools. It was only in July 2008, for instance, after much labor, that the Obama campaign, BSD, and party staffers figured out how to add a calling functionality to Neighbor-to-Neighbor so that supporters could access the voter file and targeted scripts online.

## Conclusion: Market Success

With the strain of Rospars and Self working for the DNC, in early 2006 BSD's founders brought in Thomas Gensemer as the managing director to replace Roy Neel, the firm's first managing director who helped the founders think through the business model. Like many of his new colleagues, Gensemer got his start in the commercial sector, working for a venture capital firm specializing in technology start-ups before joining the online communications team of the Clark campaign. Gensemer subsequently became the director of Internet strategy for America Coming Together before joining BSD, where he often served as the tie-breaking vote between the four founders and helped to make many of the day-to-day operational decisions.

Gensemer was an important addition to the firm, and by the end of 2006 Blue State Digital had crossed a threshold. In addition to its work with ProgressNow and the Democratic Party, BSD worked with 22 candidates during the 2006 midterms, and 20 of them won their elections. As Franklin-Hodge describes it, this "was a point where we went from being a few guys that were trying to install themselves around a town that we didn't know to being the people you talked to if you were looking for vendors."[42] At this point, BSD's success in 2006 and high-profile institutional clients enabled the firm to become the widely acknowledged leader in providing digital campaign services.

Success changed the culture of the firm. Throughout much of BSD's early history, the founders were always wary that their firm would fall apart at any moment. After 2006, this was less of a concern, given the firm's rapid growth and large institutional clients. During the course of this growth, many of BSD's operations became formalized. As Johnson describes the transition:

> In 2006 it was like me working with a bunch of friends from D.C. In 2008, we have 50 employees. This is a company. Now we have HR, we had all this stuff, and it wasn't just hanging out with friends during the day making cool web stuff.[43]

With this new prominence, the firm landed two early presidential clients: Tom Vilsack, former governor of Iowa, and Bill Richardson, former governor of New Mexico. It was the firm's work for the Obama campaign, and Rospars's assumption of the role of new media director, however, that helped usher in a historic presidency.[44]

# 5

# Organizing the Obama Campaign

Joe Rospars's work at the Democratic Party through the 2006 midterm elections provided him with invaluable experience organizing a new media campaign operation. Rospars subsequently carried this experience with him to the Obama campaign, which he joined as the new media director in early 2007. Rospars was responsible for much of the vision, goals, strategy, staffing, and day-to-day management of a New Media Division at Chicago headquarters that, by the end of the campaign, had grown to encompass approximately 100 paid staffers, 20 full-time volunteers, and more than 100 other project-based or temporary volunteers, in addition to the new media teams ensconced in the headquarters of the battle-ground states. Rospars and his team fashioned the New Media Division into a central component of the campaign, driving substantial amounts of its fund-raising, messaging, and volunteering. This role for new media "to capture and empower interest and desire" and to deliver financial, symbolic, and organizational resources to the campaign was not somehow dictated by the tools themselves.[1] The campaign's embrace of new media and its many successes in doing so were organizational and technical achievements that had been forged through the long hours, in-depth planning, complicated negotiations, and meeting of technical challenges that characterized much of the day-to-day work of its staffers.

This chapter is about the organization of Obama's New Media Division. New media staffers created the organizational processes and technical infrastructure that helped translate the extraordinary interest around Obama's candidacy into the staple electoral resources enshrined in the ubiquitous phrase that staffers used to refer to their goals: "money, message, and mobilization." With the goal of utilizing new media to garner these resources, from the earliest days of the primaries Obama's staffers meticulously planned the division's role in the larger campaign organization and its staffing and work practices. In other words, out of the media spotlight and well before the crowds of supporters arrived, the campaign's principals engaged in the hard work of organization building necessary for a presidential run. Judith Freeman, the cofounder of the New Organizing Institute who joined the New Media Division's online organizing team during

the general election, describes a *lack of* attention to the organization of the campaign among many observers of Obama's run:

> Maybe there's not an under appreciation of it, maybe people always
> think it is magic, but it just took really serious work. It was the kind of
> thing where people were like "oh it's so magical and fun and there's rev-
> elations happening every day." But it really was just writing out plans
> and it was very serious work.[2]

To reveal how organizational structure and management helped give rise to
the new media practices of Obama's campaign, this chapter proceeds in three
parts, which roughly correspond to the progression of the primary campaign
during 2007. It begins by showing how the structure of the overall campaign and
New Media Division took shape during the early months of 2007. The chapter
then turns to a detailed discussion of staffers' use of e-mail, the blog, and design,
three primary areas of new media practice in the run up to Iowa. Finally, it
concludes by detailing the "computational management" style of Rospars and
his staffers that developed over the course of the year and the sociotechnical
practices upon which it was premised.

# Organizing the Obama Campaign

To have any chance against Hillary Clinton, Obama's senior strategists believed
that the campaign needed to expand the electorate. While Obama was attracting
media attention typically only accorded to the top tier of candidates as a result of
his 2004 speech at the Democratic National Convention, he was running against
two better known opponents. Hillary Clinton enjoyed the greatest name recognition, the backing of many party elites, and a campaign staff drawn from the
party's top tier of consultants. John Edwards was a decided underdog to Clinton
but a former vice presidential nominee who enjoyed broad support among lib-
erals and much of the online netroots drawn to his newfound populism. Faced
with this primary field, from the very beginning the campaign's senior staff
placed an emphasis on reaching unregistered voters and those groups who
historically have had low rates of voter turnout: youth and African Americans.

## ORGANIZATIONAL STRUCTURE

During the earliest days of the primaries senior staffers planned to invest in
new media to help expand the electorate. In January 2007, Jim Brayton, the
Internet director for Obama's Hope Fund political action committee, reached

out to Joe Rospars to let him know that Obama was planning to run and to inquire whether he might be interested in interviewing for a position on the campaign. As the former web developer and systems administrator for the Dean campaign, as well as co-founder and chief technology officer of EchoDitto, Brayton was familiar with Rospars's work since 2003.

Brayton's call took Rospars by surprise. Heading into the 2008 elections, Rospars could imagine himself working for only two candidates, Gore or Obama. He thought that neither would run. Rospars found the possibility of working for Obama intriguing. Rospars believed that Obama, unlike the other major candidates in the race, would adopt the position of the insurgent and "run like he had nothing to lose."[3] And, he saw it as an opportunity to go up against a front-runner, establishment candidate with what was widely regarded as the "A" team of Democratic Party consultants.

This included Clinton's Internet team. Much of the political consulting industry offering new media services is relationship based. Just as Brayton reached out to his former colleague on the Dean campaign, Clinton's Internet Department employed a number of staffers who had worked together on the Kerry campaign. They included Clinton's Internet director Peter Daou, an online communications advisor for Kerry and former author of Salon's influential blog the "Daou Report." Mayfield Strategies, the firm of Josh Ross, Kerry's director of Internet strategy, provided Clinton's website design and campaign tools. SolutionSet, a behavioral data and marketing firm that provided services to the Kerry campaign, furnished the back-end tool set for the Clinton campaign.

Campaign manager David Plouffe made it clear to Rospars in their initial meeting that he wanted new media to be "at the center of the campaign."[4] The location of the New Media Division within the organizational hierarchy was a key indicator of whether it would have this role. After some negotiation, Plouffe organized the New Media Division as a separate, stand-alone division, with Rospars as its senior staff head. In terms of the campaign's organizational chart, this meant that Rospars was on a par with the heads of the other divisions, including field, finance, and communications. This decision had a number of significant consequences for the use of new media by the campaign. Rospars was a participant in key campaign decisions, representing the needs of the division's staffers. The division could also advocate for resources and had autonomy with respect to other divisions. As the former deputy director of new media and chief technology officer of the campaign Michael Slaby describes, having Rospars as a senior staffer meant that:

> We could say no to communications and that was a huge, incredibly important thing because it meant that when we would try to make a case for something it wasn't getting filtered to Plouffe. Joe would walk directly into Plouffe's office and said this is why this is important.[5]

After coming on board in January, Rospars negotiated with the other staffers of the exploratory committee over the scope of the division's activities. As Rospars describes, as the organization began taking shape there was "a series of skirmishes along the edges of responsibility across the whole campaign. Not just with us, everybody was sort of figuring that out and seeing who is doing what."[6] New media pose a particularly acute problem, given that networked technologies are a central part of the infrastructure for all contemporary campaign activities. The problem, in essence, is that a host of organizational divisions can legitimately make claims to handle campaign functions conducted with new media, from advertising to fund-raising. For example, the campaign's communications staffers could easily argue that they should have authority over Internet advertising given their responsibility over all the candidate's television, radio, and print spots.

To resolve any potential conflicts between divisions, and to clearly delineate organizational responsibilities, Plouffe asked Rospars to choose activities that the New Media Division would unequivocally handle. Rospars chose e-mail and online advertising, based on his belief that specialized new media staffers could better utilize them than the staffers of other divisions. When coupled with online organizing on the MyBO platform and other communications over the Internet (such as the campaign's blog, web videos, and web design), which were unequivocally the domain of new media from early on, as well as merchandising (run with the Finance Division), these activities encompassed the scope of the division's work. Rospars's choices reflect considerable changes in new media practice since 2004. Through the work of MoveOn, the Dean campaign, and firms such as BSD, e-mail had evolved into a distinct genre of campaign communications with defined content and format norms and data practices. Meanwhile, online advertising had changed dramatically in four years, becoming a highly specialized practice with more complex pricing and buying schemes and sophisticated targeting mechanisms.[7]

E-mail, in particular, was a central component of the New Media Division's work and a source of its considerable organizational power. For one, the division was responsible for *all* communications between the campaign and its supporters using the e-mail list. This meant that every mass e-mail had to be cleared by the New Media Division first. Meanwhile, Rospars tightly controlled access to the e-mail list to avoid inconsistent messaging among the various divisions of the campaign, which he believed would jeopardize the careful cultivation of supporters detailed below. In practice, this control over e-mail meant that the division shaped the campaign's communications and the candidate's image on a daily basis for the 13 million individuals who, by the end of the campaign, had signed up for the e-mail list. This entailed new media staffers presenting the daily messaging, determined by David Axelrod and Robert Gibbs, in a compelling way online, which differed from the traditional communications of the campaign in its often informal and explicitly mobilization-focused tone. Meanwhile, along with e-mail, online advertising and merchandising generated significant revenue for the campaign by mid-summer 2007. These revenues grounded many of the division's requests for additional resources for staffers and new organizational responsibilities. During the early months of the primaries, when everything was focused on Iowa, there was a "constant relative justification of resources for more field, versus more media, versus more new media people."[8] Fund-raising was an early way in which new media proved its worth to the rest of the campaign. As Neil Sroka, state new media director for South Carolina, describes:

> I think that's constantly the struggle of new media operations within organizations — trying to prove yourself and trying to prove your niche and traditionally that niche has always been murky. When the new media department rose and became powerful was when it was able to provide a ton of money and that's also true with the first half of the Obama campaign. You know although the Obama campaign thought about things differently and wanted to have new media have an impact on all of these other things, the real value as far as the campaign is concerned up until February [2008] was it was a cash register. It was a way to prove its legitimacy and you saw that in July of 2007 when the first numbers came out. That's when new media really secured its place within the Obama campaign and secured its ability to spend money on things like video that were really expensive that the campaign didn't want to spend money on if they couldn't get any money from it.[9]

As Sroka suggests, until February 2008, when the division proved its value for the field operations of the campaign (detailed in the next chapter), the metric of organizational effectiveness was fund-raising. This success in fund-raising, meanwhile, also furthered intra-organizational collaboration. As numerous staffers across three presidential election cycles attest, new media and Internet staffers are often treated skeptically by field, finance, and communications staffers. These domains of campaign activity are highly codified, with a more professionalized group of staffers and more formalized practices that date back decades. The Obama campaign was no different, although having what staffers roundly describe as an organizational environment that was markedly focused and professional helped to mitigate any conflicts between organizational divisions. Part of this skepticism toward new media is cultural. As numerous staffers attested, the cultures of the divisions on the Obama campaign were radically different. Among new media staffers, while their work habits were not quite as quirky as those found in many Silicon Valley offices, there were norms of starting late, working late into the night, and casual dress, and alcohol was not unheard of. Staffers of other divisions had their own ways of carrying themselves, from the more formal office work of finance staffers to the mission-driven field staffers.

And yet, new media played a central role in the work of all of the campaign's divisions. Staffers across the campaign both used new media routinely in their work and sought to use the division's tools (such as the e-mail list) for their own purposes. As such, the New Media Division had many demands from outside staffers placed upon it. To coordinate this work, the division tasked Gray Brooks, a veteran of the Dean campaign and the new media ombudsman for Obama, with serving as a liaison for staffers of other divisions, among his many other responsibilities. Brooks managed the inflow of requests to Michael Slaby, at the time the deputy director of new media. The challenge that Brooks faced was that "the new media effort was just constantly swimming in work" introduced by people bringing requests to staffers.[10] Brooks had to evaluate these requests in terms of what was in the division's purview and how they fit in terms of its organizational priorities.

The Obama campaign's approach to new media stood in contrast with the approach of the Clinton campaign. Clinton's former Internet staffers describe a fundamentally conservative campaign in terms of its new media use throughout much of 2007.[11] Staffers recall that Clinton's senior advisors argued internally that the candidate's base was fundamentally different from those of Obama and Edwards and that Iowa caucus goers "do not look like Facebook."[12] A former staffer describes how "their philosophy at the time [early 2007] was that 'we are not the Internet candidate.' They thought it [the Obama campaign] was a very Dean situation all the way into Iowa."[13] Given the candidate's front-runner status, the campaign had little incentive to innovate. The campaign's senior leadership essentially tasked Internet staffers with not doing anything to jeopardize the candidate's significant lead in polls, elite and institutional support, and extensive fund-raising network. This cautiousness, in turn, led to the Clinton campaign's emphasis on using new media as an implement of communications, not field or finance, strategy. Indeed, while this was not reflected on organizational charts, staffers cite that in practice the campaign's Internet staffers reported to the communications team throughout much of 2007 and the early primaries. In this, Clinton's Internet staffers lacked the autonomy of Obama's new media staffers.

## NEW MEDIA DIVISION STRUCTURE AND STAFFING

Shortly after joining the campaign, Rospars, in consultation with Brayton, developed a staffing plan for the New Media Division. As noted above, the Internet Department of the Dean campaign was staffed with little in the way of a formal plan—or even a clear assessment of needs in the context of electoral goals. The planning that went into the organization of Obama's New Media Division, in contrast, unfolded in a very different manner. In part, this was because Rospars had fewer technical issues to initially confront, given the dedicated campaign technologies developed by firms such as BSD in the wake of the 2004 elections. To organize the New Media Division, Rospars drew from the accumulated knowledge gained during his experiences on the Dean campaign in 2004, with BSD, and at the Democratic Party. Without the resources to fully staff the division during those early months, which led to staffers initially taking on many roles, and without foreknowledge of the additional responsibilities that the division would assume over the course of the campaign, such as design and analytics, Rospars sketched out a markedly stable plan for the organization of the New Media Division.

Rospars organized the division around a set of departments responsible for specialized new media campaign practices. One of the important differences between the Obama campaign and those of earlier cycles, such as Dean's, was the degree to which staffers engaged in specialized new media work within a clear organizational hierarchy. While at the beginning of the campaign staffers multitasked given resource constraints, as resources came in Rospars was able to staff these departments, with director-level positions managing each. The New Media Division consisted of departments of staffers working on e-mail, online advertising, video, and the blog. As described in greater detail in the next section, Rospars also made the decision to create two distinct departments for internal (My.BarackObama.com) and external (sites such as Facebook) organizing in order to "grow them separately."[14] Later in the primaries, Rospars created separate design, analytics, and state new media departments, the latter of which was responsible for maintaining the individual state pages on My.BarackObama.com.[15]

With the basic framework for the division in place, Rospars turned to staffing, determining the levels of seniority and types of skills required for the positions within these departments. Similar to the Dean campaign, which had a number of its staffers cross between professional fields, the Obama campaign hired individuals with diverse work experience.[16] Many staffers joined the campaign after working on new media for campaigns or advocacy organizations. For example, Scott Goodstein, the external online director, had a long career as a communications consultant in Democratic politics. Stephen Geer, the director of e-mail and online fund-raising, managed online advocacy efforts for the Center for American Progress—a progressive think tank founded in 2003. Others had extensive experience in the commercial technology industry. Chris Hughes, a cofounder of Facebook and the campaign's director of Internet organizing, was the visionary behind much of the campaign's use of MyBO. Dan Siroker, a former engineer with Google who worked on the Chrome browser, developed the division's analytic practices. During the general election, a number of former field staffers in early primary states also joined the division to work on the state new media operations.

The directors of each department were responsible for their core area of operations and for hiring the people underneath them, although Rospars had final say over the allocation of the division's resources. One persistent challenge for the division was hiring, as the staff grew rapidly over the course of the campaign (from Brayton and Rospars to the approximately 100 paid staffers by the end of the general election). To find qualified individuals, Rospars and his management team often relied on their social and professional ties. This was particularly the case given many staffers' work in the field and knowledge of the key players in it who could fill particular positions. Other positions were harder to staff, and staffers circulated job postings (in some cases without specifying that it was the Obama campaign) within their extended networks and on relevant job lists. Meanwhile, individuals could advance or take on new roles, depending on the campaign's needs and their skills. One example is Michael Slaby, who was hired as technical support within the division and ended up becoming Rospars's deputy and later CTO of the campaign.

Rounding out the staffers on the campaign were the volunteers based at Chicago headquarters, a number of whom played critical roles in the division. One of Gray Brooks's responsibilities was vetting and managing an ever-increasing number of volunteers and interns. Brooks actively recruited these volunteers through the campaign's MyBO database, which enabled him to query the skill sets that supporters listed when they indicated their willingness to get involved. For example, depending on the needs within the division, Brooks looked for certain programming or design skills among the tens of thousands of supporters who sought to volunteer at the campaign's Chicago headquarters. The sheer number of names meant that the campaign had a deep reservoir of support upon which to call. A number of these volunteers with specialized skills played an important role in the campaign, and volunteering was also at times a path toward a paid staff position. Siroker, who as noted above helped develop the analytic practices of the campaign, started out as a volunteer and subsequently became the director of analytics. The ethos of the campaign was that "if you are not willing to actually consider volunteering then that is definitely an indication of the type of staffer they [sic] would be."[17]

## THE TECHNICAL INFRASTRUCTURE OF THE CAMPAIGN

The campaign needed an online toolset and data back-end to support its new media operations. Despite Rospars's role as cofounder of Blue State Digital, a position from which he took a leave when he joined the Obama campaign, the campaign vetted a range of providers in January 2007, including Convio, the firm that provided the back-end for the Dean campaign. Rospars recused himself from the process to avoid any conflict of interest. After viewing proposals from a

number of providers, the campaign selected Blue State Digital and signed an ex-
clusivity contract with the firm, precluding it from taking on any additional presidential clients. (The firm was already working with Bill Richardson and Tom
Vilsack.) The firm was in the process of negotiating with John Edwards's presidential campaign when it signed the contract with Obama and subsequently withdrew
its bid.[18] The initial contract between Blue State Digital and the fledgling Obama
campaign was for the licensing and use of the firm's basic platform. The campaign
provided very little money for the license fee up front, approximately $60,000,
with BSD being paid a percentage of all donations.[19] This arrangement was advan-
tageous for the campaign at the outset, when it struggled to get off the ground;
later, it renegotiated the contract to lower the transaction fees, given Obama's
extraordinary fund-raising.

The strength of the BSD platform is that it can be "turned on" for clients in a
very short period of time. One of the reasons that the campaign chose BSD was
that staffers wanted to launch the organizing platform when Obama announced
his candidacy in Springfield, Illinois, on February 10, 2007. This meant that the
time period from finalizing the BSD contract to My.BarackObama.com going
live was approximately a week. Staffers at the campaign and BSD worked
around the clock to get the system ready, including designing the visuals, producing the content, and integrating everything at the back-end, especially the
complex contributions and e-mail systems, along with the events tools. For
veterans of the 2004 campaign cycle, launching the platform and back-end
system in seven days was a novelty, as was the ability to turn to one speciality
political vendor to do it. As Rospars compares his experience on the Dean and
Obama campaigns:

> We were inventing stuff in house and having multiple vendors through
> the Dean campaign; when Kerry became the nominee they had to build
> a mailer—and so the fact that it was cheap and quick, just the fact that
> we had a site at all and that people could make 1,000 groups on the first
> day we announced, was a dramatic shift.[20]

BSD was able to launch MyBO for the campaign so quickly because this was
not a custom system. Initially, the MyBO platform generally had the same functionality as PartyBuilder. Indeed, through its contractual work with BSD, the party
financed improvements to the platform that subsequently benefited the campaign,
such as the "Grassroots Match" fund-raising application. While at the outset the
campaign wanted some custom features, it lacked the resources to commission
them. However, as detailed in the next chapter, over the course of 2007 and 2008,
the campaign went far beyond the basic platform, investing a considerable amount
of money in its further development. (Just as with PartyBuilder, BSD retained

ownership in these modifications.) For example, beginning in the fall of 2007, the campaign paid BSD to hire full-time developers, housed at the firm, to do custom development. The decision to house these developers at BSD grew out of staffers' knowledge that it was really difficult to build new tools in a high-pressure campaign environment. By the general election, the campaign had hired more than 10 Blue State developers to work on specific projects. These developers helped build the capacity of the platform, created new and added functionality to many applications, and integrated the BSD and VAN data for a host of online voter registration and canvassing applications.

Unlike many of BSD's clients, the firm's work for the Obama campaign required much close collaboration, particularly on development projects. Staffers at both BSD and the campaign recognized this early on, and created practices to support this work. At the beginning of the campaign, for instance, Jascha Franklin-Hodge from BSD spent time at Chicago headquarters brainstorming the needs of the campaign, the new media strategy, and priorities for adding functionality to the tool set. On the campaign side, Kevin Malover, the campaign's first CTO and former Orbitz executive, served as the liaison to BSD. (Michael Slaby played this role during the general election.) Throughout the duration of the campaign, Franklin-Hodge and his counterpart at the campaign had multiple phones calls everyday, in addition to a scheduled meeting that took place every day for two years. The campaign also invited field staffers to these meetings to brainstorm how the platform could further the on-the-ground efforts. As Franklin-Hodge describes:

> There was tremendous awareness on the part of the senior management of the campaign as to the critical role the Internet was playing in their operations and there was tremendous buy-in from other parts of the organization. I remember we were starting to think about field tools and field organizing in the early part of this year [2007] and meeting in Chicago with Jon Carson, the national field director, brainstorming ideas for technology and the way that things should work, the way that it should interact with the rest of the organization. . . . You had real engagement between the field people and the technology people and my sense is that you had real engagement at the most senior levels of the organization with the new media program. That the new media folks were doing the brainstorming work for the whole organization and that the new media team defined its place, that said to me that there was a necessary high level buy in as to the value of this.[21]

Meanwhile, after Obama became the nominee, Ben Self, the technology director for the Democratic Party, joined this group. With an official nominee, the party could now formally work with the campaign, particularly on projects related to integrating the voter file and BSD's online tools, described in greater detail in the next chapter.

With the division organizationally situated and the basic technical platform in place, Rospars turned to setting out the priorities for his fledgling division. The mantra of "money, message, and mobilization" became the guiding force behind the division's work throughout the campaign.

## Money, Message, and Mobilization

Much of the work of the New Media Division's staffers was focused on garnering the electoral resources necessary to put Obama into office. Staffers were focused on three goals: money, message, and mobilization. To fund-raise, drive their message, and mobilize supporters, the division's staffers used the broad range of new media tools at their disposal. The campaign's e-mails drove much of its online fund-raising, while staffers used the blog as a symbolic resource to define Obama's run through the lens of his supporters' actions on-the-ground. Meanwhile, the campaign's graphic design encoded staffers' interpretations of the larger themes of Obama's candidacy and his place in American history.

### E-MAIL

E-mail was the chief communication and cultivation tool of the campaign. New media staffers had direct access to the over 13 million supporters who had signed up for the e-mail list by the end of the campaign through the website and at candidate events across the country, where an e-mail address was often the price of admission. It drove much of the campaign's small-donor fund-raising, and served as the key vehicle for mobilizing supporters to perform the electoral activities that it desperately needed during the primaries, such as voter identification. At the same time, e-mail also played a key role in the division's strategy of directly communicating with supporters and routing around intermediaries such as the press and interest groups.

Through his work on the Dean campaign, with Blue State Digital's clients, and the Democratic Party, Rospars had become among the foremost practitioners of e-mail communications within party politics. From the start, Rospars had a clear vision of how he wanted to approach Obama's e-mail operation. For Rospars, the most important element of e-mail and the reason that control was so important was narrative consistency. As Rospars explained:

> Everything fits together and if you go look at the very first e-mail that
> we sent out from the Obama campaign which launched February 10th

all the way up to the thank you on election night that says 'I am going down to Grant Park right now' tells the story of the campaign. You understand everything, you understand the relationship with people, you understand the big moments, you understand all of this stuff and they sound the same. It is the same story. . . . It can't be "Here finance you take the e-mail list for this week and on this day and then communications you are going to send out your press release to the e-mail list this other day and then well we have all this field stuff going out so let's send all CAPS e-mails about these events that are happening in Portland." It has to fit together.[22]

Rospars was directly responsible for all of the campaign's e-mail during the early primary months. With the division growing, however, in May 2007 Rospars placed the e-mail team under the direction of Steve Geer, who as noted above became the director of e-mail and online fund-raising. While Geer was a veteran of online advocacy, the e-mail staffers under him were mostly young and new to electoral politics. For example, Teddy Goff became the third person on the e-mail team when he joined the campaign after finishing college in June 2007. In a fast-paced campaign environment, staffers such as Goff received only a brief crash course in political e-mail writing. This training mostly involved learning by doing and being heavily edited initially by gurus like Rospars—whom everyone watched closely, given his deep experience and distinct style.

Throughout much of the summer, fall, and winter of 2007, the campaign used e-mail primarily to push for funds. During the early months of 2007, Rospars made few fund-raising requests via e-mail, creating tension with the finance staff. Thanks to Rospars's role as a senior staffer on the campaign, he had the ability to approach e-mail in his own way. The delay in asking for money was deliberate, part of Rospars's strategy to cultivate donors by making them feel more invested in the campaign. By September, however, the continual solicitation of funds was a central part of the division's e-mail efforts. Staffers directed e-mails on a national basis, according to a structured calendar that had been strategized in advance (for example, around FEC quarterly reporting deadlines). The campaign also came up with a number of fund-raising incentives, primarily to encourage small donations. One particularly successful initiative, for instance, was "Dinner with Barack," in which the campaign selected five small donors randomly to have dinner with the candidate. E-mail pitches also revolved around the rhetoric of using small dollar donations to mitigate the influence of special interests and lobbyists. Staffers tied other fund-raising e-mail appeals to external events (such as when Sarah Palin mocked community organizers at the Republican National Convention, resulting in over $10 million in donations within 24 hours).

All of these strategies proved successful in terms of raising funds, especially in the crucial first half of 2007, when fund-raising was a test of viability for political journalists. For example, in second-quarter fund-raising (April–June), the campaign raised over $32 million, far outstripping its rivals. More importantly for the New Media Division, over $10 million of this haul came online. This fund-raising, meanwhile, legitimated Rospars's approach, justified the expenditures of the division, and grounded staffers' requests for more resources. As Slaby notes, "at the beginning we fought hard for resources and lost a lot until we started to raise more money. . . ."[23]

As importantly, the campaign used e-mail as a tool for messaging that extended the larger communications strategy of the campaign. Rospars was the key drafter of all e-mails that were national in scope or important in terms of the campaign's general communications. For these e-mails, Rospars consulted with Plouffe in terms of their tone, approach, and timing, and sometimes made modifications, particularly to soften the tone of an e-mail. On a more routine basis, division staffers used e-mail to circulate what the candidate and senior campaign officials said in the press. As Rospars saw it, e-mail messaging was about using the candidate and staffers' voices to provide context for the campaign:

> In a political climate where things could get very stormy and turbulent it's a rope from the shore to your people and so in a world where they otherwise would have been tossed like a cork and thrown all around, you can make it a little bit less turbulent, it is not like people don't know what is going on but if you can provide context that is honest and authentic and focused it is an opportunity to provide leadership for people.[24]

For Rospars, then, e-mail was a way to anchor supporters during the day-to-day changes in a presidential campaign. Even more, his reflections suggest just how much staffers thought deeply about the narratives and context they provided to supporters about the campaign.

While e-mails generally extended the larger narrative themes and communications strategy of the campaign, they also provided new opportunities for messaging. For instance, the e-mail team created voices for a number of campaign personalities, including Barack Obama, his wife Michelle, David Plouffe, and Joe Biden, along with other figures relevant to the message or action that the campaign wanted supporters to take (for example, Jon Carson, the national field director during the general election). These individuals did not write the e-mails purportedly from them. Division staffers developed their personas and used rhetorical techniques in the attempt to make communication from them seem authentic. For example, during the primaries, the e-mail team devised the strategy of sending a "math" e-mail detailing electoral strategy to supporters "from" Plouffe. (During the general election, the division actually shot web videos of Plouffe narrating the state of the race over PowerPoint slides.) E-mail staffers had three main goals for these rhetorical techniques, such as those used in the Plouffe e-mail. The first was to create supporter buy-in and investment in the campaign by seemingly offering an honest assessment of the state of the campaign and providing sup-porters with a sense that they had access to the campaign's inner circle. The second was to speak directly to supporters and to provide the campaign's interpretation of events in the race. The third was using e-mail as an alternative means of setting the press agenda, given that staffers knew that journalists were on the e-mail list.

Meanwhile, the e-mail team developed many of the analytic practices that staffers later deployed across the entire division. For example, e-mail staffers continually segmented their supporter lists on the basis of personal information and closely tracked the effectiveness of appeals by monitoring click throughs. The campaign tailored e-mails to supporters based on the demographic, involve-ment, and geographic characteristics of supporters, and sent trial missives to small groups of these segmented supporters to test their effectiveness in terms of content and design. Segmentation based on geographic region, in particular, was crucial for e-mail's utility as a tool for mobilization. The campaign communi-cated the needs of state field campaigns to supporters. Staffers also publicized organizing events and visits by the candidate, as well as issued calls for volunteer help, using these state e-mail lists.

## CREATING A SENSE OF OURSELVES: BLOGGING ON THE OBAMA CAMPAIGN

Sam Graham-Felsen joined the Obama campaign in March 2007 after writing a series of articles for *The Nation* about Obama's young supporters. At the time, the New Media Division had fewer than 10 employees, and Rospars was looking for someone to become the storyteller for the campaign through the blog. Rospars wanted the blog to become the "voice of the grassroots movement" by highlighting the work of supporters and articulating the reasons they backed Obama.[25] More than mere description, the blog helped to create the notion of a "grassroots movement" itself. Obama's bloggers strove to enable supporters to see themselves in the campaign, to connect with one another, and to create a collective sense of purpose. The blog was also a cultural resource intended to help staffers imagine and pursue their work in particular ways. Rospars wanted the blog to be the "central nervous system" that injected supporters' voices into the campaign, set the tone for the entire division's communications strategy, and helped staffers to stay inspired and to value their work in terms of supporter empowerment.[26]

To help the blog play these roles in the campaign, Rospars actively created the organizational conditions that enabled its writers to imagine the campaign as a broad, empowering social movement driven by supporters. The conditions that shaped the content of the blog had three primary dimensions. First, the division had the organizational autonomy to use the blog to craft its own public narrative of the campaign. Second, Rospars insulated the blog staffers from the rest of the division so that they would orient themselves toward the campaign's supporters. Finally, the campaign made hiring decisions that ensured that blog staffers were a diverse group with little professional communications experience. Taken together, these organizational conditions helped keep the focus of the blog on supporters and their efforts, not the backstage workings of the campaign.

Similar to the division's e-mail team, staffers enjoyed considerable autonomy over much of the content and style of the campaign's blog. This autonomy was contingent, however, on the blog's content not running counter to the larger communications strategy of the campaign. As Graham-Felsen, who served as the director of blogging and blog outreach for the campaign during the primaries, recalls, in the spring of 2007 he wrote a subtle critique of another candidate. This was an accepted, and expected, style of writing on polemical sites such as *The Nation* and the group blog Daily Kos. For the campaign, however, it cut against the communications strategy of the candidate. The critique caught Plouffe's attention, and he wanted to have the Communications Division vet all future blog posts. Rospars resisted the loss of the New Media Division's autonomy. In the end, the division remained in control of the blog, but the message was clear. From that point forward, Graham-Felsen knew the limits of his position and that he could not say anything that would cause controversy. Instead, he pursued projects that "delved into details of people's lives that might have been a little muddier or messier than you would normally see in a campaign TV commercial—like a man on the street thing."[27] To pursue these stories, Graham-Felsen and Kate Albright-Hanna, the campaign's videographer, who had worked for CNN prior to joining the campaign and had produced a documentary called "True Believers: Inside the Dean Campaign," flew across the country to detail the local, grassroots efforts of supporters. As Graham-Felsen describes:

> Our strategy was don't attack a fan or don't attack Hillary or don't attack anyone and so basically . . . I had this experience doing documentary film and being a journalist but I was really inspired by James Agee for example, who took ordinary people's lives and tried to get as deep as possible into their lives and show that they were interesting and meaningful just like anyone else's.[28]

The work that resulted helped bring supporters' stories more fully into the public narrative of Obama's candidacy. Graham-Felsen approached his work in terms of providing an amalgam of compelling human stories that would create the meaning of Obama's candidacy. To this end, the campaign actively solicited stories from supporters relating why they backed Obama and provided them with a way to upload their narratives onto the campaign's website. Graham-Felsen and Albright-Hanna then selected the most compelling, contacted the supporters responsible, and interviewed and filmed them for the blog. In the process, the blog became the central vehicle for communicating the stories of supporters and the key platform that enabled them to gather around the campaign. Staffers from other divisions, in turn, often drew on these stories in their own campaign work. For example, Obama's speechwriters used these supporter stories to humanize the candidate's policy platforms, particularly around health care.

As Graham-Felsen and Albright-Hanna curated these stories, they connected them to what was, at the time, a relatively underdeveloped aspect of the candidate's public biography: Obama's work as a community organizer. For Graham-Felsen and Albright-Hanna, the candidate's decision to move back to Chicago and work with community groups after finishing a law degree at Harvard embodied the volunteer ethos that was taking shape around the campaign. The candidate himself told this story vividly in narrating his experiences on Chicago's South Side in the autobiographical *Dreams from My Father*. To capture the spirit of the book, Graham-Felsen began interviewing people with whom Obama had worked during these years. This was unorthodox for a political campaign; the candidate's biography is typically the provenance of the research staff. Through Graham-Felsen and Albright-Hanna's efforts, the story of Obama as a community organizer became a more central public narrative for the campaign. Extending the themes of Obama's 2004 convention address, during the early days of the primaries the campaign mostly focused on the candidate's record as a bipartisan reformer. The community organizer aspect of the candidate's biography, however, fit well with the supporter participation that the division's staffers were trying to cultivate through the online electoral platform and field efforts. Graham-Felsen and Albright-Hanna drew on this aspect of the candidate's biography to anchor their reports from the field. As they highlighted volunteer efforts, particularly during the late summer and fall months when the campaign developed a host of field organizing events, they situated this work in terms of the organizing efforts that Obama had led in Chicago. Importantly, this helped inject a new narrative of the campaign into public discourse. As Graham-Felsen describes:

> So, it was really like there were two stories on the campaign. There was
> the official story coming out of the communication shop which was
> Obama is this great uniter and this great man of hope and change and

then there was this other story coming from the new media team and from Marshall [Ganz] and from the field team which is Obama is a community organizer and power gets built from the bottom up.[29]

Importantly, Rospars sought to create the organizational conditions that would enable Graham-Felsen to produce this content. To protect a very fragile suspension of disbelief in the authenticity of the Obama campaign and its supporters, Rospars repeatedly told Graham-Felsen to "stay in this bubble [with supporters] and not get too close to the sausage making and all this other stuff."[30] In other words, Rospars insulated Graham-Felsen from much of the day-to-day work of the campaign and the New Media Division. This was the work described in greater detail below that helped give rise to and coordinate supporter participation, from targeting persuasive communication to processing enormous amounts of data on the electorate. Indeed, Graham-Felsen attributes his belief in the campaign as a supporter-driven movement, as well as the way that he wrote and acted as if everyone else shared this belief, to this sequestering. As such, the ability of Graham-Felsen to represent the campaign as a supporter-driven movement was contingent upon his removal from the complicated, day-to-day strategizing and data work that challenged overly romantic narratives of Obama's run. While Graham-Felsen's role changed during the general election, when he joined the "rapid response" team tasked with rebutting charges from McCain and Palin, coordinating projects such as FightTheSmears.com to counter rumors and attacks, and providing opposition research to journalists, during the primaries his only role was to craft and sustain this idea of a supporter-driven campaign.

In addition to the comparative isolation of the division's bloggers, Graham-Felsen explicitly hired staffers who could cultivate these narratives of the campaign. The blog team grew to half a dozen over the course of the primaries. Rospars and Graham-Felsen tried to avoid hiring people who had worked in politics for a long time and who might:

> have a degree of jadedness and, frankly, smoothness that would not have worked well on our blog. We were looking for political rookies— people who weren't versed in PR and old-school political communication skills. Who didn't know what "talking points" were, but who knew how to tell a story. Basically, people without D.C. experience.[31]

The campaign's former volunteers in swing states such as Iowa proved to be a key source of talent for the division, especially given that they could write about their native states.

These bloggers were not, of course, critical of the campaign or candidate in any way. Nor did they attack rivals. These bloggers also did not develop much in the way of their own voices, as their roles were defined in terms of writing about the efforts of supporters. Indeed, as a number of staffers on the campaign cited, among the veterans of the Dean campaign who worked for Obama there was a deep distrust of letting staffers cultivate their own voices online, given the danger that they may overshadow the candidate.

The blog was not just an external resource; it was also crucial to sustaining the motivation of the campaign's staffers. As many staffers cited, the stories of supporters provided, maintained, and renewed the meaning of Obama's candidacy on a daily basis. Staffers also incorporated these stories into their own work, translating many of the themes of the blog into the rhetoric of daily e-mails and even the design of the campaign's website.

## DESIGN AS A SYMBOLIC RESOURCE

Staffers in the New Media Division spent as much time thinking about the content of the campaign's blog as they did the design of the overall web presence. While crafting political messages has long been part of political practice, campaigns have historically paid less attention to graphic design, except for logos. This has been true over the past decade and a half of Internet campaigning, where design is often an outsourced afterthought for political staffers.

The New Media Division, however, approached design as a symbolic resource that staffers used to help construct and reinforce the meaning of Obama's candidacy and inspire collective action. The division did so quite deliberately, developing a distinct, meaning-laden "aesthetic of Obama" that pervaded the campaign's web presence, from the main BarackObama.com site and My.BarackObama.com platform to the Facebook application and individual e-mails.[32] For staffers, design was about architecting an experience that would shape perceptions of the candidate and mobilize and motivate supporters, helping to construct a sense of historical agency around the campaign.

In the summer of 2007, the division began a search to hire staffers dedicated to design. Hiring in-house designers was unusual for a political campaign. The Obama campaign was the only one of the cycle to have dedicated art and design director positions; most campaigns contracted with outside firms for their graphic and usability design. The division's leadership conceived of design as a fundamental part of messaging strategy early on, yet the campaign had few resources until the summer to hire in this area. Michael Slaby, who became the deputy director of new media in September, served as the division's de facto designer throughout the spring and summer while carrying a full portfolio of additional responsibilities, given that he was the most technical person on staff at that point. Rospars and Slaby wanted to hire a designer to work in-house so that the design would mesh with the ethos of the division and would be consistent with messaging strategy and what the campaign was trying to accomplish internally. They also believed that an in-house designer would be able to more quickly and efficiently turn projects around, since the division's leadership would not need to deal with an outside web agency.

Slaby hired John Slabyk as art director and Scott Thomas as the design director in September after seeing their freelance portfolios online. Slabyk and Thomas were both commercial designers and developers with no previous political experience. As Slaby relates, he and Rospars deliberately reached outside the established political design shops: "They are experts in their fields and not in politics which was key to our success. There is this tradition in politics that people hire the people they know, and they end up hiring the best designer in politics which, guess what, is not the best designer in the world."[33] By all accounts, it was not hard to sell Slabyk and Thomas on working for the campaign, given the high profile of the project and the candidate's reputation for innovative new media work.

Slabyk and Thomas immediately set out to develop a coherent aesthetic for the campaign. The goal, as Thomas describes, was to "communicate the excitement that this candidate offered the United States of America and that this election season really offered to the country."[34] Design, in this sense, became an important "sales tool" for the new media team.[35] Staffers sought to use design to encode the meaning of Obama's candidacy and to shape the experience of Internet users so that they could enact their historic roles in the campaign. Thomas describes the designers' approach as one in which they drew on their commercial branding experience and their intuitions as designers to create this aesthetic:

> This is what popular brands do all the time. They walk in and they are trying to position themselves in some industry and the first thing you need to do is step back and say "ok well, what are we going to try doing? What is our messaging? And, what are we going to try and do visually?" We could have come in with 100 different approaches of what we thought—how we should present the brand or the aesthetic of Obama. John Slabyk and I tinkered around with it for a long time and there are things that he took from me and things I took from him back and forth constantly where we were like "ok that is right, that is feeling good, this is kind of in left field, this might be a little too minimal, this might be a little too immediate" and we just kept working with each other and I think that evolved into that aesthetic that we know of as the Obama look.[36]

The vehicle for thinking about this aesthetic was a full revamp of the campaign's website, which Rospars and Slaby made a priority for the division in the late fall. They anticipated that if Obama did well in the Iowa caucuses, people who had been inattentive to the race would immediately go to the campaign's website to seek out more information about the candidate. The goal of the redesign was to appeal to these uncommitted but curious voters, as well as to inspire new supporters to get involved with the campaign. At the same time, the redesign needed to be responsive to the needs of other divisions. Throughout the early months of the campaign, the design team was constantly inundated with requests from other divisions about featuring events or news on the homepage—which had resulted in a cluttered BarackObama.com homepage.

For the staffers working on this project, the first task was to systematically flesh out the mission and purpose of the site and then to prioritize elements of the redesign based on them. The designers were inheriting a site (reproduced in figure 5.1) built in haste and launched before the candidate formally announced his intention to seek the presidency. The original design was highly functional and was tied to the electoral priorities of the campaign. For example, the site was packed with information about upcoming events and was oriented around the campaign's activities in the four early primary states. It invited donations and otherwise pushed information out to supporters ("In the News" and "Barack TV"). The link to the "My.BarackObama.com" portion of the site was not prominently displayed. Meanwhile, there was little consistency in the site's use of color, typeface, and imagery. This lack of consistency extended throughout the entire campaign, being well before the division assumed control over all of the campaign's design, printing, and production of promotional materials.

The division launched the new site over Christmas, when there was relative down time in the campaign. Staffers worked feverishly around the clock for days to complete the project, with many sleeping under their desks. As is clear, the redesign dramatically overhauled the original site (see figure 5.2). On one level, it imposed simplicity and clearly prioritized the functionality that the campaign wanted supporters to use on what had previously been a sprawling site. The site was much less crowded, and the red "donate" buttons, meanwhile, jump off the screen to attract the eye. The My.BarackObama.com platform (under "Make a Difference") is more prominent, and its features are easier to understand, with more declarative statements such as "join group" and "find events." Even more striking are the markedly different stylistic elements. Designers replaced the jumbled color palate with shades of blue and gray. Obama was nowhere to be found on the original site, whereas his stylized portrait gazing into the heavens now graces the top of the page (and a small head shot promoting "Dinner With Barack" appears below). A motivational quote from the candidate clearly situates supporters' roles and calls upon them to help Obama get elected. In the top right corner, the stars fashion the campaign logo into something resembling a presidential seal. Meanwhile, an etherial light emanates from Iowa and also outlines the candidate's image at the top of the screen, suggesting the deliverance of a religious movement.

*Figure 5.1*   Screen Capture of BarackObama.com from July 18th, 2007

*Figure 5.2*   Screen Capture of BarackObama.com from January 10, 2008

The designers subsequently developed elements of this redesign into their core "brand groups," or themes intended to create particular understandings of the candidate and campaign among the public. The first of these brand groups was the "general" campaign brand, which featured the iconic Obama blue, the campaign logo, and Gotham font, a typeface selected for its "truly American qualities."[37] Designers hoped that the consistency of this brand would provide the visual impression that the candidate, the young junior senator from Illinois, was an efficient, experienced, and competent executive. To create this brand consistency, the division gradually assumed responsibility over the design for the campaign. In the fall of 2007, Slaby noticed that the campaign's events staffers were paying a lot of money to outsource the creation of materials for rallies with the candidate. Slaby offered to save these staffers money by having the New Media Division handle the design in-house. From this start with placards at candidate events, the division's staffers eventually maneuvered to have authority over nearly all campaign materials, including what was used in state field campaigns. The division designed these materials in-house and then sent them to regional printers, saving over $19 million for the campaign. The division also developed the style guide for the campaign. This created one consistent Obama "look" across the campaign's media and at all public gatherings for the candidate throughout the country. For example, the division was able to match the font and color blue used on the website, placards, podium signs, door hangers, the wrapper around the campaign's plane, and even Obama's necktie.

In addition to this standardized general campaign brand, designers worked on creating brand groups relating to Obama, his campaign, and the historical moment. These centered on helping voters imagine Obama as president, his run as the historic extension of the founders' vision and the civil rights movement, and their own roles in American democracy. As Thomas describes, their goal was to create the design elements that communicated these themes to users:

> You have an individual who much of America believes is never going to be president and could never be viewed as being presidential and there was a certain responsibility that we had to overcome that. . . . We knew that if we used imagery from the past and if we used fairly presidential imagery that it would appear presidential. Also note that John Slabyk thought a lot of that imagery was kind of awesome because it is. It is beautiful, it is historic, it has a lot of—it feels like America, it feels American. Innately American. And that's one of the beauties that design offers, is that when you design something you design it to function in a certain way, you design it to work and in graphic design I think you design things to work, that way you directly communicate with the minds of your viewers as effectively as possible. That's what good design is about.[38]

For example, designers created the "timeless" theme to help citizens imagine Obama as president. This theme entailed the explicit design of materials to resemble official state documents and to evoke state imagery, such as the white textured background on the website that designers used to suggest the governmental buildings in Washington, D.C. The designers used the "instant vintage" brand group to evoke the American past and to suggest, through imagery, the historic nature of the campaign. To do so, they went through archives of historical documents and images and pulled elements into the campaign's design. Designers, for instance, presented materials in the style of the Declaration of Independence and drew upon imagery of the civil rights movement, including the creation of stylized and prophetic images of Obama.

Finally, the campaign crafted a "supporter" theme that involved tailored versions of the campaign's logo for different supporter demographic and affinity groups such as African Americans for Obama, Obama Pride, People of Faith for Obama, and Kids for Obama. In this sense, staffers used design to convey that the campaign was as richly polyglot as America itself. The designers, in turn, coupled this work with rhetoric on the site in order create a sense of supporter agency around the campaign. Similar to how the division used the blog, the art and design directors made a decision to frame the campaign in terms of the collective action being taken by Obama's supporters:

> I think it partly came from the message "Change We Can Believe In," but I think that within the core group of new media the thing that we kept finding is that we should not focus on Barack Obama the man but we should definitely be focusing on the people because that is actually what our platform is about. And so for us, community, building online community doing these things it was all focused around "we". . . . If we were crafting the headlines for e-mail, or trying to write something for the blog, we were definitely always trying to focus it around "we" rather than "he". . . . Whenever we had the moment to deliver something based on 'we,' we would. For example we did a t-shirt contest a la threadless style where it was a democratic voting kind of process where the top t-shirt that got designed, we could print it and sell in-store, and instead of calling it something like "threadless for Obama" or something along those lines it turned into "Tees by people for the people," right, so it is about the people, it is about "we" not about "he."[39]

Even as the division's designers performed cultural work to cultivate a sense of agency among supporters, they engaged in analytic work that rigorously measured whether it was working. Staffers married rhetoric and design to computation, which enabled the division to determine the optimal content for fund-raising and mobilization and to allocate resources effectively. As the next section reveals, these practices of "computational management" not only shaped user experiences by creating continually tailored spaces of interaction with the campaign, they provided the metrics that drove much organizational decision making.

## Computational Management

Underneath nearly all the new media work lay a sophisticated data back-end and analytic practices that furthered staffers' goal to create "a customized, highly productive individual relationship with every person in the country."[40] The aim of this relationship was to move supporters up what one staffer on the e-mail team described as a "ladder of involvement."[41] While the idea of a "ladder" of political engagement is an old one in political organizing, the campaign used new media to computationally map the general progression from the first initial attempt to persuade a voter to join the e-mail list, to fashioning a supporter into a donor and then a repeating contributor, and finally to more involved forms of mobilization, from making phone calls to voters online to traveling to a swing state or becoming a precinct captain.

Data and analytics underlay much of the work of the division, from the optimal design of the campaign's webpages to the content of e-mails. The division rigorously gathered and analyzed information on the use of all its communications media. What staffers learned, meanwhile, was a key determinant of organizational decision making. Data lay behind decisions of where to allocate resources, how to staff and organize new media work, and grounded claims for resources from the larger campaign organization and the authority of the division. The division's leadership conducted rigorous analysis of the returns on investment that every new media expenditure produced, from dollars to voter registrations, to both be efficient in its own work and to garner organizational resources. The division could do this because, unlike other media, online media "is a closed loop, you can measure from displays to clicked versions with no, basically zero externality, because it happens so accurately—the measurement is enough."[42]

This emphasis on—or what many staffers describe as an "obsession" with—data and analytics resulted in what I call a "computational management" style of organizational decision making within the New Media Division. This involved the delegation of managerial, allocative, messaging, and design decisions to analysis of users' actions made visible in the form of data as they interacted with the campaign's media. This use of data and analytics was a qualitative change in the management of new media campaign work, akin to shifts in the commercial sector.[43] As a result of the development of much more sophisticated data gathering, storage, and analytic tools and practices, the division was able to project its revenue flows and to adjust its allocations down to the minute, enabling it to more effectively control its *internal* operations. Staffers also used data as an *external* management tool to generate the actions they desired from supporters. Through the data and analytics that enabled such practices as website optimization, the division translated the mobilization around Obama's candidacy into millions of additional volunteers and dollars by increasing the probability that supporters would take the actions that the campaign wanted them to take. These millions were highly consequential for the campaign. As Slaby notes, generating higher conversion rates over the lifetime of donors meant significantly more resources for the campaign:

> That optimization is worth 57 million dollars—right, hard to argue with. Forty percent conversion rate based on the lifetime value of those people can be understood pretty well—that's 57 million dollars. That is more than our entire state budget for the entire general election in Florida. The Florida state budget was about 35 [million]. We basically paid for Florida and Ohio by fixing the optimization.[44]

## DATA AND INTERNAL ORGANIZATIONAL MANAGEMENT

New Media Division staffers recount that the emphasis on data and analytics began in the summer of 2007. Alexander McCartney started volunteering after participating in one of the "Camp Obama" organizing training workshops that the campaign hosted around the country that summer. Given that he had programming skills, McCartney, who later worked for the Democratic Party, wound up volunteering with the New Media Division in Chicago. McCartney and Rospars began talking about data and analytics, particularly the possibility that they would be able to calculate the returns on investment (ROI) of nearly all the division's activities by generating more and better data. Together, McCartney and Rospars began working on developing metrics relating to the performance of e-mail in terms of meeting the campaign's electoral goals.

The first stage in the process was having clearly defined and measurable conversion goals for all of the division's new media work. Staffers identified what electoral actions they needed performed and then linked these to the various ways they communicated with supporters. In December 2007, Dan Siroker joined the campaign as a volunteer after taking a leave of absence from Google, where he was an engineer working on the operating system Chrome. Siroker, new to politics, subsequently joined the campaign full-time as the director of analytics during the general election. When Siroker arrived in December, he found that:

> New media in the campaign had very clear conversion goals, very clear goals for our operations. It was to get people to sign up for e-mail, get

people to donate, get people to register to vote, get people to volunteer, and at the end of the day get people to vote - and so all of those things were very clear, very measurable, very concrete objectives.[45]

The campaign then measured all of its returns on investment from the perspective of meeting these goals. Generating ROIs, in turn, helped the division to allocate its scarce resources. Rospars developed and implemented a system wherein the division was constantly assessing ROIs for each of its domains, comparing where spending additional dollars would best further its overall progress toward these electoral goals. This involved a host of complicated calculations. For example, staffers used this approach in their attempt to register voters through the "Vote for Change" application developed during the general election. The division started out by assessing the campaign's priorities for voter registrations, which involved a number of state and demographic targets laid out in the field plan. The division then assessed the online tools at its disposal to help meet this goal of registering voters, from e-mails, online advertising, and polling place lookups to running "vote by mail" online programs. The key was the attempt to find the optimal way of reaching different categories of potential voters so that staffers could spend their resources accordingly. To do so, the campaign ran a series of experimental trials, such as assessing whether an individual responding to an online advertisement or e-mail actually registered to vote. Staffers did so by matching the names of individuals who signed up online to published lists of new voters issued by many secretaries of state. Where matching names was not possible, the campaign also looked for other signs of engagement, for instance whether individuals using a polling place lookup also donated to the campaign.

These data practices not only shaped how the division allocated resources and hired staff, they also defined the daily work of staffers. The division's leadership used ROIs to make staffing decisions, such as hiring staffers for e-mail or advertising, depending on what was most effective for particular projects. This approach to rigorously setting goals and generating data, in turn, filtered down to the decisions that staffers made on a routine, daily basis.

Staffers, for instance, constantly tracked their expenditures and evaluated them against the returns they were generating for the campaign. As Thomas describes:

> That came from everything from banner ads down to the printer. I remember buying the printer, I was like, "here, this is how we are going to have a return on investment." Instead of paying $100 for podium signs we are going to pay about $10 in materials so we can print 10 podium signs for what we are paying for one. That pays the printer off in about

three or four hits, and that is why we should do it. So I mean everything was about how do we make a return on investment. If I am going to spend my time doing something how can I show that my time is now valuable and how do I show that my time is actually making money?[46]

The New Media Division also used its detailed metrics as tools to achieve organizational resources. The division demonstrated the returns generated on nearly every dollar of its budget. For a money-conscious campaign devoted to running a large field operation, the division's ability to demonstrate its value was crucial to securing organizational resources. In asking for additional staffers, for example, division staffers presented the leadership with figures demonstrating that they would pay for themselves, and even had developed estimates of how much these new staffers would profit the campaign. The ability to demonstrate these returns was particularly important, given that division staffers felt that "though new media was raising a lot of money that money wasn't being facilitated back into new media for the most part."[47] As a number of staffers noted, traditional media advertising absorbed the bulk of the resources of the campaign—even though it lacked the metrics that would demonstrate its effectiveness. Slaby, for example, contrasts the New Media Division's work with that of traditional advertising:

> I can tell you the exact dollar amount to the penny of what a new e-mail address was worth to us on the campaign and the cost per acquisition— to the penny. We got to the point where we had to optimize our online buying so far that we paid for the people that we acquired, before we had to write the check we had already received the money.[48]

## OPTIMIZING CONTENT AND DESIGN

The New Media Division entwined rhetoric, design, and computation. As the campaign watched "people click and move from space to space" through the data generated on their online actions from cookies (information stored in browsers that communicates with websites), staffers learned the most effective content and design in terms of money, e-mail sign-ups, and volunteer hours.[49] These data practices required a significant amount of organizational capacity, given the degree of complexity in the processing of ROI calculations. When there was limited time and resources, staffers tested content and design for optimal results only once, such as when a new application launched. The standard practice, however, was to run more complicated analytics. The campaign's e-mail operations, for example, routinely generated 30-day fund-raising metrics to figure out optimal messaging to move an individual who signed up for the e-mail list to become a donor to the campaign.

In other words, at every step in the process, staffers measured user engagement and refined their messaging and approach accordingly. For example, staffers tested nearly all imaginable content and design in e-mails through A/B testing, which entails measuring response rates of a control e-mail against a host of different manipulations to find the optimal content for different categories of user. Staffers segmented the 13 million person e-mail list based on the extensive information it had on its supporters, from demographic and geographic information collected at sign-up to the history of interactions with the campaign. At times, segmentation was more complex, such as sending a particular e-mail to supporters of a particular race residing in an early primary state, but screening out donors who had already given more than $100.

The team then continually ran numbers on response trends through the BSD database for online contributions based on small differences in content and came up with new manipulations to be tested. For example, as noted above, the campaign sent hundreds of e-mails over the course of the election to each supporter. The cast of characters signing off on these e-mails—from Michelle and Barack Obama to David Plouffe and surrogates at the state and federal level—were all tested in terms of the effectiveness of appeals, as were the subject lines, format, and content of these e-mails. Staffers also tested whether hyperlinks versus URLs, and their respective order on the page, resulted in more contributions. Staffers did not, however, personalize these e-mails beyond the name of supporters and donation amounts (in large part because any additional tailoring had to be performed manually; the campaign could not generate tailored paragraphs in e-mails to supporters). The division even tested optimal sequences of e-mails, down to a 72-hour basis. For instance, on the first day a supporter who just signed up for the e-mail list might receive a state-specific e-mail detailing all the programs the campaign was running. On the second, it may be a general fund-raising request. On the third, it might involve a fund-raising request that had a donor offer to match the donation. Depending on the response, or lack thereof, to this sequence, the division then knew what to send next. The fourth e-mail, for instance, might offer merchandise or a different incentive.

While the division's e-mail team was segmenting its lists and testing design early on, the campaign did not develop full-scale analytic testing on its web design until 2008. For example, when Dan Siroker joined the campaign as a volunteer in December 2007, he realized that the campaign was doing a good job driving traffic to its website and raising money from e-mails. The problem, however, was that people were visiting the website but failing to sign up for the campaign's e-mail list. To address this bottleneck, Siroker created a number of variations of the "splash," or landing, page. This involved creating a matrix of different designs based on alternative combinations of candidate videos, images, sign-up buttons, colors, and content. The result from this relatively simple test was that an optimal combination of images, content, and design resulted in a 40% higher e-mail sign-up rate for the campaign. Over the course of the election, this translated into millions of additional supporters on the e-mail list and, as revealed by metrics from e-mails, millions of dollars and thousands of volunteers for the campaign.

The power of analytics for all aspects of the campaign's website content and design was at that point readily apparent to staffers within the division. The initial testing of the splash page sent a clear message to staffers that their instincts seldom revealed what was optimal in terms of producing the numbers that the campaign desired. For example, nearly every staffer in the division preferred a long, introductory, and inspiring video of the candidate to the static images on the splash page. Yet, e-mail sign-up rates with the video were abysmal. It was the power of this demonstration, in part, that led to Rospars's decision to create an analytics team within the division. After finishing up at Google, Siroker returned to the campaign full-time as its director of analytics in June. In the interim, e-mail staffers continued to run split testing based on segmentation of the e-mail list. Siroker started out with one full-time staffer, McCartney, and by the end of the campaign the team had grown to six staffers and a couple of volunteers. The team grew, in part, because it was easy to justify additional hiring given how high the returns on investment for each analytic staffer was. Similar to other sites of innovation in electoral politics, many of these analytic staffers and volunteers came from careers outside of politics. Other than one former Clinton staffer, the rest of the Analytics Department either came from industry as engineers or had specialized computer or data management skills.

Under Siroker's direction during the general election, the analytical practices of the campaign grew much more sophisticated. For example, the back-end analytics around the splash page changed dramatically (see table 5.1). Staffers began segmenting visitors to the website into different user categories, based on knowledge they gleaned through data on all the actions that users took on BarackObama.com, which was stored in the BSD database. This included five different categories of user, based on their previous involvement with the campaign. Visitors also received different appeals based on the campaign's electoral priorities for the location where they accessed the website. To maximize the likelihood that users would make a first-time or repeat donation or volunteer, the campaign displayed different, optimized content tailored to these categories of users. The campaign chose this content based on design and content experiments with these different subsets of voters.

As detailed above, these small differences in design and content, such as whether to present a video or static image to first-time website visitors, generated millions of additional e-mail addresses for the campaign. Outside the efforts

*Table 5.1* The following tables present a reproduction of the 2008 Obama campaign's spreadsheet detailing a proposed splash page redesign.

**Current splash page behavior**

| *Characteristics of visitor* | | | | | *Geolocation of visitor* | | | | |
|---|---|---|---|---|---|---|---|---|---|
| *Visited site previously* | *Signed up* | *Made a donation* | *Ordered a t-shirt* | *MyBo account* | *Strong Democratic* | *Strong Republican* | *Leaning Democratic* | *Leaning Republican* | *Battleground* |
| yes or no | no | no | no | yes or no | sign up and make a donation of $15 or more for a car magnet | | | | |
| | yes | no | no | yes or no | make a donation of $15 or more for a car magnet | | | | |
| | | yes | no | yes or no | make a donation of $30 or more for a t-shirt | | | | |
| | | | yes | yes or no | make a donation now without merchandise incentive | | | | |

# Proposed splash page behavior

| Characteristics of visitor | | | | | Geolocation of visitor | | | | |
|---|---|---|---|---|---|---|---|---|---|
| *Visited site previously* | *Signed up* | *Made a donation* | *Ordered a t-shirt* | *MyBo account* | *Strong Democratic* | *Strong Republican* | *Leaning Democratic* | *Leaning Republican* | *Battleground* |
| no | no | no | no | no | welcome and sign up to learn more | | | | |
| yes | no | no | no | no | sign up and make a donation of $15 or more for a car magnet | | VFC | | |
| | yes | no | no | no | make a donation of $15 or more for a car magnet | | | | |
| | | yes | yes | no | make a donation of $30 or more for a t-shirt | | | | |
| | | | no | no | make a donation now without merchandise incentive | | | | |
| | | | yes | yes | N2N | | | | |

Other potential characteristics: registered to vote, skipped splash page many times around sign-ups for e-mail, much of the optimization work of the campaign focused on increasing donations, given that it was both easy to measure and crucial to the division and the campaign. Even more, the analytic staffers knew that much of the campaign's persuasion efforts, such as actually convincing a voter to support Obama or to turn out, were best handled in the field, through the online organizing on MyBO, or in television advertisements seen by a wider range of the electorate. Siroker's challenge, then, was moving the online fund-raising from a system in which everyone coming to the website generally saw the same content to the personalization of content and design on the basis of individual characteristics, campaign involvement, and geolocation, similar to the splash page. Siroker discovered, for instance, that if a visitor had never donated, she was most likely to respond to an appeal that said "donate now and get a gift," whereas the most effective appeal for a supporter who had already donated was simply "contribute." As Siroker describes:

> the difference between those two [phrases] was so staggering in terms of looking at the statistics, looking at everything, that I think that is an opportunity where if we had learned that earlier instead and said we really need to customize everyone's experience, based off of who we know, what we know about them—there is such an opportunity to raise more money and to get more people to engage and volunteer.[50]

The search for ever higher conversion rates, or the fashioning of users into donors, through personalization led to the ever expanding scale of analytic testing. The campaign generated over 2,000 slightly varying contribution pages and ran trials on them all. It also tested the width, color, and page placement of donor buttons as well as the images and content on the contribution pages based on different categories of individuals. Staffers themselves marveled at the work of the analytics team. As Goff describes: "It was the coolest thing that I ever saw, different audiences actually peaked at different responses to colors."[51]

## Conclusion

Like much on the Obama campaign, these analytic practices were premised upon productive collaborations between the analytics team and others within the New Media Division. As Thomas describes:

> So, we can test things on the website based on button colors on the types of content that we put in certain areas. We could do testing on web pages so we know where people are clicking. A lot of these analytical

tools informed what we were already doing design wise. There were certain ways that we could test a lot of our decisions early on. . . . And I think the analytics team, I call them the linebackers of our organization, because they were the ones really making the tackles, delivering us the information that we needed in order to best come out with the design that we know was also the most effective.[52]

Computational management was not without its limitations, however. While it helped the division allocate resources and staffers and make decisions about content and design, much new media work did not lend itself so easily to quantification and computation. Thomas, for example, believed there were aesthetic decisions best left to intuition and experience: "The way people think about typography. . . . They don't know anything about typography and if you focus group something you might walk out using Comic Sans because it is on everyone's computer. That might not be the best choice, that might not be the astute choice, the informed decision."[53]

A similar mix of science and art underlay staffers' work with volunteers on the My.BarackObama.com platform, which was a key component of the division's work in the run up to, and throughout, the primary nominating contests and general election.

# 6

# Mobilizing for Victory

At the close of 2007, the New Media Division's staffers found themselves almost entirely alone in Chicago. The campaign's strategists knew that Obama needed a victory in Iowa on January 3 to have any hope of winning the nomination and that the result in New Hampshire five days later would shape the dynamic of the primaries. While the campaign had field operations running in Nevada and South Carolina, they paled in comparison to the resources directed toward these first two contests. Indeed, so much was riding on Iowa that Dan Siroker, the director of analytics, remembers that when he joined the campaign as a volunteer in December "almost everyone in the campaign was actually in Iowa."[1]

With the approaching nominating contests, the Obama campaign entered a new phase. While staffers spent much of 2007 preparing for the voting to actually begin, the time had come to test the volunteer mobilization and voter turnout operations in the early primary states for which the campaign had meticulously planned. This new electoral phase meant changes for the New Media Division. The division not only needed to keep its online messaging and small-donor fund-raising growing, its ability to deliver volunteers and voter identifications took on a new importance and urgency. This was especially important in states outside the first four. In what turned out to be an extraordinarily long and hard-fought primary campaign, an outcome few had predicted, mobilization became central to the work of Obama's new media staffers.

This chapter is about the New Media Division's mobilization work and the tools, practices, and organization that supported it. Although its staffers were far removed from ground-level battles over electoral turf, the division played an important role in them as a result of staffers' success at leveraging their new media tools for the ends of the field efforts. New media staffers provided supporters with tools for organizing on-the-ground months in advance of the arrival of active field staffers, created a distributed online canvass operation that involved thousands of volunteers, and registered thousands of new voters online. The chapter opens by looking at attempts to integrate new media and field operations on the campaign during 2007, paying close attention to the role of external sites such as Facebook and internal sites such as MyBO during the primaries. It then turns to the general election, showing how the division developed a distributed field operation and created new tools to register voters. The chapter concludes with a consideration of the "Get FISA Right" protests that took shape around the campaign after Obama became the nominee.

## Integrating New Media and Field

The division used its BSD-provided organizing platform as well as external sites such as Facebook to gather and channel supporters toward the electoral work that furthered the campaign's field operations. To do so effectively, however, required organization. From early in the primaries, the campaign made the integration of new media and field operations a central goal for staffers. High-level field staffers were engaged in the new media and technical side of operations early on, as in the meetings between the campaign's staffers and Blue State Digital during the early months of 2007 detailed in the previous chapter. With knowledge of field staffers' electoral priorities, the New Media Division invested heavily in its external and internal organizing departments and created practices to further the ground efforts. In other words, the campaign did not simply make tools available for supporters to use. The campaign created effective organizational processes that helped staffers to actively cultivate supporter participation and channel it towards electoral priorities. This was a complex sociotechnical project. As Rospars describes, it involved:

> understanding the field plan and the goals and priorities of each state because they were very different from state to state . . . in the primaries it was the rules of participation, but in the general election, voter registration deadlines and handling voter registration in the states. . . . Understanding the demographics of who we were targeting, understanding how they [the Field Division] organized their field staff, which was different for different states, so we would understand how to plug all the existing people and the new people coming into the campaign into specific initiatives in different states, whether that's about organizing volunteers that they need, whether that's phone calls or traveling to the state from nearby states.[2]

### ONLINE ORGANIZING

In February 2007, shortly before Obama announced his candidacy, the campaign hired Chris Hughes, a cofounder of Facebook, as the director of Internet organizing. At the time, Hughes was working on an application for the social networking firm that enabled candidates to extend their presence on Facebook by setting up dedicated pages to connect with supporters. In working on the application, Hughes got to know Obama's bodyman (or personal assistant) Reggie Love and Jim Brayton, the Internet director for Obama, who were exploring using Facebook for a possible presidential campaign. The prospect of Obama running resonated with Hughes, who was drawn to the potential candidate's message. In conversations with Brayton, Hughes began thinking more deeply about how to go beyond a Facebook profile to the use of the "participatory web" more generally and what this would look like for a presidential campaign.[3] Hughes soon took a leave from Facebook and joined the campaign. With Rospars and Hughes in place Brayton, whom many described as paving "the groundwork for the new media team in the spirit and substance," stepped down.[4]

Rospars and Hughes were really reactive to campaign events during their first couple of months on the campaign, given a lack of staff and resources for the division. Obama announced his candidacy within weeks of these staffers starting and, as noted above, the campaign launched the MyBO platform at the same time. When MyBO went live, supporters launched hundreds of groups nearly instantly. As Hughes recalls:

> We opened up the platform, people flood in, we've got groups all over the place, we've got events, you've got people calling the office, there's no space. So really, for the first, at the very beginning it wasn't like "here's our vision of how technology should be used in a political campaign."[5]

In the weeks that followed, new media staffers worked to sort out issues with the MyBO platform and launched and promoted the candidate's pages on social networking sites such as Facebook and MySpace.

With the basic technical infrastructure up and running, Rospars and Hughes began to think more proactively about the role of supporters in the campaign. Instead of just putting tools out there for supporters to use as they saw fit, staffers took a much more active role in mobilizing volunteers and channeling their efforts toward the fund-raising and early field efforts that would help make Obama a viable candidate. To help accomplish this, Rospars created two distinct departments for "external" and "internal" organizing that were later integrated during the general election. While there was overlap and coordination between these departments, Rospars wanted them managed and staffed differently in order to:

> grow them separately because there is organizing on our site like the groups, the events stuff, and integrating all of that with field. But then there is MySpace, Facebook - all those things which we need to take seriously too. I didn't want to put one person on that because depending

on who you pick they will prefer one or the other so I put a wall between those two to try to make them cooperate but grow up separately. Once they were grown they became an integrated organizing crew for the general election.[6]

With this organizational structure in place, Rospars and Hughes thought deeply about how new media technologies could further progress toward the campaign's field goals and how the division's staffers could coordinate their efforts with those of the field staffers. This meant developing rapport with the field staff and identifying their priorities so that new media work complemented work on-the-ground. To do so, early in the primaries Rospars and Hughes met with high-level field staffers to show them the MyBO organizing tools and to begin a conversation about how they could further the efforts of field staffers. As a result, Rospars describes how the division modified the MyBO platform to provide the functionality that field staffers desired:

> [In the beginning] it was very like one foot in front of the other; us learning how they needed to work, they are learning how we can help and also changing tools to facilitate things— little things like when you rsvp for an event and the host, depending on the event, should be able to, if they want, require a phone number from the person who rsvp'd.... Something like that for certain types of events makes a big difference and for a field organizer it makes the difference about whether they can have their volunteers use the tool at all which then in turn will make a big difference about who will be able to see and find the event and etc. etc. and whether we will ultimately collect all the data about it and everything else.[7]

In addition to meeting with the leadership of the field team and modifying the functionality of the platform, on a more general level division staffers worked to introduce field staffers to the campaign's networked tools. As Teddy Goff, the staffer who oversaw the state-level new media teams during the general election, describes: "[Field] is just a tougher shell to crack. You're introducing new people, you're introducing new techniques."[8] Even though general familiarity with the Internet had grown among field staffers, there was an established set of field organizing practices honed over many electoral cycles and passed down through "learning by doing" to each new generation of campaign organizers. These practices made little use of new media other than VoteBuilder, which meant that new tools would alter established ways of doing things.

As such, new media staffers needed to make the case for how the campaign's technical systems could facilitate the work of field staffers. To this end, Rospars and Hughes created a pilot program to demonstrate the successful integration of new media and field efforts. Early in the campaign, Rospars and Hughes met with Jon Carson, the Illinois state director who later became the voter contact director for the Super Tuesday states and field director of the campaign during the general election. They sought out Carson because they identified early on that a very large number of potential volunteers in Obama's home state of Illinois had signed up on MyBO, and the state's proximity to neighboring Iowa made these supporters a tremendous asset. Even more, Carson and his field director were grouped in a couple of cubicles near the new media offices at headquarters. All of this made Illinois a convenient state for a pilot program. Rospars, Hughes, Carson, and their staffs worked together to deploy the volunteers from Illinois signing up on MyBO to Iowa. In addition, they created a host of fund-raising and volunteer events in Illinois throughout 2007. Through this work, Illinois fueled the early growth of the campaign, becoming a crucial source of financial and volunteer support.

After this Illinois pilot, in June 2007 the New Media Division organized a national canvass. The field staffers of Iowa, New Hampshire, South Carolina, and Nevada had all organized their own large-scale canvass events to take place on different dates in June. Looking to get Obama supporters who lived outside these states more involved with the campaign, Rospars and Hughes approached Temo Figueroa, the national field director at the time, Steve Hildebrand, the deputy campaign manager responsible for field organizing in the early states, and Plouffe about having these four states host their canvass events on the same day. The idea was that this canvass would become the basis for a branded, national "Walk for Change" event that provided supporters across the country with the opportunity to participate in a national field effort. With the campaign's go-ahead, the New Media Division did all the branding for the national event and provided many of the printed materials for the canvass.

While the scale and rigor of this canvass was drastically different in the early primary states from the rest of the country, the event both demonstrated the division's capacity to decentralize the execution of a national canvass and helped to define supporter participation in the campaign. Already well staffed, the "Walk for Change" event in the early primary states was very sophisticated, with target lists generated in the VAN and organizing events planned by the field teams. For the rest of the states, most of which lacked paid staffers and field offices, the New Media Division provided support and resources for efforts organized by volunteers. This was a role that the division reprised in states without much of an official presence by the campaign during the run-up to the Super Tuesday contests. The division mailed a box of materials for the canvass to all self-identified "Walk for Change" organizers who used MyBO to organize an event and had a minimum of 34 people sign up. Division staffers also provided logistical support to the supporter organizers of these canvasses.

The event proved to be highly successful in some states. For example, supporters in North Carolina, a state that played a large role in the primaries and the general election, held approximately a dozen events with hundreds of volunteers. For the division, the national canvass both demonstrated the effectiveness of new media tools for field staffers and created a sense of ownership in the campaign among supporters. At the same time, it enabled staffers to set expectations for the types of electoral activities that the campaign needed performed, laying the groundwork for independent supporter efforts in Super Tuesday states, such as Colorado, and those with later contests, like Idaho.[9] The event also helped the campaign create relationships between staffers and supporters, and among supporters themselves.

## STATE NEW MEDIA STAFFERS

To facilitate collaboration with field, the New Media Division embedded staffers in the four early primary states and in other battleground states during the primaries and general election. Their task was to "stick like glue to the field people."[10] Working from state headquarters, these staffers fulfilled key roles online and on-the-ground in being responsible for all aspects of state new media operations. Staffers, for instance, worked from state calendars, using targeted e-mails through their access to the BSD database to solicit volunteers for particular field events. They also helped funnel volunteers coming to the campaign online into state field efforts. While the Chicago New Media Division ultimately added the polish and pressed "send" on these e-mails, these state new media staffers strove to communicate with supporters in a distinct, local voice. There were no formal talking points handed down from the national campaign to the state staffers, but one staffer described the campaign's message as being like "pornography, you know it when you see it."[11] The national campaign expected state new media staffers to exercise their good judgment. State new media staffers also managed the state blogs on MyBO and social networking presences on external sites such as Facebook. The state new media staffers also provided national staffers with insight into what was happening in the states. Staffers in Chicago would often pull compelling content from the state blogs onto the national blog so that supporters across the country could get a sense of what was happening on-the-ground.

The work of the state new media staffers in South Carolina during the primaries illustrates their role in the campaign. Neil Sroka was the state new media director for South Carolina, working out of headquarters in Columbia. Jeremy Bird, a key architect of Howard Dean's highly lauded New Hampshire field campaign and the field director for South Carolina during the primaries, hired Sroka. (Bird would also work in Maryland and Pennsylvania during the primaries and served as the general election director of Ohio.) With the intensity of field efforts in an early primary state, Bird had little time to invest in new media, and he was looking for someone who could build an online presence for the state campaign and who "would work really well with the field program."[12] Sroka's work complemented and extended the field effort. Sroka produced regular blog reports on the state field efforts and played a large role in pushing the field offices to capture e-mail addresses so that the campaign could remain in touch with its supporters. With access to the BSD database, Sroka targeted e-mails to these supporters by region, demographics, and their history with the campaign to encourage them to turn out to events that field staffers planned. Shooting video of the campaign's field activities was also an important part of Sroka's job. Video was powerful in offering Obama's national supporters a rich look into what was happening in the early primary states between candidate visits (which Chicago's staffers were responsible for filming). Sroka, for example, filmed the woman who delivered the famous "fired up, ready to go" line that became the unofficial slogan for the campaign.

In addition to crafting much of the online presence of the South Carolina campaign, Sroka also worked to connect the volunteers signing-up online to the field efforts on-the-ground. This was a significant accomplishment. The campaign had no automated way of providing field staffers with immediate access to the information of supporters signing up online until the general election, a problem described in more detail below. As the only person who could access the BSD supporter database in South Carolina, Sroka was responsible for manually generating these lists and providing them to the field offices across the state. Sroka explicitly contrasts his experiences on the Obama campaign with those of new media staffers during earlier electoral cycles, where online volunteers were often treated with skepticism by field staffers. On the Obama campaign, field staffers "would acknowledge what new media could bring to a field campaign in a way that I don't think was appreciated in the Dean days."[13]

State new media directors also managed the social networking presences for the campaign in the early primary states, reaching out to geographically local supporters and groups on commercial platforms. Facebook, in particular, played an important role in the run-up to Iowa and the other early voting states. The site was the primary means through which the campaign's state new media staffers and youth organizers reached out to college and high school students. In the months before the caucuses, new media staffers set up Facebook groups for every high school and college in Iowa. The Iowa youth organizers then used these groups to communicate with students and to publicize campaign events, volunteer opportunities, and caucus rules and locations, as well as offer opportunities to share videos from the campaign trail.

As importantly, capturing data on supporters from sites such as Facebook was a key part of these staffers's work. Field staffers needed to know who their supporters were in order to coordinate their activities and to ensure that they turned out to vote. However, during the primaries, new media staffers lacked a systematic way of generating the individually identifiable information the field operation needed from sites such as Facebook, and did not have a way of synchronizing data from these sites with the voter file or BSD's online database. In the face of such challenges, state new media and field staffers created informational work-arounds, manually cobbling together spreadsheets for this organizing work. As Hughes describes:

> So if we had people coming in through the Facebook applications, what we would do is we would have zip materials and we would put them all in the online database and then we would take those lists and what would happen is any new constituents would technically go into the VAN as Obama supporters, although that didn't start until the fall of 2007, before that it was manual. But what we would also do to make sure the [Obama] youth organizers . . . we would also send lists manually to the youth directors and then they would actually cut them up and then send them to the youth organizers. . . . That was really, really quite dirty stuff. We did this Facebook piece for all of the early states not just Iowa, we did it and this was really important in South Carolina for the youth vote.[14]

Facebook was an important organizing tool throughout the primaries and general election. Campaign staffers cited how nearly all the student groups active on college campuses used the platform for their organizing activities. For the campaign, however, this was not an ideal situation, given that it had little access to the data on these supporters and their activities. Similar to the Dean campaign, Obama's staffers faced a challenge in the large numbers of supporters who used Facebook and Yahoo! and Google Groups to organize instead of the MyBO platform during the primaries and general election. The new media staffers therefore strove to bring these organizational efforts inside the campaign by getting "everyone's e-mail lists and everyone's activities and everything tracked through [MyBO]."[15]

As the primaries wore on, a number of other states received state new media directors. After Obama's victory in South Carolina, for instance, Sroka went to Ohio, where he had a staff of four people doing all the blogging and video production for the campaign's local efforts. During the general election, every swing state had a new media team and blog. Other states, such as California and Massachusetts, had blogs as well, mostly geared toward mobilizing in-state supporters to travel across state lines to swing states such as Nevada and New Hampshire. There were also blogs for affinity groups, such as Americans Abroad for Obama and African Americans for Obama.

The role of the state directors changed significantly during the general election. While the state new media staffers enjoyed a considerable amount of autonomy during the primaries, Chicago staffers centralized their control over new media during the general election. The former state directors became "new media organizers" who were essentially bloggers and troubleshooters for MyBO but had little substantive power, with all e-mails and social networking being centrally coordinated from Chicago.

In part, this centralization occurred because of ever-present management challenges regarding the state new media staffers. For Sroka, it was never quite clear to whom he was ultimately accountable. Sroka's immediate boss was Bird, a reporting relationship that reflected the campaign's desire to integrate field and new media. Yet, this was complicated by the fact that Bird often had little sense of what Sroka was doing, and a lot things, such as producing videos from South Carolina for the national website, had little to do with the state campaign. At the same time, Sroka had no formal reporting relationship with the state communications director, even though he was supposed to get approval for his new media messaging. Meanwhile, Sroka was accountable to the New Media Division in Chicago, which ultimately provided the resources for his position and vetted all his e-mails. This dilemma of management, never fully solved, resulted in a "fair amount of bad blood by the end of the campaign" between Sroka and the field staff in South Carolina, as he more often than not had to defer to the priorities of the New Media Division in Chicago.[16]

## EXTERNAL ORGANIZING

Scott Goodstein, a communications consultant long active in Democratic politics, served as the external online director for the campaign during the primaries. In this capacity, Goodstein was responsible for establishing and maintaining the campaign's presence on commercial sites such as Facebook, MySpace, and Twitter, as well as social networking platforms for affinity communities, such as Black Planet. Goodstein's department also coordinated the campaign's mobile messaging efforts. During the general election, after the division combined the external and internal organizing departments and placed them under the direction of Hughes, Goodstein was solely responsible for mobile messaging. The external organizing department operated on the premise that the campaign had to "engage people where they want; you have to go to your audiences online."[17] In other words, the division's staffers realized early on that not everyone supporting Obama would set up a MyBO account. Yet, staffers still wanted these supporters to further the campaign's electoral ends, such as by becoming conduits of strategic messaging in their online social networks. Obama's supporter networks were very large; upwards of 80,000 individuals "friended" Obama on

Facebook shortly after he announced that he was running for president, and over 2 million more joined them by the end of the campaign.

The external organizing department's mission was to cultivate these supporters in order to get them to take action and to leverage their social networks for the ends of the campaign. This work had little precedent. Sites such as Facebook and MySpace had not been around during the 2004 elections, and their use by campaigns was only halting during the 2006 midterms. As such, the work of these staffers was experimental, as opposed to formalized and routinized. Gray Brooks, one of the earliest hires in the external organizing department, describes his work during the early days of the primaries in terms of trying to extend existing work routines with new tools, "and then you try to see possibly what else you could do that you couldn't do before."[18] The general approach among the external organizing staff was to view the campaign's official presence on these different social networking sites as "embassies," spaces where the campaign was embedded within a set of existing social relationships, interaction norms, and local "customs."[19] In keeping with this metaphor, Rospars describes the goal of external organizing as "trying to encourage tourism and immigration back home, whether that was a sign up for e-mail or 'check out this event' on MyBO."[20] The campaign wanted to establish as many points of contact with supporters as possible, even as staffers always attempted to move supporters to the "home" MyBO platform. Like the state-level new media staffers, external organizers wanted to bring supporters "home," given that there were defined uses for and limits on what the campaign could do with these external sites. In contrast, the campaign had much more flexibility in how it designed, used, and collected data from MyBO.

New media organizers used these external "embassies" to extend the division's money, message, and mobilization work. These embassies were gateways to the wider universe of the campaign's web presence for supporters and a means of lowering the barriers to certain actions that the campaign needed accomplished, such as donating or registering to vote. Staffers, for instance, used MySpace to publicize the fund-raising and volunteer campaigns in which the division as a whole engaged, integrating content across various platforms. When the campaign stressed early voting, its communication on Facebook dovetailed with messaging in e-mails and online advertising. In sum, the division tied all of its channels to a "march of different important dates and initiatives that . . . would transform all of our communications whether it was on MyBO, alerts popping up on people's dashboard or e-mail or social networks or text messages, or whatever it was, all those initiatives would go everywhere."[21] External organizing staffers also used these sites as tools to facilitate the electoral actions that they needed accomplished, such as adding donation buttons and volunteer sign-ups on the candidate's Facebook and MySpace pages. Meanwhile, particularly important for these new platforms, the campaign used the computational management practices detailed in the last chapter to continually measure the value generated by and to develop a sense of what works and does not on these external social networking sites. Staffers collected data ranging from how many sign-ups occurred on these sites to how much traffic appeals on these sites drove back to the campaign and how much fund-raising these sites generated.

External organizing staffers also used a number of different Facebook applications over the course of the campaign. During the primaries, if a supporter used the campaign's Facebook application, it sorted their friends according to a set of categories. For example, the application displayed the images of friends who went to the University of Iowa or listed cities in Iowa as their hometown. It then encouraged supporters to contact these friends and urge them to help the campaign in Iowa. It also included a news feed from the campaign that publicized its messaging as well as fund-raising and volunteer appeals. Later versions of the campaign's Facebook application made it easy for supporters to contact friends who lived in early voting states and appeal to them to turn out. During the general election, the campaign's Facebook application supported the voter registration tool Vote for Change and polling place lookup tool. The campaign also called on supporters to devote their Facebook status to Obama on Election Day.

Ironically enough, for all the popular celebration of and scholarly speculation about how social networking sites and mobile technologies have lowered the costs of communicating with supporters, the New Media Division had an enormous staffing infrastructure dedicated to maintaining the campaign's presence on these sites. Throughout the primaries and general election, dozens of low-level staffers, volunteers, and interns within the campaign's headquarters were devoted to approving Obama's friends on MySpace and Facebook and to dealing with questions and responding to posts on these sites. The mobile program, for instance, let supporters respond to texts with questions, which would then be answered by these staffers.

## INTERNAL ORGANIZING

During the primaries, Chris Hughes and his deputy Nikki Sutton headed the internal organizing department of the division. Hughes and Sutton were responsible for overseeing all the supporter organizing conducted on the MyBO platform and coordinating what became a distributed field operation that complemented what was taking place on-the-ground in the states. The internal organizing work was closely tied to the campaign's overall electoral strategy through the collaboration of new media and field staffers. Meetings between senior staffers from new media and field, as well as initiatives such as the national canvass event, helped create the mutual respect among divisions, day-to-day work practices, relationships, and technical systems that enabled staffers to specify how new media could further the goals of the field program and operationalize metrics for success. Judith Freeman argues that it was precisely such work that enabled the campaign to overcome the pitfalls of the 2004 campaigns, where new media were largely separate operations from field:

> I think that is one of the biggest lessons that we learned in 2004—and they obviously did it way better in 2008 then they did it in 2004—if you don't create a structure and give people a way to get engaged people are going to figure it out on their own. They are going to create their own Google Groups or their own neighborhood block party, or whatever. And so it is up to you as a campaign, especially a presidential campaign, where everyone wants to get involved, to create the structures and give people ways to get engaged and help the campaign with their strategy. Otherwise everyone is just going to be running around doing anything. And I think they did a really good job overall both on the field and offline. . . .[22]

From early 2007, Hughes and his team focused their efforts on working with supporters in states that lacked field offices and staffers because of the concentration of resources in Iowa, New Hampshire, Nevada, and South Carolina. Hughes saw that the MyBO platform would play little role in the four early primaries, given their extensive field operations and canvass efforts. The goal, then, was to have supporters fill gaps in field resources by using MyBO to organize for the 23 state primaries held on February 5, 2008, otherwise known as Super Tuesday. These states included a number of large traditionally Democratic states, such as California and New York, along with smaller Republican states such as Utah and Oklahoma, only some of which received field staffers well in advance of their primaries. In addition, a number of these states would also play central roles as battlegrounds during the general election, including Colorado and Missouri.

The campaign began explicitly discussing its strategy for Super Tuesday in July and August 2007. Representatives from each of the campaign's divisions met during morning meetings. Chris Hughes was the campaign's new media representative. At these meetings, staffers went through all the states in play on February 5 and discussed the prospects for Obama, as well as their respective strengths and weaknesses from an organizational perspective. This planning occurred in the context of staffers knowing well that the dynamics of the race would change drastically after Iowa, the outcome of which had the power to make Obama a real contender or to effectively end his candidacy. Indeed, Obama would have to win Iowa to have any realistic chance of moving forward. At the time, polling in these early primary states revealed consistent 30 point margins for Hillary Clinton.

In this context, one variable that staffers used to plan the allocation of field resources for after the Iowa caucuses was the location and number of supporters signed up for the division's e-mail list and MyBO platform. For example, the number of active supporter groups on the MyBO platform in Super Tuesday states informed decisions of where to send staff. Connecticut, for instance, was a strong Obama state on MyBO from very early in the primaries. Supporters in the state planned scores of events for Obama and recruited hundreds of volunteers. In contrast, comparatively few supporters were using the MyBO platform in New Jersey. Given the proportional nature of the Democratic delegate race, where candidates benefited greatly from finishing close in states' popular votes, even if they did not win these primaries, the campaign looked for states where only a few staffers would have an outsized impact. In states such as New Jersey, with few independent supporter efforts prior to February 5, a couple of field staffers would make a great deal of difference in turning out Obama's voters. Alternatively, with phone banking and canvassing already going on, fewer field staffers would be needed in states such as Connecticut.

This planning laid the groundwork for what happened during and after what was, by all accounts, the hectic and emotionally intense month of January. Many staffers described how the four early state contests in January defined the psychology of the campaign through November 2008. Staffers always had the prevailing sense that victory was precarious, grasped but never firmly held. Few staffers predicted the emotional tide that crested with Obama's victory in Iowa on January 3 and crashed with his surprise loss in New Hampshire just days later. New Hampshire rocked the confidence of staffers who had been told that Iowa was the key to victory, to Obama running the table as Kerry did four years earlier. Obama's loss prompted the campaign to send everyone not in South Carolina, including much of headquarters, to Nevada. The result there was a numerically solid, but psychologically flimsy, gain in delegates over Clinton but loss in the popular vote, which further rattled the campaign. After Obama's crushing victory in South Carolina, the campaign turned to the Super Tuesday states. It was the first big test of whether the campaign would be able to compete in a multistate primary against an established and well-known front-runner.

With 23 states set to vote on February 5, the campaign needed to hold its own against Clinton. Supporters using the MyBO platform played a large role in helping the campaign meet the immense organizational challenge of running canvass operations in these states (more than are typically at play during a general election). While some electorally important large states such as California had active field operations, other states only received substantial investments of field resources and staffers after South Carolina's primary on January 26. To compensate for the absence of field resources, in the months before Super Tuesday division staffers mobilized thousands of supporters around the country to use an online BSD tool to call voters in these states. On-the-ground, local supporters used the tools offered on MyBO to plan their own volunteer events such as canvassing their neighborhoods and gathering in public places to provide visibility for the candidate. These events were important conduits of sign-ups to the campaign's e-mail list and additions to the pool of volunteers, as the MyBO tools enabled supporters to find nearby events. Some of these supporters even opened their own campaign offices in lieu of an official field presence, guided by a manual of legal and financial information for doing so that was provided by the campaign.

While these independent efforts were valuable, even more important was the fact that the new media staffers could quickly mobilize supporters in these states to participate in field efforts. MyBO offered new media staffers what was essentially a LISTSERV through which to contact all the local groups of supporters active in primary states. The division also segmented its e-mail list by state. As such, the MyBO platform and e-mail offered new media staffers a way to quickly contact and drive supporters to on-the-ground canvass events planned by field organizers.

Many field organizers in Super Tuesday states came from "Camp Obama" trainings, which trained over 3,000 organizers during the course of the election. The longtime labor leader and social movement scholar Marshall Ganz, Obama field staffer Joy Cushman, and Liz Pallatto from the Sierra Club, along with other field staffers from the Obama campaign, developed the Camp Obama trainings based on work that Ganz had done for the Sierra Club. Central to this method of organizing was a team approach, in which organizers learned to create local volunteer leadership groups that operated independently from one another and the campaign but had defined metrics for their work and therefore were held accountable. Once trained, these organizers traveled across the country as volunteers and staff to start and join field offices.[23]

The different constituencies within the campaign—field organizers, new media staffers, and supporters—had to collaborate to get ground efforts up and running. As newly minted organizers traveled to the Super Tuesday states at different stages in the primaries, they utilized the campaign's new media tools to organize the extant independent supporter efforts. As Ganz recalls:

> With Super Tuesday what was happening in all of those states is that the people we trained were going to those states and were organizing them. And, of course, they were taking advantage of whatever they could take advantage of including new media stuff. . . . The beauty from my point of view of the whole thing was the fact that the organizers and the new media people had to get along with each other, had to figure out together how to make this stuff work. . . .[24]

New media staffers had to coordinate e-mails and outreach to the MyBO groups with field organizers to integrate supporters into the state campaigns. For their part, supporters had to cede much of their autonomy and control to the field offices.

According to many accounts, collaborations between field organizers and supporters went smoothly. For one, the field campaign explicitly trained their organizers to work with supporters according to the tenets of their ubiquitous motto: "Respect. Empower. Include." At the same time, it was evident during my participant observation on-the-ground as a precinct captain in California in the months before Super Tuesday that victory over Clinton was the goal for Obama supporters. Supporters generally saw their roles in terms of furthering the electoral strategy of the campaign as dictated by the field offices—with markedly little conflict. And yet, this buy-in among supporters did not just come about on its own in response to the primary challenge from Clinton. The campaign carefully set its expectations for supporter involvement. This direction was important to ensuring that the campaign was not a "crazy state of nature," while at the same time providing supporters with a clear indication of what would further the ends of the campaign in advance of the primaries.[25]

For example, Hughes and Sutton worked with supporters to communicate the priorities of the campaign and to define their roles. After the launch of MyBO, Hughes held a conference call with a few hundred of the campaign's active supporters on the site. Hughes and his team also kept in touch with these supporters, providing answers to questions and resources. Staffers intended these communications to send the message that supporters were being listened to and valued, but also set the expectation that they were not part of the campaign's inner circle. There were some questions that supporters did not get answers to, and the overall message was one of "trust us, we know what we are doing."[26] The online tools themselves also defined legitimate supporter activities and roles. Tools that supported event organizing, fund-raising, visibility, and voter identification, for instance, made the campaign's priorities explicit. As one highly active volunteer for both the Dean and Obama campaigns makes clear in contrasting his experiences during the two primary cycles:

> They [Obama's campaign staff] made it very clear that they wanted you to do what you can do to become your own organizer, to use the tools to organize locally in whatever way you wanted to. Things were much more rigidly defined [than on the Dean campaign], so that people could very quickly recognize what role they might bring to the table. . . . They were much clearer about what they wanted out of their community, because they set the parameters for what the community could do as well—more specifically in language and in the actual tools.[27]

Obama's integration of new media and field during the primaries stands in sharp contrast to accounts that Clinton's former staffers tell of their campaign's failure to capitalize on the candidate's New Hampshire victory and prepare for the February contests. As one former Clinton Internet staffer argued:

> Until Hillary found her voice there wasn't much of a voice on the online program. We can talk about the chicken or the egg on that one, but I think the online program could have been there too when she found her voice in New Hampshire and accelerated her far past the Obama campaign with her years of experience and brand name and dedication that her supporters have. But it wasn't there. I see online campaigns as building buckets so when it rains we can collect the water.[28]

Clinton staffers argue that the reason this bucket was not there was because of strategic and technical missteps on the campaign throughout 2007. As detailed above, Clinton's senior leadership never saw new media as being central to the campaign, arguing that Iowa caucus voters "do not look like Facebook."[29] Even when the campaign did take new media seriously, staffers suggested that its leadership learned the wrong lessons from the Obama campaign. Former staffers cite that throughout 2007, Clinton's senior staffers were continually surprised by the growth of Obama's online fund-raising and field operation, especially after Obama out-raised Clinton during the first quarter. Internet staffers argue that the Clinton campaign's leadership disregarded their advice that Obama's success was due to the effective narrative use of e-mail that fostered supporter investment in the campaign and fund-raising programs tied to deadlines and featuring social incentives such as "Grassroots Match." Instead, the campaign's leadership accepted the theory of powerful donors that Obama's success was attributable to a social networking platform. The campaign subsequently decided to implement its own platform. A number of Internet staffers made the internal case for developing a powerful, custom platform with more functionality than MyBO and explicitly designed to support field organizing. Mark Penn, the campaign's chief strategist, overruled these staffers in favor of implementing a cheaper, faster to develop system designed for fund-raising.

All of these missteps meant that when it did rain after New Hampshire, the Clinton campaign missed its chance to fully capitalize on the moment. Because there was little connection between the Internet and field staffers, the campaign could not fully leverage the human resources of its online supporters. Even more, there was often not much of a field campaign to channel these supporters into. Staffers recall that Penn overruled those on the campaign who wanted to open field offices in the Super Tuesday states, following the lead of the Obama campaign, because he did not think they were necessary. As another former staffer details:

And so that [the lack of a February 5th presence] to me was a big puzzle of the whole thing. That, plus the strategic mistake of not counting delegates from the beginning. But the reason why David [Plouffe] thought he could count delegates from the beginning was because he had this grassroots field campaign and he could say "hey let's organize in the caucuses in these random states." And we [the Clinton campaign] looked at it as "oh we are never going to win the caucus states and if we don't win the state then what is the point to contest that place?" The numbers showed that if we had just, if we had activated . . . the fraction of our e-mail list that typically does field volunteer action that we want to do then we would have twice the number of delegates. There actually would have been a race after February 5th and that is the untold story. The biggest frustration that I had . . . is that we started a phone calling program, we worked with an online calling tool as a way to try to activate volunteers in the states, but there was never a commitment to it so it always kind of fell through the cracks. I really think the race could have been close if they had, even if it wasn't on fund-raising even if we lost the fund-raising race, if we had just focused on activating our volunteers using these tools I think it would have been a lot closer of a race and it was already a close race.[30]

It was only after Obama racked up a significant lead in delegates over the course of February that Clinton's former Internet staffers argued that they were able for the first time to run a more innovative new media operation. This was not about changing personnel so much as the internal focus and dynamics of the campaign. Whereas the campaign used new media as an arm of communications strategy for much of 2007, in the wake of Iowa and the campaign's subsequent financial issues as the primaries wore on, Internet staffers gained autonomy and became more independent. One reason is that Internet staffers had demonstrable success fund-raising—which in turn enabled staffers to gain organizational authority and implement their own programs and strategies. No longer was the Internet team reporting, for all practical purposes, to the communications staff.

## Rebuilding the Technical Infrastructure for the General Election

Obama held his own on Super Tuesday, narrowly garnering more "pledged delegates" than Clinton, according to the party's proportional representation rules.[31] As the campaign redeployed its field staffers from the Super Tuesday states to those with upcoming contests, new media staffers followed the same model of e-mailing their state lists of supporters and recruiting MyBO groups to turn out for field events. Through these efforts and extensive field organizing, the campaign produced a string of 11 victories during the month of February, which provided the candidate with a nearly unassailable numerical lead in pledged delegates over Clinton.

In this context, on March 4 the Obama campaign faced symbolically important contests in Ohio and Texas, and two other primaries in Rhode Island and Vermont. Clinton was seeking to turn her campaign around after the string of losses in February and the resignation of her campaign manager, Patti Solis Doyle. Facing demographically unfavorable terrain in three of these four states (Vermont being the exception), the Obama campaign sought to minimize its delegate losses by taking advantage of Texas's unique primary and caucus process. Texas had the largest number of delegates at stake among the remaining state contests. It awarded delegates through a unique mixed system, in which they were allocated based on both the overall share of the vote in a primary and a separate series of precinct caucuses held immediately after the polls closed, which were open to everyone who voted in the primary.

Staffers believed that they had an opportunity to out-organize Clinton in the caucuses, even though Obama might lose the primary. To this end, Joe Rospars, Jon Carson, and Jeff Berman, the national director of delegate operations, met to discuss strategy around the Texas primaries. The three came up with the idea of branding the unique primary and caucus process as the "Texas Two-Step," something easily digestible for supporters to understand. Through online advertising, targeted e-mailing, and scripts that volunteers across the country used when contacting Obama supporters in the state, the campaign sought to educate supporters about the process and turn their voters out at the caucuses. Meanwhile, the division reconfigured its polling place lookup application to provide information to Texas supporters on their caucus locations. The effort was successful. Obama lost the primary but won the caucuses by a margin that resulted in a net gain of five pledged delegates. And, even with high-profile primary losses in Texas, Ohio, and Rhode Island, with wins in Vermont and subsequent March contests in Wyoming and Mississippi, Obama added to his delegate lead.

Meanwhile, as it became increasingly clear that Obama would win a majority of pledged delegates, both campaigns turned to contesting the unpledged "superdelegates," given the outside possibility that they could decide the race. Superdelegates made up approximately 20% of the total 4,233 delegates awarded during the Democratic primaries, and included sitting state and federal officeholders as well as past and present national and state party leaders. As the race continued throughout the spring and early summer, the New Media Division leveraged its tools and detailed supporter database to make a finely tailored set of appeals to these superdelegates. Staffers did so in much the same way that they approached the "Texas Two-Step": using new media to educate supporters, mobilize them, and define concrete actions in which they could engage. For example, the division identified superdelegates who might be persuadable and then asked targeted groups of supporters to contact these individuals via e-mail or phone calls with their own stories about why they were supporting Obama. Meanwhile, Berman hosted periodic calls with the campaign's active superdelegate volunteers to update them on the state of the numbers, as well as keep them motivated and invested in their work.

The division also leveraged its database in innovative and powerful ways. The division produced packets of materials about the districts of superdelegates who were members of Congress. These materials detailed the number of voters on the campaign's e-mail list, events planned by Obama supporters, active volunteer groups on MyBO, and the amount of money raised from supporters in these members' districts. The division then coupled this data with narratives about the activities taking place on-the-ground in the district contributed by local field staffers and people uploading their stories on MyBO. The campaign also published the stories that did not make it into these packets on the state websites.

In the end, by early June the superdelegates fell in line behind the results of the primaries. Obama declared himself the presumptive nominee on June 3, after the final two primaries, and major press outlets followed suit. Clinton followed by conceding on June 7. Meanwhile, as the campaign's field staffers closed out the final primaries, new media staffers began addressing technical issues and forecasting needs for the general election.

## TECHNICAL CHALLENGES

Shortly after the February contests, the New Media Division formed a group to take stock of current operations and to brainstorm the technical and organizational systems that the campaign would want for the general election. This planning was born of the division's experiences during the primaries. While division staffers convincingly demonstrated in February that they could deliver field resources for the campaign, the new media infrastructure was overwhelmed at points by the demands placed upon it by supporters. For example, for much of the week leading up to Super Tuesday, the BarackObama.com site ran in "core mode," providing only the home and donation pages, those absolutely crucial to the campaign.

During the primaries, the campaign was the victim of its own success. Campaigns are similar to start-up organizations in that they can grow rapidly if candidates are doing well. Even though BSD had developed one of the most sophisticated online platforms in electoral politics, MyBO suffered under the weight of interest in Obama's candidacy. Many campaigns have faced similar issues as a result of the growth of online political engagement and the nature of the political technology business. The number of individuals visiting candidate websites and donating money online has grown exponentially with each presidential cycle. Meanwhile, similar to other firms, Blue State Digital relied on a number of small clients to fill the intervening years between presidential elections. And, while BSD also worked with large clients such as the Democratic Party, these organizations did little to test or extend the capacity of the platform at the scale at which the Obama campaign ultimately ended up needing it. Compounding the problem was the fact that few previous campaigns had experienced such rapid growth as that which occurred among Obama's active supporter base, which exceeded the expectations of nearly all the campaign's staffers.

Capacity challenges were particularly apparent given the sheer unprecedented volume of financial transactions that occurred on the campaign's site and occasionally overwhelmed its servers. At key moments in the campaign, such as after a primary victory or a big speech, Obama took in as much as a million dollars in small donations per hour, so much that the number of transactions per second put serious strains on the system. To address these scale issues, the campaign continually made investments in the capacity of the BSD platform, since it was the firm's only client that placed these demands on their multi-tenanted servers. In advance of the August 2008 Democratic National Convention, for instance, CTO Michael Slaby and BSD's Jascha Franklin-Hodge built three different layers of redundancy into the contribution system to keep the site running after Obama accepted the nomination. This additional capacity, in turn, proved to be ample for the rest of the general election. In addition to these capacity issues, new media staffers had a wish list of technical improvements and new applications. Hughes cites how new media staffers had some basic development needs, such as further website optimization, more reliable e-mail delivery, and better contact management.[32] Meanwhile, staffers continually sought new applications for the platform. Trying to do development on a live platform is difficult, which is what the campaign ended up doing.

The campaign had so much traffic, and such considerable resources, that some prominent Obama supporters in the technology industry believed that it needed to create its own technical infrastructure for the general election. In April 2008, when it became evident beyond a reasonable doubt to senior staffers that Obama was going to be the nominee, the campaign convened a secret meeting in Chicago. The meeting brought together representatives of Blue State Digital, Voter Activation Network, and Catalist, the private data firm, under the auspices of laying the groundwork for the general election. There was an ulterior motive. A group of technology industry backers of the campaign that had the candidate's ear, gathered under the moniker of "Silicon Valley for Obama," was making the internal case that with its hundreds of millions of dollars in fund-raising, the campaign should commission a Valley firm to build an entirely new, custom online platform and voter file interface. Despite putting together what was widely recognized as the best package of political technologies in electoral politics, these industry supporters argued that what BSD offered was inferior to what Valley firms used in commercial contexts. Meanwhile, knowing full well the failures in the data operations of previous presidential candidates, these supporters and some campaign staffers had a persistent lack of confidence that the party's data and vendors were up to the task of the field operation that the campaign hoped to mount for the general election. In essence, BSD, VAN, and Catalist were called upon to make the case for why the campaign *should not* spend something on the order of $25 million to develop new systems.

After this meeting, the campaign decided to remain with the providers that had carried it through the primaries. The decision was based on a number of factors. For one, Obama's leadership recognized that these firms had unique knowledge of how technological systems needed to work in political contexts and that a firm specializing in work for commercial clients would lack experience in electoral politics. In addition, the time and cost of commissioning something new and training staff in the midst of planning the general election run was daunting. As such, the campaign committed to continuing to work with VAN and BSD, with the party's voter file supplemented by data provided by Catalist. The campaign did, however, have a number of priorities for development, particularly around running a large-scale distributed field operation in battleground states. This meant opening the voter file to increasing numbers of volunteers, both through the VAN interface and the online MyBO platform.

## THE CHALLENGES OF DATA INTEGRATION

Given the number of Obama supporters involved in electoral efforts during the primaries, the campaign had high hopes for mobilizing thousands of additional volunteers during the general election. To this end, after their April meeting, the campaign, VAN, and BSD engaged in extensive planning for ways to best leverage the energy of the volunteer base. It became readily apparent that to maximize this support, the campaign would need to synch the VAN and BSD systems and provide unprecedented access to the voter file. Opening the voter file to greater numbers of volunteers than any campaign had done previously would ensure that supporters spent their time making contact with, and generating data on, individuals whom the campaign identified as priorities. Doing so, however, posed challenging technical problems, particularly around the need to provide thousands of individuals with simultaneous access to the voter file and to integrate the data housed in VAN and MyBO.

To open the voter file to additional volunteers, the campaign commissioned VAN to build in another layer of access to VoteBuilder. As detailed in the last chapter, VAN originally built VoteBuilder to provide different levels of access to campaign staffers depending on their position, with the platform's functionality determined by organizational role.[33] When staffers created new users in Vote-Builder, they assigned them different profile categories, which provided prede-termined levels of access. At the highest levels of campaigns, staffers could see all the information on voters and volunteers stored in VoteBuilder. Lower level staffers had limited access to certain categories of information. For example, a state field director could develop target universes on the basis of voter modeling and could monitor the data generated by canvasses. A field organizer, mean-while, could only "cut turf" (or walk lists) from those universes and enter the data generated by volunteers.

The Obama campaign wanted its trained "super-volunteer" precinct cap-tains to be able to access the voter database to generate walk lists for canvasses and to direct other volunteers. In previous campaigns, and those of Obama's rivals during the 2008 cycle, these activities were generally the domain of the paid field staffer. To add this additional layer of access and standardize user privileges across states for the general election, approximately a week after Obama became the nominee, Mike Sager, the national VoteBuilder adminis-trator for the party, Matthew Loveless, a campaign field staffer, and approxi-mately eight other campaign representatives sat in a converted field office in Portland, Oregon, and came up with a new data structure for the Obama cam-paign, creating it live in VoteBuilder. First, these staffers detailed all the dif-ferent user profiles used in the primaries to map one set of permissions that the campaign required at each user level. They then added the data access that the campaign wanted volunteers to have during the general election. Finally, these staffers generated a universe of survey questions across all states that volunteers would need to ask in canvassing. The result was a uniform set of defined access permissions for all users, including volunteers, as well as standardized data col-lection across all states. In other words, during the general election field direc-tors saw exactly the same categories of data and had the same functionality based on their role, whether they were in Missouri or North Carolina. Stan-dardizing the data from the states made it easier to run national level reports on the ground campaign.

Based on input from field staffers, during the general election the campaign also created an application that fed online volunteer sign-ups on the MyBO plat-form directly to field staffers through the VAN's "MyCampaign" volunteer man-agement database. Working with hired developers at BSD, campaign and VAN staffers created flows between the various databases used on the campaign. This meant that field staffers had instantaneous access to the e-mail addresses and phone numbers of volunteers who were signing up for the campaign online in their regions, something that had eluded the campaign throughout the primaries. Field organizers could contact these supporters quickly and schedule them for meetings or events. As Slaby describes the importance of this application:

> There were a lot of different ways that the data got integrated and flipped back and forth but I think the most important one that really made the biggest difference was the volunteer integration. . . . One of the most important things you get from online, especially in the campaign, is that it is where people find you and so those lists of people that came in online, those people got sent directly into the queue for volunteer prospects and the field organizers had their phone number, e-mail, everything right away.[34]

Meanwhile, the campaign sought to achieve a more comprehensive integration between MyBO and VoteBuilder. The object of this integration was Neighbor-to-Neighbor (N2N). As detailed in Chapter 5, N2N was initially a project of the Democratic Party. Working with Blue State Digital, party staffers had the idea to enable volunteers to access parts of the party's voter file online so that they could generate and print their own walk lists and go door to door to canvass voters. The party piloted a demonstration version in a 2007 special election in Virginia. In this version, volunteers were also responsible for entering the results of their canvasses back into the system. These voters were "checked out" to volunteers for a limited time, and if they did not return the data their access would expire.

After Obama became the nominee, the campaign requested that the party add calling functionality to Neighbor-to-Neighbor, with the tool to be hosted on MyBO. Having a calling tool synched to the voter file had long been a goal of division staffers. During the primaries, the campaign used a BSD-developed online calling tool that proved to be of limited utility because it was not integrated with the voter database. This meant that new media staffers under Hughes had to go into the VAN, manually generate a target list of phone numbers, upload them into the calling tool, and create a series of questions. Meanwhile, after online volunteers made their calls, the data needed to be downloaded from the calling tool and then manually entered into the VAN. As a result of how labor-intensive this system was, and the fact that data could not be recorded instantly, the universe of targets used for this calling tool were generally a low priority for the campaign. Staffers knew that an online calling tool synched to the voter file would drastically improve the utility of these supporter efforts for the campaign. It would also reduce the need to open field offices in expensive urban areas to capitalize on concentrations of Obama supporters willing to make calls. Finally, it would also improve the quality of data by standardizing response categories (and eliminate scribbled notes on walk sheets) as well as enable the campaign to generate more targeted scripts to categories of voters.

Fortuitously from a technological standpoint, the Obama campaign happened to also use Blue State Digital tools. PartyBuilder already had limited integration with VoteBuilder through the party's work on N2N in 2007. That said, adding a calling tool to N2N required significant new pathways between the BSD online database and the voter file. The challenge lay in the web data, the most active data set with the sparsest information, because the campaign needed to keep the barriers to volunteer entry as low possible. For example, the campaign often only required an e-mail address or Facebook ID to log into MyBO, without requiring that supporters enter all of their information. Given this, VAN would have to radically open up its interface to a much wider universe of users. As Sullivan describes, the challenge lay in creating:

> the ability to distribute voter contact to essentially the anonymous user, practically anonymous users. Everything that we'd ever done we'd only worked in the sort of private logged-in space. We have never done anything until this current election cycle [2008] actually, where we are now very focused on web stuff, but we never worked outside of the logged-in space and of course that's Blue State's specialty is the open space, the public space. The priority was to deliver these. There's an ability where you can go set up a campaign to the target universe of a million people . . . and let people on the public website get lists of 25 people and call them up. . . .[35]

In the end, while staffers were able to create this functionality, N2N never quite had the utility that staffers hoped for when they dreamed of gaining "100,000 employees" for a distributed field operation.[36] Launched over July and August 2008, N2N facilitated distributed calling in opening portions of the voter file to thousands of volunteers who could access this system from their own homes. And yet, despite more integration between the BSD and VAN back-ends than many other tools used on the campaign, the problem with N2N lay in the mismatch between the needs of field staffers and online volunteers. The work flows that opening the voter file to this extent required did not fit with the practices of field staffers. Field staffers generated lists of voters that online volunteers using N2N called. The problem was that once these lists were "checked out" by online volunteers, they could not be changed, as the campaign wanted to prevent duplicate calls. Field staffers had to wait until online users checked the lists back in before doing anything with those voters. For its part, the New Media Division was very cognizant of the fact that the utility of this tool lay in online volunteers having their own set of voters to call at their leisure, which meant that checked out voter lists took a while to expire. The upshot was that these lists of voters were out of circulation from the field program for a while, not an ideal process for field staffers who needed the flexibility to discard, reassign, and create new lists.

Meanwhile, the data generated from these calls was not automatically reinserted back into the voter database in real time (although staffers no longer had to do it manually, as with the previous calling tool). Because these lists were "checked out" by volunteers, the division had to update the voter file from N2N calls in batches of returned lists every 24 hours. Timing these updates proved challenging. Across the campaign, volunteers in the field conducted canvassing phone calls and door knocks until 9 P.M. Soon after, field staffers generated daily reports for their regions and started cutting lists for the next day based on these reports. New media staffers could not upload data from N2N while field organizers were cutting lists, so they updated the voter file from 2 to 6 A.M. This then created a 24-hour lag in the N2N data, where it would not inform the cutting of walk lists until a full day after it was entered. As Slaby explains, this situation meant that in field staffers' "minds they could not rely on the universe [of voters] that was on the online calling tool getting called . . ." As a result, similar to the printed lists, only the least essential calls made it into the N2N universe. Online volunteers made approximately 30 million of these calls using N2N. This number was comparatively small (the campaign's field organization made 70 million voter contacts in the last weekend of the campaign alone) but far beyond what any campaign had accomplished online up to that point.

These calls were also more targeted than in previous Democratic campaigns, as voter modeling had grown much more sophisticated since the presidential election of 2004. The Obama campaign hired the voter modeling firm Strategic Telemetry in 2007. Strategic Telemetry began its work of modeling voters by taking a poll of a random, representative sample of the electorate. Based on the candidates whom these polled voters supported, the firm then worked backward to find correlated variables for Obama supporters and undecideds. As Sullivan describes: "We throw a ton of stuff in the black box, and it spits out which things have correlations."[37] Strategic Telemetry then created combinations of these correlated variables that corresponded to the characteristics of the candidate's supporters and undecideds. The campaign's data consultants then layered these models onto the electorate using the voter file's public and commercial voter data, generating a composite score of likely support for Obama on a 0–100 scale for every member of the electorate. The firm then continually polled and incorporated the results of field canvasses to test the accuracy of and update its models.

This approach to voter modeling helped the campaign to better identify its supporters and those leaning in the candidate's direction to target its fieldwork. Targeting is about finding people who lean toward a particular candidate and are less likely than others to show up at the polls. Unlike the Democratic efforts in 2004 detailed in  Chapter 4, the Obama campaign targeted priority individuals who resided in heavily Republican precincts. The campaign also focused on neighbor-hoods with low voter turnout and favorable likely supporter demographics. Meanwhile, with early voting increasingly common in many states, the campaign attempted to bank as many votes as possible in advance of the election. These early voting efforts were predicated on knowing who had already voted in order to free up campaign resources to concentrate on those who had not.

To facilitate its field operations and online phone banking, as noted above the campaign also ran a simpler and cleaner version of the VAN with tiered data to remove functionality and hide raw data from all but the senior level staffers. In the place of many categories of data, the Obama campaign dis-played only the numerical scores of likely support. Only higher-level field staffers could directly access the more detailed data and generate target uni-verses. On-the-ground field organizers then pulled these target universes down to create canvass walk lists, which they then used to deploy volunteers. As Sullivan relates:

> So the number of people who are using the micro data has shrunken over time to the people who are using it informed by all that we have learned over the years about what is successful and what is not and how to use the models and which models are useful.[38]

These more sophisticated voter-modeling techniques made N2N calls more effective for the campaign, even as the tool's utility was ultimately limited by the data entry issues. Regardless of the overall utility for field operations, however, N2N kept the distributed network of Obama supporters engaged and included in the campaign, and thus likely to contribute in other ways, such as financially or through volunteering. In other words, quite apart from the data it generated, staffers perceived the returns from N2N as valuable in terms of relationship building with a community of supporters.

## VOTE FOR CHANGE

The Obama campaign also leveraged new media tools in its voter registration efforts. The conventional wisdom among presidential campaigners is that it is rarely worth the expense required to register individuals only remotely likely to vote. Senior strategists on the Obama campaign, however, believed that the cam-paign needed to expand the electorate to win the primaries and then the general election, and that Obama had the unique potential to do so, since he was a young African American candidate. To further this effort, the campaign invested in developing tools that enabled staffers to manage data on voter registration and made it easier for individuals to register.

Voter registration projects posed a large data management issue for the campaign. During the primaries, the campaign did not have a way to add unregistered individuals to the voter file. This is because the foundation of the voter file is public data on registered state voters. Field organizers needed to find ways to manage data on unregistered voters both to track who filled out registration forms and to check back to make sure that they were actually sent in. For these reasons, it was crucial for unregistered voters to be on canvass walk lists. In the absence of a dedicated way of marking these individuals in the voter file, field organizers were constantly creating work-arounds to collect data on these individuals. For example, throughout the primaries, field organizers often dumped new registrants in the MyCampaign volunteer section in VoteBuilder. Organizers would create lists in MyCampaign of individuals who had received registration information and then follow up with them to see that they had actually registered. In 2008, VAN began developing a solution to this problem by creating a dedicated voter registration file within VoteBuilder. This involved creating a single national file for all new registrants, where every field organizer would enter his or her data in bulk uploads.

While the back-end was far from perfect, this data solution helped the campaign to develop its "Vote for Change" application during the general election. Launched in conjunction with a 50-state voter registration drive, the Vote for Change tool enabled individuals to either register online or print a form to mail in to register to vote, depending on state law. Vote for Change was a deceptively simple tool that masked its impressive design and engineering. The application had a markedly simple interface designed by Scott Thomas, the campaign's design director. In doing preliminary research into online voter registration tools, Thomas noticed that applications often had long and daunting forms with questions that individuals had to fill out in order to register. In contrast, Thomas designed Vote for Change to only ask registrants one question at a time, and then in an iterative process have answers determine the next relevant question (see figure 6.1). What counted as a relevant question was markedly challenging to determine. Behind this simple interface lay a complex organizational and technical back-end. The campaign's staffers researched the online voter registration requirements for all 50 states. Division staffers then programmed the interface to ensure that individuals filled in the forms correctly and that all the required information was collected so the state had what it needed to register these voters. Vote for Change also combined online voter registration with polling place lookup, an additional layer of complexity.

Meanwhile, the campaign integrated the Vote for Change application with the VAN. This enabled campaign staffers to access voter registration data and then act upon it in important ways. As individuals registered to vote online, for instance, which for many states involved generating forms that had to be printed and

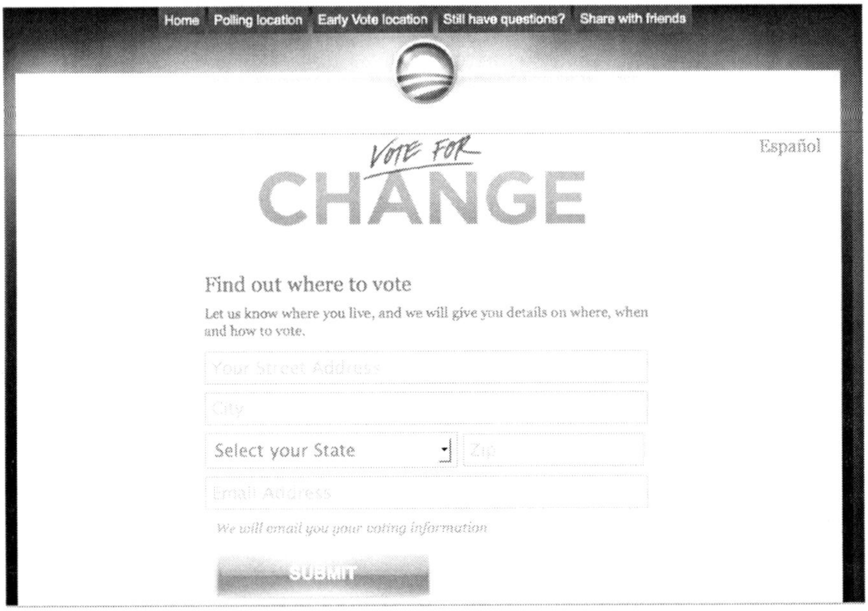

*Figure 6.1* Vote for Change Application Screen Capture, October 29, 2008

mailed to governmental offices, the campaign transferred the information on these individuals to the dedicated voter registration file detailed above. Field staffers then had volunteers call these individuals to follow up and make sure that they sent their forms to the appropriate state agency. Meanwhile, if people opted to provide their e-mail address as they were registering to vote, it went to the BSD-maintained database for MyBO.

Despite the success of tools such as Vote for Change, large-scale data integration on the campaign between BSD and VAN remained a complicated task. This is evident in the challenges that the campaign faced with what it termed the "Houdini Project." The campaign intended the Houdini Project to be a way of systematically updating the voter file as individuals went to the polls on Election Day. The plan was for the campaign's poll watchers, individuals who monitored the vote at locations throughout the country, to update the voter file remotely after they discovered who turned out through on-site public voter rolls and overhearing declarations of identity. In essence, the campaign wanted to build a national system for real-time voter roll updates so that it could more effectively deploy resources, such as not sending volunteers to the homes of individuals who had already voted.

Shortly after Obama became the nominee, the campaign contacted VAN to build a system that could support these real-time updates to the voter file. VAN had some experience with this approach to real-time updates, although not at the same scale the campaign desired. Indeed, real-time vote tracking had long been a "holy grail" for many campaigns. In 2004 VAN piloted a system based on bar codes, where voters who had turned out were scanned into a Palm Pilot and uploaded into a database. During the 2006 midterms, the firm used four-digit voter identification codes that were recorded on-site and then uploaded into the voter file. Neither system, however, was able to update the voter file in real time. For the Obama campaign, VAN developed an Interactive Voice Response phone system, in which volunteers could call an 800 number and punch in the four-digit codes of voters who had turned out. They also built another system that featured a mobile application for volunteers to do the same updating. All of this was premised on volunteers identifying the correct precinct codes and then individual voter codes. The campaign and VAN dispensed with a log-in, figuring that this would prove too high a hurdle for volunteers to participate. Given the potential for abuse, the system would automatically not enter data if the precinct codes or if a percentage of voter IDs were wrong—the accuracy of which essentially validated the user. Once the data was approved, it was then processed into the voter file. All told, this system was designed to have a mere three-minute delay between when the data entered VAN's servers and when it made it to state databases.

Despite the popular attention that the Houdini Project received, the ability to process data in real time remained a dream not quite achieved. At 8:30 in the morning on Election Day, the phone system crashed. As a result, national field director Carson abandoned the program, except in states such as Indiana and Virginia that were primarily using the mobile system. In Virginia, the system worked successfully, while in Indiana, the campaign was collecting enough data that it was making resource allocation decisions on the basis of other numbers. The Houdini Project showed enough promise that the development of similar systems continued in subsequent years.

## Conclusion

Despite the effective organizing, symbolic work, and targeted communications, there were extraordinary moments when Obama's online supporters mobilized to challenge the campaign. The most prominent episode was the online opposition to Obama's general election shift from his stance during the primaries of opposing retroactive immunity for the telecommunications firms that assisted the Bush administration in its warrantless wiretapping program. The "Get FISA Right" (Foreign Intelligence Surveillance Act) activists used the MyBO platform, sites such as Facebook and YouTube, and many blogs within the netroots to gather resources and garner press attention in an attempt to get Obama to change his new position. The MyBO Get FISA Right group alone swelled to over 15,000 members, making it the most popular group on the campaign's platform.

Meanwhile, these supporters raised enough money to produce a YouTube video and a national cable television advertisement.

On one level, this mobilization using the campaign's own tools was frustrating for many staffers. New Media Division staffers saw the Get FISA Right organizing as distracting volunteers and staffers from their electoral work. Yet, there was also the acknowledgment that this independent supporter action was facilitated by the very tools that the campaign deployed and leveraged to get supporters involved. From the campaign's perspective, however, participation was not absolute. As one staffer noted, it was not "campaign by committee."[39] Much of the division's work involved expectation setting. It was always, in the words of a staffer, a "delicate dance" to "make sure people feel like they are involved in the campaign without giving them a sense that they are actually setting strategy." This expectation setting was always an art, as was staffers' work as coordinators of citizen participation. With participation taking place outside formal organizational structures, achieving effective coordination was about providing:

> signposts and training for people to successfully go bottom up and sort of rise up and grow and lead, but in the end it is up to them to do whatever they want. What we saw was that when you provide that public utility and a strong framework . . . a strong and obvious and transparent framework for what needs to be done, the vast, vast, like 99.99% of people want to be as efficient as possible with their time and want to make sure that they do everything they can to help, and so pretty much everybody is on the same page.[40]

Obama's supporters generally accepted this framework for their participation, so long as the goals of the individuals taking distributed action and those of the campaign were aligned. This was the norm for most of the campaign. Supporters expected the campaign to do everything it could to win, wanting staffers to maximize their financial and volunteer contributions and extend the candidate's base of support. Supporters wanted Obama's opponents to be defeated, and were generally willing to serve in that effort as best they could.

And yet, the FISA organizing reveals what could happen when the basic terms of electoral participation became contested. Expectation setting and more tacit forms of coordination on the campaign such as goal-setting and the designed functionality of tools had real limits, and supporters had powerful new capacities for action. Given the very low barriers to signing up on MyBO, launching an event for Obama, and even contacting voters on the candidate's behalf, control was not absolute. Staffers ultimately knew that they "created a system that if anyone is a smart organizer like those FISA people were, they could have built enough momentum around their group that would have forced us to respond."[41] Indeed, upset with the campaign for its abrupt policy shift on FISA during the general election and demanding accountability, some members of the larger group of Obama supporters developed an independent sense of themselves, defined their own purpose for collective action, and used the campaign's own platform to mobilize.

The campaign did have to respond to the Get FISA Right mobilization, but Obama did not change his position on the bill. The candidate addressed the Get FISA Right supporters directly through a written statement explaining his position. The campaign also made two senior foreign policy advisors available for an online discussion. Staffers defended this response as providing supporters with channels to express their views in ways that were officially acknowledged by the candidate, even if it stopped short of a policy change. For many staffers, this reflected Obama's valuing of having a respectful debate in which each side has its say—with the candidate ultimately deciding the outcome based on political strategy and policy preferences. A less charitable view, voiced by a few staffers, saw this airing of debate as a "safety valve," giving "up control below, to increase control above."[42] In other words, the campaign increased the legitimacy of decisions by letting supporters have their say. Staffers ultimately knew that supporters had little bargaining power, and there was little risk in the candidate's minimal response. Supporters had nowhere else to go, knowing that if they left the Obama effort they would contribute to McCain's candidacy. After eight years of Bush, Obama's supporters were not about to derail the campaign.

In the end, the moment passed and the campaign's response defused the Get FISA Right protests. While staffers interpreted the Get FISA Right events differently, it was both a genuinely disruptive event on the campaign, even as it reveals the limited degree to which supporters had a voice in the legislative platform of the candidate.

# Conclusion: New Media Campaigning from Dean to Obama

On the night of Obama's election, new media staffers hit "send" on a final "thank you" e-mail to supporters and raced down to Grant Park to hear the president-elect declare that "change has come to America." It was a euphoric moment for those who endured months of 20-hour days in a committed effort to elect the nation's first African American president. These staffers helped achieve what to most political observers was a long shot in the early days of 2007. Together, they endured a bruising and exceptionally hard-fought primary battle against the party's most well-known and well-resourced candidate, Senator Hillary Clinton, and faced down the campaign of their Republican rivals, John McCain and Sarah Palin. Through it all, new media staffers transformed the inchoate desire of those inspired by the candidate's powerful rhetoric into concrete resources, from the funding that opened field offices to the volunteers who contacted millions of voters through online calling tools. They also helped to register thousands of voters, countered the wild rumors propagated by Obama's detractors, and coordinated thousands of supporters crossing state lines to canvass in contested states.

This book reveals how the active crafting of Democratic networked politics over much of the last decade helped to put Obama in the White House. In doing so, the book shows how campaigns do not simply exist within a social and technological context that determines the form of online politics. Campaigns, as well as parties, consultancies, and advocacy and social movement organizations, actively shape that context through their new media work. The Dean campaign was not simply the product of shifting online social practices and new networked applications that helped millions of Americans become more comfortable with purchasing commercial products and taking political action online. While these factors were important, the Dean campaign was an organizational and technical achievement. Staffers' appropriation and modification of existing tools and development of new ones shaped the extraordinary success of the campaign at raising funds and recruiting volunteers and helped to propel Dean to the front-runner position, albeit before any voting actually took place. Staffers developed the internal organizational structures to support this technical innovation, as well as the online organizing practices to coordinate the participation of supporters toward the financial and volunteer resources that Dean needed in order to compete.

Through this sociotechnical work, on the Dean campaign the Internet became a central organizing tool in electoral politics for the first time. During previous cycles, political staffers had used the Internet to engage supporters in electoral activities, but these efforts were generally halting and at a remove from the center of campaign strategy. In contrast, on the insurgent Dean campaign, the Internet was at the heart of electoral strategy and a central organizational tool, vital to efforts to garner human, financial, and communication resources. This was a significant electoral innovation, and one that the challenger Obama embraced in many respects four years later in his own bid for the presidency. The successful use of the Internet in both of these campaigns, meanwhile, was premised as much on the extraordinary mobilization behind these candidates as on the work of staffers who translated enthusiasm and energy into money and volunteers.

On both campaigns, much of this innovation was the product of the creative assemblage and application of knowledge and skills from spheres outside politics to these electoral runs. Drawn to electoral politics by the powerful social, technological, and political vision that the Dean campaign represented, many staffers and volunteers brought understandings and skills honed in commercial technological contexts and the worlds of open source politics technical production to the campaign. Staffers' abilities to recognize back-end technical and data needs, to cobble together new systems, and to design new social networking applications that stood as innovations, even in the commercial sector at the time, reflect these specialized technical skills. Even more, with little in the way of developed best practices for new media campaigning in 2004, Dean's staffers were open to and looked everywhere for new ideas. MoveOn staffers helped Dean's Internet Department develop the more proactive and data-driven use of e-mail. As they adapted these practices to the electoral context, Dean's staffers developed an entirely new—and now widely adopted—genre of campaign communications. In the Obama campaign, a number of key figures also came from the technology industry and crafted new modes of campaign work, even as the campaign drew talent from a new generation of political consultancies and trained new media campaign staffers that emerged after the 2004 cycle. Chris Hughes implemented new ways of coordinating supporters for a distributed field operation on MyBO and Facebook, while Dan Siroker helped the campaign to refine its analytical practices.

Staffers on the Dean campaign also pioneered the online organizing practices that now define networked electoral campaigning and carried them to other sites, such as the Democratic Party and the Obama campaign. Staffers engaged in projects of network building—working to create, cultivate, and maintain ties with supporters who could be mobilized for electoral social and symbolic action. Dean's staffers developed communicative practices to build relationships with and to coordinate the actions of supporters and key bloggers in the netroots. These practices entailed creating agendas for MeetUps and posting on blogs to signal the campaign's priorities and to set expectations for participation. The Dean campaign also delegated much of its coordination work to the structured interactivity of tools to facilitate certain forms of participation, such as fund-raising. Dean's former staffers carried these practices and tools of organizing to many sites in electoral politics through the consultancies they joined and founded after the 2004 election. Nowhere were these organizing practices more powerful, however, than on the Obama campaign, given a candidate who inspired tremendous mobilization. Adopting ways of working with supporters online and applying them to complement an unprecedented field effort, Obama's staffers vastly extended the online organizing first developed on the Dean campaign. In the process, the campaign achieved the unprecedented integration of its new media and field efforts. The campaign used new media to register tens of thousands of voters, to coordinate a vast, distributed volunteer operation, and to mobilize supporters to donate millions of dollars and thousands of hours of volunteer time.

Obama's new media staffers were successful in part because many of the technical and organizational challenges faced by Dean's staffers were addressed in the years between the presidential elections. Too often, scholarship on new media and politics leaves the impression that campaigns quickly and easily adopt existing new media tools for their electoral purposes. As this book has shown, however, the realization of a successful new media campaign is premised on much hard work, false starts, and overcoming immensely challenging social, technical, and institutional issues. With little in the way of dedicated tools that could function on the scale of a presidential effort, Dean's staffers developed many of their tools as needed, while still actively campaigning. As a result, the applications and systems that many scholars have heralded were actually quite limited in their utility for staffers and volunteers. On the Dean campaign, applications and their data were often siloed at both the login and the back-end. Technical systems crashed frequently under the strain of the mobilization around Dean's candidacy. Organizational routines developed very slowly as new needs continually arose in the high-stakes pressure of a presidential primary. In short, there was a very messy and complex world of mundane, daily new media work in which staffers engaged through long days and nights spent sleeping under desks. Up close, the Dean campaign resembled little of the frictionless, peer-to-peer collaboration and "open source" politics that so many popular and scholarly accounts suggest.

The work of Dean's former Internet staffers between elections was crucial for addressing many of these challenges and for enabling Obama's new media staffers to have much of the basic technological infrastructure in place when the candidate announced that he was running for the presidency. What takes place in the interstices of presidential politics has generally been ignored by scholars who focus narrowly on electoral cycles. Yet, as this book demonstrates, the years between the 2004 and 2008 presidential elections were crucial for the extension, formalization, standardization, and dissemination of the practices and tools developed on the Dean campaign. The network of consultancies and training organizations founded by many former Dean and, to a lesser extent, Clark staffers after the 2004 primaries created an infrastructure for Democratic new media campaigns comprising knowledge, practices, dedicated campaign tools, and trained staffers. A number of campaigns in 2006 and 2008 drew on these resources in their electoral contests.

The history of the consulting firm Blue State Digital and the work of its four founders illustrates just how important this infrastructure-building was to Democratic campaigning and Obama's victory. During Howard Dean's tenure as chair, BSD cofounders Ben Self and Joe Rospars played a leading role in two massive infrastructural projects that directly benefited the Obama campaign: the construction of VoteBuilder, the national voter file and interface system, and the development of the online campaign platform PartyBuilder.

The voter file project provided Chairman Dean with an occasion for completely overhauling the way in which the party conducted its elections and the relationship between the national and state parties. Dean made rebuilding the party's voter file a priority given the high-profile failures in Democratic field efforts during the 2004 elections and his promise to contest all 50 states and to reinvigorate their local party organizations. As the book detailed, this proved an extraordinarily challenging and complex infrastructural project. To build this voter file, Self had to coordinate the back-end technical work necessary to support a national database, and he commissioned Voter Activation Network, a private firm, to customize their voter file interface for the party. This entailed rebuilding much of the technical infrastructure of the party to make the data systems more robust and to allow access to voter files through an online system. As importantly, Self and his team engaged in the backstage organizational and negotiation work necessary for accessing, integrating, and standardizing 50 separate voter files maintained by distrustful state parties. The result was a national voter database and interface system called VoteBuilder, which subsequently became the core of the party's data infrastructure and was central to all of the major Democratic candidates' field campaigns in 2008. As a result of this work, Democratic candidates at all levels of office and across the 50 states have much more powerful voter files and volunteer management systems.

Meanwhile, as Self was reorganizing the party's voter file, his fledging firm was honing its campaign platform and new media strategy services through its work for a number of Democratic clients. Through a licensing model that managed the firm's technologies as a type of partisan "club good," BSD transformed the Dean campaign's tools into a powerful and integrated election platform. The party invested in the capacity and extended the functionality of this platform, and Rospars helped to implement it before the midterm elections of 2006. PartyBuilder provided supporters with new tools, while Rospars helped ensure that they were effective in electoral terms by integrating much of the field and Internet operations at the party for the midterms. This work served as the template for Rospars's work as the new media director of the Obama campaign in 2008.

All of these developments meant that when the Obama campaign launched in early 2007 with the candidate's announcement, much of the core technical infrastructure was in place for staffers to begin soliciting donations, communicating with supporters, and coordinating independent supporter actions on-the-ground. The importance of this is clear when the Dean and Obama campaigns are compared historically. At the start of the 2004 cycle, there was little in the way of dedicated tools with the capacity to function at the scale of a presidential campaign. This meant that for much of the primaries, Dean's staffers faced technical limitations and spent much time developing work-arounds for tools built with the needs of the nonprofit sector in mind and new systems with the functionality that the campaign needed. In contrast, through a chain of technical development stretching from Democracy for America, MoveOn Student Action, and ProgressNow to the Democratic Party, BSD developed its platform to overcome the problems of control and capacity that its founders experienced on the Dean campaign. While Obama's staffers faced their own challenges with respect to wanting new tools and needing more capacity later in the election, at the outset the campaign had the core of what it needed in place to begin accepting donations and facilitating supporter actions. As a result, the principals behind the fledgling New Media Division could devote time to strategic planning, the organization of technical operations, and the development of collaborative work practices with other divisions.

As such, this infrastructural history in turn suggests much for analytical accounts of new media and politics. Accounts that attribute changes in political organization and participation to the lowered costs of organizing and engaging in collective action leave much out of their frame of reference. For one, the Obama campaign's ability to effectively organize collective action was premised upon years of massive investments of human, technical, and organizational resources in developing practices and tools for online campaigning. Without these investments, the Obama campaign would have encountered many of the issues enumerated in the discussion of the Dean campaign. This includes the lack of developed practices for working with supporters online and the metrics for doing so. The campaign also would have lacked the capacity to reliably perform basic functions such as accepting donations and e-mailing supporters. The time between presidential elections, away from the pressure of being in the middle of a campaign, was central to the ability of consultants and staffers to rebuild their tools and to refine their practices of online campaigning. Building, maintaining, repairing, and crafting new infrastructure is much of what these political staffers inside party bureaucracies and organizations did in the years between elections. The form of online politics, what campaigns and citizens have the capacity and are organized to do during elections, is the outcome of this work of infrastructure building. As this book demonstrates, the most taken-for-granted forms of online collective action, such as donating money and contacting voters, are often premised upon years of technical development, organization building, and staff training.

Even as new media campaign infrastructure has largely remained outside of scholarly view, the internal workings of campaign organizations also receive rare treatment in the literature. While there is a robust literature on the consultants who run campaigns and market candidates through television advertising, the mundane, day-to-day work that constitutes electoral politics is much less well understood. In the context of new media campaigning, only a few works examine the internal workings of organizations or interview new media staffers about their practice.[1] This is a significant oversight. As this book reveals, there is much more to campaigns than the consultants who advise them at the highest levels on messaging and electoral strategy. Indeed, the story of the Obama campaign's New Media Division reveals that organizational decision making is very consequential. The campaign's senior leadership invested in new media early in the primaries and had the foresight to make Rospars a senior staffer on a par with the heads of traditionally powerful divisions such as Communications and Finance. This structure helped to ensure that the division had access to organizational resources. As importantly, the division enjoyed both significant clarity in its role and responsibilities and the autonomy to pursue its work according to the best practices of online organizing, from day-to-day e-mail communications with supporters to running online advertising.

Capturing former staffers' reflections on their work, meanwhile, reveals how these new media practices were achievements in their own right. From afar, the Obama campaign seemed to seamlessly integrate its new media and field operations, flawlessly adopt social networking tools, and easily coordinate massive online fund-raising drives. Closer to the ground, however, the contingency, planning, organizing, and setbacks of the massive new media operation come into view. On the other side of the sophisticated design and polished interface were staffers' coding struggles, work-arounds for the lack of data integration, daily challenges with the functionality of tools, and reactivity to events such as "Get FISA Right." Much of our retrospective understanding of the success of Obama's new media operations was far from apparent to the staffers involved in actually assembling the organizing and technical practices of the campaign.

The campaign's innovations were also forged through much hard work and trial and error. New media staffers spent much energy developing intra-divisional work practices to coordinate the development of tools with field staffers. Through this work, the campaign developed entirely new tools, such as the Vote for Change registration application, and improved old ones, such as allowing field staffers to instantaneously receive information about supporters signing up to volunteer on the MyBO platform.

The computational management style that Rospars and his colleagues honed in late 2007 also developed over time to help ensure that the division was efficient in its operations and rigorously focused on its metrics for new media organizing. Outside the blog and design, which served as important tools for the symbolic representation of the campaign for supporters and staffers alike, much of the division's work was rigorously quantified to serve the electoral ends of the campaign. On one level, this was an internal management tool that allowed the division to be efficient in its own work and to demonstrate its effectiveness to the larger organization to garner resources. Staffers knew the comparative value of different aspects of their new media work, and they could allocate resources and personnel effectively. Even more, staffers could probabilistically anticipate flows of resources down to the minute. Staffers also used data as an external management tool. Data transformed supporters into abstract entities that staffers could then manipulate to gain the resources that the campaign needed. Website optimization and targeted e-mail messaging reveal these processes of tracing, and acting upon, data representations of users. The actions that staffers sought to induce were contingent upon both electoral strategy and the characteristics of the targeted individual. For example, in what is a quintessential technology of probabilistic control, optimization enabled staffers to know what resources they could expect to receive from aggregate visits to the website and the optimal targeting of content and design to achieve their goals.

## New Media Campaigning and Democratic Processes

Political campaigns matter. They help determine electoral outcomes. Although other factors matter as well, such as the economy, the international context, the preferences of party elites, and the popularity of the incumbent, the dynamics of campaigns are particularly consequential in primaries and close elections. To look at campaigns as important only in terms of what happens on election day, however, is to leave much out. As the political scientist Daniel Galvin has shown, campaigns both reflect the organizational capacity of parties to mobilize supporters and actively contribute to party infrastructure.[2] In a complementary analysis, this book shows that it was the sociotechnical remnants of a *failed* campaign, that of Howard Dean, which helped build a new infrastructure for Democratic campaigning.

While many scholars have noted that campaigns still allocate expenditures disproportionally to traditional television advertising, new media also proved electorally consequential during the 2004 and 2008 elections.[3] While their efforts ultimately came up short, Dean's staffers used new media to propel their candidate to the front of the Democratic field. In the process, Dean secured a more visible platform for his critique of the Bush administration and the war in Iraq, opening up the rhetorical space for Democrats to be more critical of the incumbent president. The networked applications that the Obama campaign deployed were central to his success during the primaries. The Internet facilitated millions of small-dollar donations and purchases of campaign gear in the online store. MyBO provided a key infrastructural tool for supporters to organize their own local canvass and visibility efforts, and field staffers leveraged these efforts during the primaries. While it is impossible to know whether Obama would have emerged from the primaries without the campaign's new media operations, it is clear that these staffers and their technologies mattered in an electoral contest that was decided by the slimmest of margins.

As the above discussion suggests, both the Dean and Obama campaigns were innovative in their use of new media for the transactional ends of campaigning. Political scientist Matthew Hindman noted this, arguing in a study of Dean's run that new media revolutionized the operational back-end of political campaigns.[4] From Howard Dean to Barack Obama, new media have provided campaigns with new ways to find and engage supporters, to run their internal operations, and to translate the energy and enthusiasm generated by candidates and political opportunities into the staple resources of American electioneering. Meanwhile, as these tools and practices have grown more powerful, political staffers and new media consultants have facilitated a resurgence in political activity among the electorate. Campaigns use new media to make it easier for citizens to take social and symbolic action in electoral politics, from increasing the number of financial contributors and field volunteers to providing supporters with new means of engaging in political expression with potentially large audiences.

In focusing closely on the contexts of new media use, this book shows that theorists who see a dystopic form of elite management and network optimists who see enlightened collaboration as the consequence of changes in technologies miss the hybridity of a form of organizing politics that combines both management and empowerment. Over the last decade, a body of scholarship has with great alarm documented the increasing rise of political professionals in new media campaigns. Communication scholar Philip Howard provides the most detailed study of new media campaign professionals and argues that they have new opportunities to "manage" citizens by targeting communication, conjuring up issue publics, and providing very thin avenues to engage in politics. Social movement scholar Victoria Carty extends this work in her research on the Obama campaign, arguing that staffers used new media to create managed citizens.[5] These perspectives on new media campaigning echo a wider body of literature that argues that civic life has shifted "from membership to management" due to changes, in part, in mass media and computing.[6] In this view, centralized advocacy and campaign organizations wield the tools of mass and networked media and direct mail to narrowly mobilize the electorate and to structure civic participation.

As this book demonstrates, while the Obama campaign certainly engaged in sophisticated forms of data profiling and targeted its persuasive communications, these scholarly accounts generally overstate the control that campaign staffers and political consultants have over the electorate. Electoral campaigning, even in the most computational forms of Obama's new media campaign, is a complicated, unstable, and dynamically unfolding sociotechical affair. Despite their groundbreaking technical work, Dean's staffers struggled to develop practices, routines, and tools for coordinating the work of supporters outside the campaign's formal organizational boundaries. Staffers always had to remain responsive, at least to a degree, to the concerns of supporters given the voluntaristic nature of their participation. Meanwhile, staffers could not formally manage these supporters, and even lacked the close, in-person coordination of volunteers that is a characteristic of embodied field campaigns.

While the Obama campaign pioneered practices of computational management and leveraged the party's vast data infrastructure, control of supporters' actions was always probabilistic, not deterministic. Control was limited to increasing the likelihood that people would take particular actions for the campaign. It was confined to easily measured domains, such as sign-ups to the e-mail list and donations. While the campaign used data to coordinate its volunteers and new media applications, such as Neighbor-to-Neighbor, to script what communication scholar Rasmus Nielsen calls "personalized political communication" and improve data capture, there was plenty of volunteer agency in the interstices of these systems.[7] Supporters could, and often did, go off MyBO and use tools such as Google Groups to organize their neighborhoods. In my many observations, phone canvassing seldom adhered to scripts, as voters demanded more authentic forms of dialogue (and volunteers were often happy to oblige). Comments on the blog often deviated from the official narrative of the campaign, for example when supporters called on the candidate to more aggressively respond to the attacks of Clinton and McCain.

Indeed, many scholars concerned with the management of electoral politics have generally overlooked the fact that the interests of campaigns and the publics they mobilize are *aligned* most of the time. Supporters expect campaigns to do everything they can to win. Supporters want campaigns to maximize their financial and volunteer contributions and to extend the candidate's base of support. Supporters want opponents to be defeated and are often willing to serve in that effort as best they can. Campaigns, for their part, strive for the same outcomes and use supporters to implement electoral strategy. It is only during extraordinary moments of significant crisis that fissures appear in this alignment, as occurred when the Obama campaign lost primaries in Ohio and Texas, or when supporters feared that the candidate they had worked for would disappoint them (during the "Get FISA Right" protests). In the wake of these primary losses, supporters took to the blog to demand a strategic voice in the campaign given its perceived failures, but such a voice would have conflicted with staffers' tight control over communications and decision making. In the FISA case, supporters desired more accountability over policy positions. In each case, after supporters exercised their voice and the campaign or candidate responded to this discontent, the alignment of interest was restored, in part because there was little in the way of an alternative candidate.

In light of these empirical findings, it is clear that certain veins of the literature take an overly deterministic view of campaigns' ability to structure and control political participation. At the same time, the Dean and Obama campaigns were not robust proving grounds of democratic citizenship. A number of scholars have advanced overly optimistic claims about new media campaigns, particularly the Obama campaign. These accounts generally overstate the agency of citizens vis-à-vis campaigns and electoral institutions. Dean's Internet policy team was made up of a cadre of Silicon Valley business leaders and technologist luminaries working without any public participation.[8] As the "Get FISA Right" protests suggest, the Obama campaign set its policy agenda according to its own strategic needs, and supporters could not do much about it. Networked media have not necessarily made campaigns more responsive to supporters or their concerns. Meanwhile, grand claims for democratic transformation are only sustained if the ends toward which campaigns direct supporter collaboration are left out. As this book reveals, the Obama campaign, like the Dean campaign before it, spent much time and effort translating energy and collaboration into the staples of political campaigns: money, message, and votes.

At the same time, much suggests that networked tools can be used for different ends, and that the Obama campaign was not particularly democratic when measured against other organizations. As the political scientist David Karpf reveals, MoveOn captures data and uses analytic techniques similar to those used in the 2008 Obama campaign. For example, MoveOn tracks and analyzes the click-through rates of members without their knowledge.[9] The organization uses this data to monitor the issue preferences of members and to make decisions as to what advocacy and electoral activities to pursue. Contrasting MoveOn's real-time system with the old membership surveys of large-scale federated organizations, Karpf calls these new forms of member input and organizational decision making through analytics a form of "passive democratic feedback."[10] While Karpf shows how passive democratic feedback allows for stronger representation of members' interests, the Obama campaign made mostly transactional use of these same technologies.

That the Dean and Obama campaigns lacked substantive citizen participation in matters such as policy and strategy is not necessarily a bad thing. As temporal entities with very clear metrics for success, campaigns simply are not designed to be the training grounds of radical democratic participation that many desire. As such, they are neither as onerous as their critics suggest nor as transformative as their advocates declare. This book has shown how much of the work of Internet and new media staffers revolved around creating tools and practices for the highly transactional ends required for electoral success. Many supporters not only accept but embrace this, given the basic goal alignment between these campaigns and their supporters: the objective is to defeat rivals, not remake democracy. To do so, these campaigns had to develop new ways of mobilizing supporters and coordinating their participation. As such, the embrace of new media by campaigns is about innovating and working within electoral institutions, not subverting them.

This book maps, then, the evolution of the hybrid political organizing practices that couple sophisticated forms of computational management and democratic empowerment. It is worth returning to the quote from Michael Slaby, the Obama 2008 campaign's chief technology officer, cited in Chapter 1 of this volume, on this point: "We didn't have to generate desire very often. We had to capture and empower interest and desire . . . We made intelligent decisions that kept it growing but I don't think anybody can really claim we started something."[11] The Obama campaign, like the Dean campaign before it, created the organization, tools, and practice that translated age-old political desire fueled by values, interests, and grievances into concrete electoral resources. Citizens were empowered in the sense of having new opportunities to contribute to institutional electoral politics, but these were always bounded by the dictates of electoral strategy.

*Taking Our Country Back* therefore tells an old story of electoral mobilization, not transformational politics. Many of those who saw these campaigns in terms of transformational politics believed that the tools that powered Dean and Obama's runs and the forms of participation that they supported would change politics forever. On the eve of Obama's election, many saw the

potential for a newly participatory polity and more robust political representation, given the affordances of social media to bring the president-elect
closer to ordinary Americans. Others speculated on the potential of Obama's
"online army" as a blunt legislative tool to pressure centrist Democrats and
recalcitrant Republicans into acceding to the new president's far-reaching
agenda of reforming health care and ending the Bush tax cuts and the Iraq
War.[12] And yet, less than a year after Obama took office, many of these same
authors watched this supposed army "creak into action" to help implement
the president's agenda.[13]

Waves of electoral mobilization often break upon the shores of routine politics given the durability, stability, and persistence of electoral institutions. The
vast campaign apparatus was placed in the service of the party as Organizing for
America (OFA) and directed to the needs of the legislative agenda, which at
times meant bolstering conservative Democrats.[14] Obama ceased acting like the
leader of a social movement and assumed the role of a governing statesman, and
much of his inspirational and moral rhetoric fell away. Meanwhile, persistently
poor economic conditions and a resurgent Republican activist base challenged
the new president. As sociologist Karin Knorr Cetina had the foresight to note,
shortly after Obama's election: "Entrenched institutions and competing leaders,
charisma theory predicts, will not simply recognize charisma, they will put it to
a trial of strength, and fight."[15]

With this transition to governance, persistent unemployment, the counter-
mobilization of the Tea Party, and simple exhaustion among the president's supporters, the most powerful new media political tools in the world had very little
to translate into electoral resources. By the midterm elections, much of the campaign was a distant memory in the face of the energy of a group of Tea Party activists striving to take their country back. Former staffers sought to replicate the
campaign's success at OFA in this new electoral environment and watched as
their party was handed a historic defeat at the polls. Others, at a remove from
electoral politics, struggled to use networked media to open up hardened federal
bureaucracies and to change the practices of the White House.

As the 2012 campaign cycle got underway, Joe Rospars took another leave
from his newly acquired firm to soldier through his third presidential cycle as
the chief digital strategist for Obama's reelection bid. Michael Slaby joined up
as well, becoming the chief integration and innovation officer for the campaign. Teddy Goff became the digital director for the reelection bid. The 2012
campaign unfolded in a very different context from that of four years earlier.
Rospars, Slaby, and Goff wielded their new media tools in the service of a
president with diminished approval ratings and with America mired in steep
unemployment, facing massive budget deficits, and grappling with persistent
income inequality.

# Developing a Research Agenda

This book fills gaps in our knowledge of new media and politics in providing an in-depth look at the changing infrastructural and organizational contexts of contemporary politics. In concluding this book, I argue that this analytical and methodological approach of chronicling the work of political practitioners and technologies across many organizational sites, electoral cycles, and domains of social and technical activity suggests a number of avenues for future research. In particular, I argue that this approach is well suited to documenting and analyzing the evolving infrastructure and practices for gathering and managing data that the history presented here suggests will increasingly define the work of campaigns in the years ahead.

*Taking Our Country Back's* contribution lies in being the first scholarly, yet insider, account of the history of new media and campaigning over much of the last decade. The book moves across election cycles and organizational boundaries to detail the larger sociotechnical contexts and fields that campaigns are embedded in and the products of - even as they create and shape these contexts and fields. While there are many practitioner and a few scholarly accounts of the work of campaign staffers, most are tied to election cycles.[16] And, while there is a developed literature on political consulting, few works have closely tracked changes in the industry servicing campaigns or the shifting professional backgrounds of campaign new media staffers. This literature, for instance, seldom accounts for the launching of new firms and careers after the completion of electoral cycles, generally overlooks the movement of individuals into digital political consulting from other sectors, and too often fails to account for the wide range of organizations that help to produce tools and practices for online campaigning.

As this book has shown, what happens in the interstices between elections and at organizational sites far from campaigns in contexts from business to software development is enormously consequential for shaping the infrastructural context within which campaigns act. This analytical approach, in turn, helps open the "black box" of tools that are routinely used on campaigns and the practices that have developed around them.[17] Behind even the smallest of campaigns lies the complex world of technical development that unfolds over years and consumes much of the time of hundreds of practitioners at numerous organizational sites. From this vantage point, campaigns appear as sociotechnical achievements that are years in the making, even as they contribute back to the infrastructure for campaigning.

This analytical and methodological approach in turn opens new opportunities for research into new media and politics. Scholars can trace the connections between campaigns and parties, social movement organizations, and firms, as well as the circulation of actors between industries, as potential sources of innovation in electoral politics. The history presented in this book suggests the importance of heterogeneity in terms of knowledges, skills, and tools as being an important source of campaign innovation. The transfer of tools and skills across industries and institutional contexts, as well as protected organizational spaces in which staffers could ply their trade, were important to both the Dean and Obama campaigns. So, too, was the fact that these were insurgent candidates who had senior staff that were committed to running technologically unconventional campaigns. Scholars can draw on these insights to more systematically analyze innovation on campaigns, and to explore when these conditions and innovations fail to produce extraordinary electoral runs. For example, much anecdotal evidence suggests that Wesley Clark's 2004 and Ron Paul's 2008 campaigns featured professionals from the technology industry, new tools and organizational logics, and staffer autonomy. It seems that both campaigns were innovative technologically and organizationally. And yet, both campaigns had candidates who failed to generate energy and enthusiasm among the wider electorate. Accordingly, scholars can further analyze the sources of the political mobilization that new media captures and sustains, from the charisma and rhetoric of candidates to perceived political opportunities.

Scholarly work in this domain can take closer account of the infrastructural work of political parties and their allied organizations that train those who work on campaigns, carry knowledge and skills across election cycles, and shape the tools that candidates have at their disposal. Scholars can analyze the changing composition of "campaigns" as heterogenous and temporal assemblages of people, knowledges, organizations, and tools drawn from this infrastructural context.[18] Tracing these assemblages, and the struggle to build them, in turn opens a frame of analysis onto the historical development of campaign technologies and practice. For example, the book documents the many technologies used in the Obama campaign, the history of their development between electoral cycles, the crafting and formalization of practices around them, and the struggle to align different systems, such as the attempted integration of VoteBuilder and PartyBuilder. Similar work is needed on the development (or possibly the dismantling) of the infrastructure of the Republican Party during this time period and during the years between the 2008 and 2012 presidential elections, when it was out of power. Scholars should look to the evolution of relationships between parties, their allied organizations, campaigns, and commercial fields in the years ahead, and analyze how this affects the tools and practices that candidates have at their disposal. Even more, scholars can conduct comparative work on the composition of campaign assemblages as potential keys to understanding their successes and failures.

Scholars can also explore the lines of technological and organizational development traced in this book in studies of future campaigns. The Obama campaign was the most advanced technologically in 2008, and it tied together a number of disparate threads in electoral innovation that took shape over the last decade. For one, Obama's staffers extended practices of leveraging the social ties of supporters for electoral purposes. Digital networks facilitate campaigns' ability to transform supporters into active conduits of political messages and information to their friends, family, and affinity groups. An innovative feature of the 2000 elections, this practice has been extended considerably over time through dedicated social networking applications developed by campaigns and commercial platforms such as Facebook. In the years ahead, scholars can look to evolving techniques of leveraging the social networks of supporters to create new digital two-step flows of strategic campaign communications.

Scholars can also research the organizational and technical integration of new media and field operations that campaigns have struggled with over much of the last decade. There have been many challenges for campaigns in this domain, but the trend is clear: campaigns have continually sought to develop more effective ways for networked media to complement offline field operations. This task has been hindered by both the incommensurability of work practices among new media and field staffers and the limitations of tool sets. The Obama campaign made considerable, if imperfect, progress in coordinating the work of these disparate staffers, developing explicit organizational processes designed to facilitate collaboration between divisions and integrating its data systems so that state field organizers received instantaneous information on supporters signing up online to volunteer for the campaign. How future campaigns address the organizational and technical integration of disparate areas of campaign practice should be a subject of scholarly investigation in the years ahead.

Finally, scholars of new media and politics should have the infrastructures and practices for gathering, storing, managing, analyzing, and acting on data at the forefront of their research agenda. A central theme of the history presented in this book is the ongoing building of data infrastructures by parties, consultancies, and campaigns, the attempts to integrate various streams of data across often proprietary systems, and the growing use of analytic practices in all domains of campaigning.

In the years ahead, scholars should analyze the continual development of these data and analytic practices and the knowledges and technologies that support them. Research on future campaigns should look to the diffusion and further development of these data-driven management practices and their attendant technologies. Scholars should also seek to uncover the online, public, private, and commercial sources of data that underlie the targeting of communications and conduct of new media and field campaigns. Research should be attentive to the attempts of campaigns to integrate data on users of platforms such as MyBO, data from commercial sites such as Facebook, and the massive voter files maintained by political parties and third-party organizations. Scholars should also look to the new applications that further integration of data streams afford, such as Neighbor-to-Neighbor. Finally, scholars should consider the democratic consequences of the profusion of data in electoral politics, from the more effective transactional management of campaigns and the potential compromising of citizen political privacy to the increasingly effective narrowcasting of political messages and tailoring of information environments.

# Notes

Acknowledgments

1. Staff titles on campaigns are often inexact or left unspecified. There are often different versions of formal titles in Federal Election Commission filings, staffers themselves used many variants of titles when addressing their work, and many staffers changed positions during the course of these campaigns. I report the best approximation of these staffers' titles here when they are available, choosing the most consistent way they represented themselves in interviews and on online sites such as LinkedIn, checked against how they were represented in organizational records. When the title is unclear, I use more general descriptions to capture staff positions on these campaigns, and rely on the narrative in the book to provide more context regarding organizational roles. In addition, there is not a clear moment when primary campaigns end and general election campaigns begin, as campaigns begin restructuring and staffing for general elections well in advance of the formal nominating process. The designation of 'primary' and 'general' election campaigns should therefore be considered approximate.

Chapter 1

1. WPP Digital, a global communications firm, acquired Blue State Digital in December 2010.
2. A number of scholarly works have sought to explain the impressive mobilization around Obama's candidacy. See Alexander, *The Performance of Politics*; Formisano, "Populist Currents in the 2008 Presidential Campaign"; Castells, *Communication Power*; and Knorr Cetina, "What Is a Pipe?."
3. Michael Slaby, personal communication, August 18, 2010.
4. Schudson, *The Good Citizen*.
5. The campaign had over 3 million active volunteers, but still utilized paid phonebankers; Jamieson, *Electing the President, 2008*.
6. The trajectory of academic thought regarding new media and politics can be broken into three general periods: optimism, reinforcement, and collective action. The first dates from the early 1990s through to the collapse of the dot.com bubble and features optimistic accounts of the Internet's effect on democracy. See Barber, "The New Telecommunications Technology"; and Grossman, *The Electronic Republic*. During the second wave that emerged at the turn of the century, a group of scholars argued that the Internet reinforced extant political power. See Bimber and Davis, *Campaigning Online*; Davis, *The Web of Politics*; and Margolis and Resnick, *Politics As Usual*. For an extensive overview of the literature on new media and politics see Neuman, Bimber, and Hindman, "The Internet and Four Dimensions of Citizenship"; and Boulianne, "Does Internet Use Affect Engagement?".

7. Classic work on transaction costs includes Coase, "The Nature of the Firm"; Olson, *The Logic of Collective Action*; and Williamson, *Markets and Hierarchies*. In Olson's paradigmatic account, "free-riding" is the defining problem of collective action, in which rational actors will choose not to participate, given that they will benefit from public goods despite their lack of involvement.

8. Chadwick, "Web 2.0."

9. See Benkler, *The Wealth of Networks*; Bimber, Flanagin, and Stohl, "Reconceptualizing Collective Action in the Contemporary Media Environment"; Earl and Kimport, *Digitally Enabled Social Change*; Lupia and Sin, "Which Public Goods Are Endangered?"; and Norris, *Digital Divide*.

10. See Castells, *Communication Power*; Jenkins, *Convergence Culture*; and Jenkins and Thorburn, *Democracy and New Media*.

11. A number of works chronicle innovations on the Dean campaign without analyzing why they occurred. See Hindman, "The Real Lessons of Howard Dean"; Kreiss, "Developing the 'Good Citizen'"; Panagopoulos, *Politicking Online*; and Wiese and Gronbeck, "Campaign 2004 Developments in Cyberpolitics." An exception is Streeter and Teachout's edited collection of firsthand accounts that reveal innovation in the making; Streeter and Teachout, *Mousepads, Shoe Leather, and Hope*.

12. In *Information and American Democracy*, Bimber notes that established political entities have considerably more resources to invest in online campaign services, which has mitigated the potential of new media to level the playing field among differentially resourced organizations.

13. To tell this history, I draw on actor-network theory's methodological approach of "following the actors" as they assemble the sociotechnical. See Latour, *Reassembling the Social*; and *Science in Action*. The book follows the work of political actors as they create the information environments that many scholars focus on as the cause of changes in political collective action. I also borrow from a related body of work that takes the building and evolution of infrastructure as its object of analysis. Much of this literature proceeds from Star and Bowker's methodological work on "infrastructural inversion" in *Sorting Things Out*. As scholars such as Paul Edwards have shown, infrastructural inversion can proceed historically, showing how infrastructure both provides a background context for action and is shaped by sociotechnical action and institutions over time; Edwards, *A Vast Machine*. Drawing on this work, I document how campaigns and consultancies shaped, while being shaped by, the infrastructural contexts in which they acted. Understanding the Obama campaign required a historical approach to uncovering the background contexts of action which made it possible.

14. I draw here on work that analyzes a network mode of social organization that is distinct from both the market and the hierarchical firm. See Powell, "Neither Market nor Hierarchy"; and Podolny and Page, "Network Forms of Organization."

15. The term "netroots" eventually became more expansive, providing a compelling banner under which the entire online progressive movement organized itself. See Kerbel, *Netroots*. For a number of chapters discussing the role of blogs in the 2004 elections, see Tremayne, *Blogging, Citizenship, and the Future of Media*.

16. Aaron Myers, a longtime web developer and veteran of the Gore and Kerry campaigns, as well as both of Edwards's runs, remembers that at the start of the 2000 cycle, campaigns could not collect money online: "In 1999 it was illegal for campaigns to take contributions by credit card ... the only way to make contributions was by printing out a form and cashing a check and mailing it in. And then what changed all of that was actually a petition ... by the Bush campaign to the FEC"; Myers, personal communication, May 9, 2009.

17. For an extensive discussion of McCain's campaign, see Kaid, *The Millennium Election*.

18. The Gore campaign had multiple users of its website in mind, including committed supporters, undecided voters, children, and local Democratic officials who needed policy information; Myers, personal communication, May 9, 2009. There is evidence that there are many users visiting sites throughout campaigns for different purposes. Numerous staffers

on the Dean campaign, for instance, describe how during the last two weeks before the Iowa caucuses the web traffic on the campaign's informational pages rose dramatically, which staffers interpreted as undecided voters looking for substantive information to make a decision.

19. For a discussion of brochureware and early candidate websites, see Foot and Schneider, *Web Campaigning*.

20. In *Web Campaigning*, Foot and Schneider document the evolution of candidate web pages and the practices behind them, from speaking to undecided voters to mobilizing supporters.

21. Kreiss, "Taking Our Country Back?"

22. Howard, *New Media Campaigns and the Managed Citizen*. Howard chronicles the structure and work of what he describes as the "e-politics" community of professional political consultants trading in data and "narrowcasting" persuasive communications. Howard conducted his ethnographic work before the 2003–2004 electoral cycle, when a new group of staffers entered politics for the first time and crafted qualitatively different online campaign practices. For example, Vaccari shows how networked technologies supported offline mobilization during the 2003–2004 elections, a fundamentally different mode of campaigning than the one-way, targeted communications model; Vaccari, "From the Air to the Ground." To be sure, the Dean and Obama campaigns still used "narrowcasting" (as is clear in the targeted e-mails and online advertising), but largely developed them in house and did not turn to this e-politics group of consultants.

23. An exception was Gore's presidential campaign. Staffers cite that, in keeping with his policy interests, Gore had a commitment to using new technologies in his campaign.

24. Nicco Mele, personal communication, July 29, 2008.

25. Mele's work at Common Cause provided him with the opportunity to meet much of McCain's Internet staff. Mele cites both watching the McCain campaign closely and having a close relationship with Max Fose, McCain's Internet director.

26. For the literature on political consultants, see Blumenthal, *The Permanent Campaign*; Dulio, *For Better or For Worse*; Farrell, Kolodny, and Medvic, "Parties and Campaign Professionals in a Digital Age"; Gibson and Rommele, "Changing Campaign Communications"; Johnson, *No Place for Amateurs*; Mancini, "New Frontiers in Political Professionalism"; Medvic, "Professional Political Consultants"; Nimmo, *Political Persuaders*; Plasser, "Parties' Diminishing Relevance for Campaign Professionals"; Sabato, *The Rise of Political Consultants*; and Thurber and Nelson, *Campaign Warriors*. To date, there have been only a few works explicitly focused on new media campaign consultants and staffers. See Howard, *New Media Campaigns*; Johnson, *Campaigning in the 21st Century*; Karlson, "Fear the Political Consultant"; Sabato, *The Year of Obama*; and Tatarchevskiy, "The 'Popular' Culture of Internet Activism." Howard explicitly refers to the "e-politics" consultants as "professionals." However, as I extensively document below, the practitioner community that emerged after the 2004 elections differed significantly from this e-politics group with respect to its explicitly partisan orientation and new practices, technologies, and skill sets.

Throughout this book, I use the term "practitioners" instead of "professionals" to refer to the individuals who work with new media on political campaigns. (Following the literature cited above, I at times use the term "professional" when referring to other areas of campaign practice, such as fund-raising and communications, even though as Nielsen notes in *Ground Wars* there is at best uneven professionalism within campaigns.) I do so because most of the Internet staffers who worked in new media in 2004 on the Dean and Clark campaigns came from outside electoral politics. As the book shows, even as many of the staffers active during the 2004 cycle stayed in politics through subsequent electoral cycles, there was still a considerable number of new entrants in 2008. Staffers responsible for hiring, including veterans of campaign new media work, even stated that they looked explicitly for people outside politics in the hopes of being innovative. All of this suggests that new media campaign staffers are engaged in what Grossmann calls an ongoing "professionalizing project" across a host of different organizations, from consultancies and training organizations to the Democratic Party; Grossmann, "Going Pro?." However, there is still a marked openness to outsiders. This is in direct contrast to accounts that presume a static "profession" of new media campaign workers.

27. For a discussion of innovation arising from uncertainty, heterogenous logics, and organizational arrangements that foster creative recombinations of ideas, practices, and technologies, see Stark, *The Sense of Dissonance*. Chadwick also had the insight that campaigns and parties will "develop subunits that exhibit social movement style digital network repertoires but such subunits are sealed off from the main campaign decision makers, or are strategically channeled toward specific societal groups perceived as receptive to looser forms of political engagement"; Chadwick, "Digital Network Repertoires," 297.

28. For a discussion of the technological vision of the campaign as an inspiration for its staffers, see Streeter and Teachout, "Theories; Technology, the Grassroots, and Network Generativity."

29. Kevin Thurman, personal communication, July 16, 2011.

30. Mele, personal communication, July 29, 2008.

31. Chen, *Enabling Creative Chaos*. For other work on Burning Man, see Turner, "Burning Man at Google."

32. Chen, *Enabling Creative Chaos*, 21. For a discussion of hybridity in the political domain, see Chadwick, "Digital Network Repertoires and Organizational Hybridity."

33. Campaigns have increasingly invested in canvassing and field operations over the last decade in the face of diminishing returns from mediated communication, although they are often reliant on civil society actors to compensate for diminished party infrastructures and attachments among the electorate; Nielsen, *Ground Wars*. The Internet offered a new vehicle for candidate-centric electoral mobilization in the wake of larger shifts away formal party-based political forms. For works on changes in the nature of electoral participation, see Polsby, *The Consequences of Party Reform*; and Rosenstone and Hansen, *Mobilization, Participation, and Democracy in America*.

34. For an excellent overview of field campaigns and the "assemblages" that constitute them, see Nielsen, *Ground Wars*.

35. See Norman, *The Design of Everyday Things*. On delegation, see Latour, "Where Are the Missing Masses?".

36. For more on the limits of interactivity and the lack of policy participation on the Dean campaign, see Haas, "Subject to the System"; Hindman, "The Real Lessons of Howard Dean"; Hindman, *The Myth of Digital Democracy*; and Stromer-Galley and Baker, "Joy and Sorrow of Interactivity on the Campaign Trail." This is not to say that the campaign did not create and adop an extraordinary range of tools that supporters could use for their own ends, such as DeanSpace. For perspectives on how design structures social action, see Woolgar, "Configuring the User."

37. Andrew Bleeker, personal communication, June 30, 2010.

38. A number of firms and staffers also came out of the various "Draft Clark" efforts and the retired general's campaign, which were also technically innovative; see Feld and Wilcox, *Netroots Rising*. Brent Blackaby and Larry Huynh, former Silicon Valley executives who founded DraftClark2004.com, started Blackrock Associates, a digital political consulting firm now part of Trilogy Interactive, after the campaign. Lowell Feld was also active in the Draft Clark efforts and became a prominent political consultant. Matt Stoller worked on ClarkSphere and later went on to work as a political consultant for Connecticut U.S. Senate candidate Ned Lamont's 2006 campaign and became the president of BlogPac, an organization that supports progressive political activists. For a review of the subsequent work of Dean staffers, see "On the Download," *National Journal*.

39. Star, "The Ethnography of Infrastructure," 377.

40. Lievrouw and Livingstone approach new media as a set of technologies, practices, and social organization in their edited volume; Lievrouw and Livingstone, *Handbook of New Media*.

41. For a rich historical discussion of parties as infrastructure for electoral politics, and the far greater success of Republicans in party-building, see Galvin, *Presidential Party Building*.

42. Shirky, *Here Comes Everybody*. See also, Harris, Moffitt, and Squires, *The Obama Effect*.
43. Polletta, *It Was Like a Fever*.
44. For an extensive discussion of the Dean campaign's complex deployment of the "open source" metaphor, see Kreiss, "Open Source."
45. For work on the cultural performances of the Obama campaign, see Brown, "Conjuring Unity"; and Ivie and Giner, "American Exceptionalism in a Democratic Idiom."
46. While there is a lack of works on the building of infrastructure, a number of scholars document its importance. Aldrich argues that parties have not declined, but have transformed into "parties-in-service" to political candidates since the nominating reforms of the 1960s. These services include fund-raising (particularly for down-ballot candidates), staffers, consultants, and technologies such as voter files and targeting practices; Aldrich, *Why Parties?*. Nielsen documents the importance and processes of building party infrastructure, such as voter files, and the limits of the parties' capacities to conduct coordinated and sustained field campaigns; Nielsen, *Ground Wars*.
47. For more details on the renewed importance of field campaigns, see Nielsen, *Ground Wars*.
48. In 2011, VAN merged with NGP, another Democratic political technology firm, to form NGP-VAN.
49. A "club good" is a good that many can enjoy but that can be excludable. In this sense, BSD, the private owners, managed its platform in a way that defined the "club" as Democratic-allied organizations and excluded non-ideologically aligned groups. Investments in the good benefited all members of the club; for an extensive discussion of club goods, see Cornes and Sandler, *The Theory of Externalities, Public Goods, and Club Goods*.
50. Joe Rospars, personal communication, May 19, 2010.
51. The New Organizing Institute was founded by Judith Freeman and two veterans of the Dean and Kerry campaigns, Amanda Michel and Zack Exley, whose work is detailed in later chapters.
52. For additional discussion of the role of organizations such as NOI in formalizing campaign practice and tools, see Karpf, *The MoveOn Effect*.
53. Jascha Franklin-Hodge, personal communication, December 22, 2008.
54. Thurman, personal communication, June 16, 2011.
55. John, *Spreading the News*, 11.
56. Nye, *American Technological Sublime*.
57. O'Reilly, "Google, WalMart, and My.BarackObama.com"; and Mumford, *Technics and Human Development*.
58. Talbot, "How Obama 'Really' Did It."
59. Foot and Schneider argue that there is a "mutual shaping" process whereby tools, online organizing practices, and the practices of larger campaign organizations shape one another; Foot and Schneider, *Web Campaigning*, 18.
60. Plouffe, *The Audacity to Win*.
61. Many scholars have documented the technologies of the Obama campaign, but in being bound by the election cycle have missed their historical origins. For example, see Burch, "Can the New Commander in Chief Sustain His All-Volunteer Standing Army?"; Carty, *Wired and Mobilizing*; Johnson, *Campaigning in the 21st Century*; and Levenshus, "Online Relationship Management in a Presidential Campaign."
62. Nielsen shows how formal, bureaucratic structures help organizations overcome many problems caused by the lowered information costs of political participation; Nielsen, "The Labors of Internet-Assisted Activism." As the following discussion suggests, the planning conducted by the campaign's senior leadership and Rospars helped staffers overcome the problems of "over-communication, mis-communication, and communication overload" that Nielsen identifies.
63. For a post-campaign retrospective of where this integration failed, see Romano, "Yes We Can (Can't We?)."
64. Chris Hughes, personal communication, July 20, 2010.

65. Ibid.
66. Obama "won" Iowa and South Carolina; Clinton "won" New Hampshire and Nevada. However, "won" is a problematic concept for understanding the primaries, as these campaigns ultimately competed for delegates, not the popular vote. Obama, for instance, lost the popular vote but netted more delegates than Clinton in Nevada.
67. Neil Sroka, personal communication, December 22, 2008. Sutton was Hughes's deputy.
68. Slaby, personal communication, August 16, 2010.
69. Franklin-Hodge, personal communication, December 22, 2008.
70. A/B testing is a quintessential "control" technology in being probabilistic, not deterministic; Beniger, *The Control Revolution*.
71. Documentation of and concerns over targeting have long been a staple of the literature on new media campaigns. See Bennett, "Engineering Consent"; Carty, *Wired and Mobilizing*; Howard, *New Media Campaigns*; and Kreiss and Howard, "New Challenges to Political Privacy."
72. For an analysis of the ways that computation has transformed the internal workings of organizations, see Kallinikos, *The Consequences of Information*.
73. Kenski, Hardy, and Jamieson show that the Obama campaign (like most campaigns) devoted the vast majority of its resources to television advertising; Kenski, Hardy, and Jamieson, *The Obama Victory*.
74. A number of scholars have looked at the rhetoric, narratives, and performances of the Obama campaign. See Ganz, "Organizing Obama"; and Alexander, *The Performance of Politics*.
75. Scholars of social movements have long noted that cultural processes help give rise to and shape collective action. See Benford and Snow, "Framing Processes and Social Movements"; and Gould, *Moving Politics*.
76. For a detailed argument about design, content, and the negotiation of meaning between users and designers online, see Livingstone, "The Challenge of Engaging Youth Online." The most extensive statement on the symbolic affordances of design in the context of politics comes from Chadwick, "The Electronic Face of Government in the Internet Age."
77. Scott Thomas, personal communication, August 3, 2010.
78. For an excellent history of design in electoral politics and an analysis of the Obama campaign's design as well as the role of artists such as Shepard Fairey in framing the campaign as a cause, see Seidman, "Barack Obama's 2008 Campaign for the Presidency and Visual Design." For a collection of the campaign's design work, see Thomas, *Designing Obama*.
79. For a rich discussion of political advertising that goes beyond content to include symbolic and production practices, see Kaid and Johnston, *Videostyle*.
80. Gould, *Moving Politics*.
81. Thomas, personal communication, August 3, 2010.
82. The targets were both supporters and the staffers themselves who have to "drink their own Kool-Aid" to get through working 20-hour days for over a year; Slaby, personal communication, August 18, 2010.
83. See Skocpol, *Diminished Democracy*; and "United States."
84. Agre, "Real-time Politics."
85. See Coleman, "The Lonely Citizen," for arguments about the potential of new media to foster more robust political representation.
86. It is fundamentally an agonistic view of politics; see Mouffe, *Dimensions of Radical Democracy*.
87. Alexander, *The Performance of Politics*. See also Green, *The Eyes of the People*.
88. See Pateman, *Participation and Democratic Theory*.
89. I thank Richard John for this insight.
90. See Polsby, *The Consequences of Party Reform*; and Cohen, Karol, Noel, and Zaller, *The Party Decides*.
91. Howard, *New Media Campaigns*; and Kreiss and Howard, "New Challenges to Political Privacy."
92. Goff, personal communication, July 6, 2010.
93. Ibid.
94. These tools served as what Turner describes as "network forums" in *From Counterculture to Cyberculture*. These forums allowed aggrieved supporters from multiple communities to

find and make themselves visible to one another, hone a sense of collective identity, plan and coordinate challenges to the campaign, and take the fund-raising and publicity actions that drew attention to the protest.

95. Hirschman, *Exit, Voice, and Loyalty*. Ultimately there are few opportunities to exit in American electoral politics by backing an alternative candidate, especially during a general election which lacks the alternatives of primaries—except, of course, by not voting.

96. For a detailed discussion of the interviews conducted with Dean campaign staffers, see Kreiss "Taking Our Country Back?". For the Obama campaign, see Kreiss, "Acting in the Public Sphere."

97. The GWU Democracy in Action database is available online at: http://www.gwu.edu/~action.

## Chapter 2

1. For campaign archives of this time period, see the Howard Dean 2004 weblog at: http://dean2004.blogspot.com/2003_03_01_archive.html; and Dean Call to Action weblog at: http://www.deancalltoaction.blogspot.com/2003_03_30_deancalltoaction_archive.html#91851410. For records on the first quarter fund-raising in the presidential primaries of 2003, see the George Washington University's Democracy in Action page at: http://www.gwu.edu/~action/2004/money/1stq03summary.html.

2. Kreiss, "Open Source as Practice and Ideology."

3. Trippi, "The Perfect Storm."

4. In a highly publicized series of studies, Heaney and Rojas show how the fortunes and strength of the anti-war movement over the last decade rose and fell with the dynamics of partisan mobilization. Democrats protested against the Iraq War to contest Republican leadership, but left the movement in droves once Obama was elected. Dean's campaign served as an early vehicle for this electoral mobilization, which shifted to Kerry once he became the nominee. Heaney and Rojas, "Partisans, Nonpartisans, and the Antiwar Movement in the United States"; and "The Partisan Dynamics of Contention." For a review of the interplay between elections and social movements, see McAdam and Tarrow, "Ballots and Barricades." For a discussion of the netroots's attraction to Dean, see Farrell, "Bloggers and Parties."

5. Armstrong, "How a Blogger and the Dean Campaign Discovered Each Other," 44.

6. For a more detailed account, see Trippi, *The Revolution Will Not Be Televised*.

7. Jerome Armstrong, personal communication, November 21, 2008.

8. For the dynamics of network forums, see Turner, *From Counterculture to Cyberculture*.

9. For an account, see Armstrong, "The Journey with Trippi, Dean, and DFA."

10. Bobby Clark, personal communication, June 23, 2010.

11. Michael Silberman, personal communication, July 28, 2008.

12. Ibid.

13. Silberman argues that the Meetup organizers were demographically mixed in terms of age but not geography (as detailed below, this was because of the campaign's lack of supporters in the Great Plains states); Ibid.

14. Ibid.

15. Zephyr Teachout, personal communication, July 10, 2008.

16. Video of the speech is archived at: http://www.archive.org/details/dean-sacramento.

17. This is often a self-perpetuating cycle: journalists look to fund-raising and poll numbers to determine where to allocate coverage, while candidates find it difficult to gain either without press coverage. For a discussion of the dynamics of primary campaigns, see Aldrich, "The Invisible Primary and its Effects on Democratic Choice."

18. Mele, "A Web Activist Finds Dean," 185.

19. Teachout, personal communication, July 10, 2008.

20. Ibid.
21. Ibid.
22. Ibid.
23. Ibid.
24. See Teachout, "Something Much Bigger Than a Candidate," 68. Aaron Myers, director of Internet operations for Edwards in 2004, describes his campaign's reaction to the Dean online effort: "I remember our lawyers went crazy every time we would see some stuff that he [Dean] was doing"; Myers, personal communication, May 9, 2009. Myers recounts that Edwards's staffers faced the same legal uncertainty, and asked many of the same questions about online participation, such as whether it was legal for supporters to build their own websites for the candidate.
25. Mele, personal communication, July 29, 2008.
26. Clark, personal communication, June 23, 2010.
27. See Kreiss, "Open Source as Practice and Ideology."
28. Teachout, personal communication, July 10, 2008.
29. Ibid.
30. Dean staffer, personal communication, not for attribution.
31. Clark, personal communication, June 23, 2010.
32. See Agre, "Real-time Politics."
33. Interestingly, the Dean campaign also has a story of an innovation that *did not* happen. As Armstrong relates in "How a Blogger and the Dean Campaign Discovered Each Other," when the campaign was looking to upgrade from Blogger, Matthew Gross "wanted to base the campaign blog on the layout of Daily Kos, using the MT [Moveable Type] platform and blogroll style of a grassroots blog; meanwhile, Zepyhr discovered Rusty Foster's Kuro5hin. org website, which used Scoop to allow the community to promote the content." Gross won out, and when the campaign looked into Scoop again in the fall, the programmers said that it would not be able to scale. This is noteworthy, given Karpf's argument that the subsequent technical design of Daily Kos, which moved to Scoop in October of 2003, shaped much of the dramatic growth and community dynamics of the blog; Karpf, *The MoveOn Effect.*
34. Joe Rospars, personal communication, May 10, 2009. Also blogging at Not Geniuses were Ezra Klein and Matt Stoller, now two prominent members of the netroots.
35. Staffers later built a "Letters for America" application that enabled individuals to download Iowa voters' addresses online. The campaign did not have the ability to allow supporters to access the voter file online (a functionality which was developed by the party in 2006), so the field staffers e-mailed Internet staffers a spreadsheet of voter IDs. One problem was that there was little integration between the two departments beyond this. Staffers cite how, even though supporters sent over 100,000 letters to Iowa, no one on the national or local field campaign ever asked for data on who actually received letters.
36. For a discussion of how the campaign used its new media tools to generate professional press attention, see Kreiss, "Open Source as Practice and Ideology."
37. For work on MoveOn see Carty, "Multi-Issue, Internet-Mediated Interest Organizations and Their Implications for U.S. Politics;" and Chadwick, "Digital Network Repertoires and Organizational Hybridity."
38. Mele, personal communication, July 29, 2008.
39. "Happy Days Are Virtually Here Again," *New York Times.*
40. For a discussion of MoveOn's innovations in online organizing, see Chadwick, "Digital Network Repertoires and Organizational Hybridity."
41. Teachout, "Something Much Bigger Than a Candidate," 64.
42. Dean Internet staffer, personal communication, not for attribution.
43. For a history of the free and open source software movement, see Kelty, *Two Bits.* For the role of open source in the Dean campaign, see Kreiss, "Open Source as Practice and Ideology."
44. Mele, personal communication, July 29, 2008.
45. Myers, personal communication, May 9, 2009. At the same time, Myers describes how inside the Edwards campaign organization there was a pervasive understanding that they had a different candidate, with different supporters, from Dean.

Chapter 3

1. Kintera also had a "software as a service" model.
2. Yates, *Control Through Communication*.
3. Nuxoll, "E-mail: Sign Your Own Name," 199.
4. Biddle, "Hitting Home Runs On and Off the Internet," 172.
5. Clark, personal communication, June 23, 2010.
6. Nielsen, *Ground Wars*.
7. Direct mail raised over $10 million for the campaign.
8. To demonstrate differences between the 2000 and 2004 cycles, on the Gore campaign supporters could create personalized pages, but these were based solely around pre-packaged content templates and lacked donation systems.
9. Zack Rosen, personal communication, April 7, 2008.
10. Aldon Hynes, personal communication, April 2, 2008.
11. Rosen, personal communication, April 7, 2008. In "Drupal Nation," David Cohn argues that the Dean campaign served as the point of diffusion for this open source content management system in the United States. After the election, Rosen and Neil Drumm co-founded CivicSpace Labs, an organization that adapted DeanSpace for nonprofit use as a downloadable piece of software. Taken together, the Dean campaign's use of Drupal in DeanSpace and CivicSpace's subsequent work as a U.S.-based training organization and evangelist for the platform, along with a number of other high-profile adopters, helped diffuse the platform and create and foster a robust developer community.
12. Rosen, personal communication, April 7, 2008.
13. The three were the subject of a feature article in the *New York Times Sunday Magazine* by Samantha Shapiro, "The Dean Connection."
14. Clay Johnson, personal communication, June 3, 2010.
15. Rospars got by on a $1,000 a month salary by renting a cheap room from Macon Philips. Phillips later took over much of Rospars's role at BSD after the cofounder became new media director for the Obama campaign. Phillips also served as Rospars's deputy on the Obama campaign during the general election. Phillips subsequently became the director of new media for the transition and served as the White House director of new media in the Obama administration.
16. Clark, personal communication, June 23, 2010.
17. Convio now has an open API that enables its clients to build custom tools around its database.
18. Rospars, personal communication, June 25, 2010.
19. Project Commons is archived at: http://web.archive.org/web/20040116063621/commons. deanforamerica.com/transition.php.
20. Franklin-Hodge, personal communication, December 22, 2008.
21. Ibid.
22. Ben Self, personal communication, July 20, 2010.
23. Rospars, personal communication, June 25, 2010.
24. A few staffers suggested that the campaign's Iowa strategy was a particular point of debate among the candidate's advisors. There was discussion of pulling out of Iowa until as late as the summer of 2003. The state was never believed to be politically favorable to Dean's message, and senior staffers were aware that Kerry and Edwards were better funded during the first two quarters of the campaign in 2003, which resulted in them having more resources for early field offices. Some staffers even actively suggested that Gephardt would win Iowa, given that he had performed strongly there in previous presidential caucuses. In this scenario, Dean could win New Hampshire, and shut Kerry out of a crucial early victory.
25. Tamara Pogue, personal e-mail communication.
26. See Davis, "Presidential Campaigns Fine Tune Online Strategies."
27. Pogue, personal e-mail communication.
28. Ibid.
29. Ibid.
30. Internet staffer, personal communication, not for attribution.

31. Mordecai, personal communication, January 23, 2009.
32. Mordecai and Welch founded the political consultancy Advomatic after the election.
33. For personal recollections, see an Open Left diary at: http://www.openleft.com/diary/3193/.
34. Warshaw, personal communication, November 26, 2008.
35. Dean's former field staffers were active in a number of key states during the 2008 cycle as field directors and staffers for the Obama campaign. Jeremy Bird subsequently became the field director for South Carolina, Maryland, and Pennsylvania during the primaries and the general election director of Ohio. In 2012, Bird served as the national field director for the reelection effort. Buffy Wicks, an Iowa field staffer who worked to bring the New Hampshire model to the struggling state, subsequently served as Obama's California field director during the primaries and Missouri state director for the general election. Bird and Wicks also worked for Kerry in 2004. Karen Hicks, the New Hampshire state director for Dean, subsequently worked as the field director for the DNC in 2004 and then as a senior advisor for Clinton's campaign.
36. Marshall Ganz, personal communication, September 20, 2010.
37. Macomber, "Letting Go."
38. Bleeker, personal communication, June 30, 2010.
39. Generation Dean was a student outreach program.
40. Exley, personal communication, January 6, 2009.
41. Amanda Michel, personal communication, August 10, 2008.
42. Freeman, personal communication, July 1, 2010.
43. Kerry had the most extensive online advertising campaign in Democratic politics at the time. Michael Bassik, from MSHC Interactive, ran the campaign's fund-raising and persuasion online advertising.
44. See Carty, "Multi-issue, Internet-Mediated Interest Organizations and Their Implications for U.S. Politics"; Chadwick, "Digital Network Repertoires and Organizational Hybridity"; and Karpf, *The MoveOn Effect.*
45. See Denton, *The 2004 Presidential Campaign.*
46. For details on the MoveOn canvassing operations and estimations of its effect, see Middleton and Green, "Do Community-based Mobilization Campaigns Work Even in Battleground States?"
47. For a discussion, see Campbell, "Why Bush Won the Election of 2004."
48. For a discussion, see Vaccari, "From Air to Ground."
49. See Postelnicu et al., "The Role of Campaign Websites in Promoting Candidates and Attracting Campaign Resources."
50. Cornfield, "The Internet and Campaign 2004."

## Chapter 4

1. Michael Silberman, personal communication, July 28, 2008.
2. A number of practitioners argued that the founder of the fund-raising and compliance tool firm NGP, Nathaniel Pearlman, created the model of only working with Democrats in the political technology industry. Pearlman founded NGP in the mid-1990s. In essence, this new partisan stance after 2004 brought the new media sector in line with the overall practices of the political consulting industry; see Bernstein, *The Expanded Party in American Politics.*
3. Franklin-Hodge, personal communication, December 22, 2008.
4. Johnson, personal communication, June 3, 2010.
5. Ibid.
6. Ibid.
7. Stanton, "The Dean Dozen."
8. Thurman, personal communication, June 16, 2011.
9. For a history of the various attempts to remake the party after the 2004 electoral losses, see Bai, *The Argument.*
10. Nagourney, "Dean Enters Race for Democratic Chairman."
11. See Kerbel, *Netroots*; and Kerbel and Bloom, "Blog for America and Civic Involvement."

12. See Berman, *Herding Donkeys.*
13. Johnson, personal communication, June 3, 2010.
14. The other large firm in addition to Convio and Kintera at this point was Plus Three, which provided technologies and services to a number of Democratic organizations and interests.
15. Johnson, personal communication, June 3, 2010.
16. BSD's founders describe spending many hours from mid-2004 through mid-2005 brainstorming a business model on whiteboards at the house of the firm's first managing director, Roy Neel, the man who replaced Trippi as Dean's campaign manager. Neel was instrumental in helping the founders think through the firm's business approach.
17. Thurman, personal communication, June 16, 2011.
18. Ibid.
19. Clark, personal communication, June 23, 2010.
20. In 2006, ProgressNow began expanding to other states. It is now a network of affiliated state organizations.
21. Clark, personal communication, June 23, 2010.
22. Ibid.
23. Ibid.
24. For more details on the history of the Republican Party's VoterVault, see Kreiss and Howard, "New Challenges to Political Privacy."
25. During the 19th century, parties had national voter databases; see McGerr, *The Decline of Popular Politics*; and Kazin, *A Godly Hero.*
26. For more information, see Howard, *New Media Campaigns.*
27. Nielsen argues that there was also a leadership vacuum in Republican Party politics during Bush's second term, with little planning for the future; Nielsen, *Ground Wars.*
28. Mark Sullivan, personal communication, July 8, 2010.
29. Mike Sager, personal communication, July 1, 2010.
30. Sullivan, personal communication, July 8, 2010.
31. See Rosenthal, "Okay, We Lost Ohio. The Question Is, Why?"
32. Michel, personal communication, August 10, 2008.
33. For a discussion of Catalist's role as an independent purveyor of data to progressive groups, which has at times meant supporting challenges to the Democratic Party's elites, see Issenberg, "For Sale: Detailed Voter Profiles."
34. McAuliffe's earlier attempt to remake the party's data infrastructure failed precisely in this attempt at integration, given a range of opposition from the state parties. See Cillizza, "Critics Slam Demzilla"; and Jaquith, "The Demzilla Downfall."
35. The two state parties that do not use the national party system are Texas and California.
36. In many ways, this recalls what Gerschenkron described as the "relative advantage of backwardness"; see Fuller, *Science*, 101.
37. Sullivan, personal communication, July 8, 2010.
38. Franklin-Hodge, personal communication, December 22, 2008.
39. Sager, personal communication, July 1, 2010.
40. The PartyBuilder system was built for the national Party; the states used their own web vendors.
41. Staffers cited that this caused problems, but their impacts were generally small.
42. Franklin-Hodge, personal communication, December 22, 2008.
43. Johnson, personal communication, June 3, 2010.
44. Johnson stepped down shortly before the campaign signed a contract with Obama, citing that he was burned out with running the D.C. side of the business.

Chapter 5

1. Slaby, personal communication, August 16, 2010.
2. Freeman, personal communication, July 1, 2010.
3. Rospars, personal communication, June 25, 2010.
4. Ibid.

5. Slaby, personal communication, August 18, 2011.
6. Rospars, personal communication, June 25, 2010.
7. For a discussion of changes in online advertising in commercial contexts see Turow, *The Daily You*; and *Niche Envy*. For a look at the evolution of online political advertising see Kaye, *Campaign '08*; and Kreiss, "Yes We Can (Profile You)."
8. Slaby, personal communication, August 18, 2011.
9. Sroka, personal communication, December 22, 2008.
10. Gray Brooks, personal communication, June 29, 2010.
11. Interviewees wished their comments about the Clinton campaign to be not for attribution, as they did not want to be seen as criticizing a losing campaign.
12. Clinton staffer, personal communication, not for attribution.
13. Ironically enough, in interviews many new media staffers on both the Obama and Clinton campaigns stated that Clinton's core supporter demographic (women between the ages of 45 and 55) was a great potential strength in terms of online organizing, given that these individuals are among the most active online and especially heavy social media users.
14. Rospars, personal communication, June 25, 2010.
15. There were embedded new media staffers working out of the headquarters of the key battleground states during the primaries and general election.
16. In contrast, FEC filings suggest that with the front-runner candidate and wealthier campaign, at least initially, Clinton's team was largely and more exclusively drawn from the ranks of more prominent new media staffers.
17. Brooks, personal communication, June 29, 2010.
18. Edwards's campaign ultimately hired Plus Three, the firm that provided the e-mail and contribution systems for the DNC before Dean's tenure. Plus Three also provided these systems for Kerry's presidential bid and the Democratic Senatorial Campaign Committee and the Democratic Congressional Campaign Committee during this time.
19. In contrast, the Clinton campaign paid Mayfield Strategies over $500,000 for the design and implementation of its system.
20. Rospars, personal communication, June 25, 2010.
21. Franklin-Hodge, personal communication, December 22, 2008.
22. Rospars, personal communication, June 25, 2010.
23. Slaby, personal communication, August 18, 2011.
24. Rospars, personal communication, June 25, 2010.
25. Graham-Felsen, personal e-mail communication, April 18, 2011.
26. Ibid.
27. Ibid.
28. Ibid.
29. Ibid.
30. Ibid.
31. Graham-Felsen, personal e-mail communication. A number of staffers cite this as Rospars's approach to staffing more generally. As Teddy Goff describes, Rospars "didn't want people who were sort of infected by, his word and idea, past campaigns and cultures"; Goff, personal communication, July 6, 2010. The division also looked to hire individuals who were involved with field operations in the states.
32. Scott Thomas, personal communication, August 3, 2010.
33. Slaby, personal communication, August 18, 2011.
34. Thomas, personal communication, August 3, 2010.
35. Ibid.
36. Ibid.
37. Ibid.
38. Ibid.
39. Ibid.
40. Brooks, personal communication, June 29, 2010.
41. Will Bunnett, personal communication, April 9, 2009.

42. Slaby, personal communication, August 18, 2010.
43. See, Kallinikos, *The Consequences of Information.* For a related discussion in the context of journalism, see Anderson, *Networking the News.*
44. Slaby, personal communication, August 18, 2010.
45. Siroker, personal communication, September 1, 2010.
46. Thomas, personal communication, August 3, 2010.
47. Ibid.
48. Slaby, personal communication, August 18, 2010.
49. Thomas, personal communication, August 3, 2010.
50. Siroker, personal communication, September 1, 2010.
51. Goff, personal communication, July 6, 2010.
52. Thomas, personal communication, August 3, 2010.
53. Ibid.

Chapter 6

1. Siroker, personal communication, September 1, 2010.
2. Rospars, personal communication, June 25, 2010.
3. Hughes, personal communication, July 20, 2010.
4. Brooks, personal communication, June 29, 2010.
5. Hughes, personal communication, July 20, 2010.
6. Rospars, personal communication, June 25, 2010.
7. Ibid.
8. Goff, personal communication, July 6, 2010.
9. For a detailed discussion of the role of new media in these state primaries, see Berman, *Herding Donkeys.*
10. Rospars, personal communication, June 25, 2010.
11. Graham-Felsen, personal communication, November 23, 2010.
12. Sroka, personal communication, December 22, 2008.
13. Ibid.
14. Hughes, personal communication, July 20, 2010.
15. Freeman, personal communication, July 1, 2010.
16. Sroka, personal communication, December 22, 2008.
17. Hughes, personal communication, July 20, 2010.
18. Brooks, personal communication, June 29, 2010.
19. Rospars, personal communication, June 25, 2010.
20. Ibid.
21. Ibid.
22. Freeman, personal communication, July 1, 2010.
23. For the history behind Camp Obama, see Ganz "Organizing Obama."
24. Ganz, personal communication, September 20, 2010.
25. Rospars, personal communication, June 25, 2010.
26. Ibid.
27. Neil Jensen, personal communication, November 10, 2008.
28. Clinton staffer, personal communication, not for attribution.
29. Clinton staffer, personal communication, not for attribution.
30. Clinton staffer, personal communication, not for attribution.
31. Pledged delegates are those allocated to candidates directly or indirectly according to the results of primaries and caucuses. For extensive discussion of the campaign's strategy with respect to delegates, see Plouffe, *The Audacity to Win.*
32. Hughes, personal communication, July 20, 2010.
33. Campaigns are not the sole determinants of this access. These permissions based on profile varied by state during the primaries and general election because some states have more restrictive rules about access to their data.

34. Slaby, personal communication, August 18, 2010. There were continual data integration issues on the campaign. As Siroker describes: "It was so horrible. There was, and this essentially is a problem that all big organizations face, the problem is that every data store has its own information about individual people and it is very difficult for each data store to talk to each other. So the online aspect, the donations, MyBO all of that was on Blue State's database. We spent a lot of time looking at that data and we did queries and we used it very, very excessively. Beyond that there were four or five other sources of data that were also very valuable that we really didn't touch all that much. Things like the voter file and Catalist for consumer data and all of the information from Vote for Change, all these different data sources just weren't talking to each other. There were people who we hired whose full time job was to get integration but at that level, unless you plan for it ahead of time it is something that is very very hard to solve after the campaign gets in the swing of things"; Siroker, personal communication, September 1, 2010. Similar to the Dean campaign, the challenge throughout was that a campaign is a temporary entity scaling in a very short period of time, with different vendors and systems servicing the campaign.
35. Sullivan, personal communication, July 8, 2010.
36. Hughes, personal communication, July 20, 2010.
37. Sullivan, personal communication, July 8, 2010.
38. Ibid.
39. New Media Division staffer, personal communication, not for attribution.
40. Rospars, personal communication, June 25, 2010.
41. New Media Division staffer, personal communication, not for attribution.
42. New Media Division staffer, personal communication, not for attribution.

## Conclusion

1. See Nielsen's *Ground Wars* for participant observation within congressional campaigns. In "'Technology Is a Commodity,'" Vaccari interviews a number of new media staffers active on both sides of the aisle in 2008.
2. Galvin, *Presidential Party Building*.
3. Kenski, Hardy, and Jamieson, *The Obama Victory*.
4. Hindman, "The Real Lessons of Howard Dean."
5. Carty, *Wired and Mobilizing*.
6. Skocpol, *Diminished Democracy*.
7. Nielsen, *Ground Wars*.
8. Kreiss, "Open Source as Practice and Ideology."
9. Karpf, *The MoveOn Effect*.
10. Ibid.
11. Slaby, Personal communication, August 18, 2010. For a complementary argument, see Vaccari, "Technology Is a Commodity."
12. See, for example, Delany, "After the Election, Will Obama's Online Army Target Congress?".
13. Delany, "Obama's Online Army Creaks into Action on Health Care Reform (Or, What a Difference a Year Makes)."
14. For a discussion of this point, see Karpf, *The MoveOn Effect*.
15. Knorr Cetina, "What Is a Pipe?," 134.
16. Plouffe, *The Audacity to Win*; Jamieson, *Campaign 2004*; Jamieson, *Campaign 2008*; Streeter and Teachout, *Mousepads, Shoe Leather, and Hope*; Trippi, *The Revolution Will Not Be Televised*; and Vaccari, "Technology Is a Commodity."
17. For a discussion of black boxes, see Law, "Seeing Like a Survey."
18. For the porting of Manuel DeLanda's assemblage concept in *A New Philosophy of Society* into the study of electoral politics, see Nielsen, *Ground Wars*.

# Bibliography

Agre, Philip. "Real-time Politics: The Internet and the Political Process." *The Information Society* 18, no. 5 (2002): 311–331.

Aldrich, John. "The Invisible Primary and its Effects on Democratic Choice." *PS: Political Science & Politics* 42 (2009): 33–38.

Aldrich, John H. *Why Parties?: The Origin and Transformation of Political Parties in America.* Chicago: University of Chicago Press, 1995.

Alexander, Jeffrey C. *The Performance of Politics: Obama's Victory and the Democratic Struggle for Power.* New York: Oxford University Press, 2010.

Anderson, C. W. *Networking the News.* Philadelphia: Temple University Press, forthcoming.

Armstrong, Jerome. "How a Blogger and the Dean Campaign Discovered Each Other." In *Mousepads, Shoe Leather, and Hope: Lessons from the Howard Dean Campaign for the Future of Internet Politics,* edited by Thomas Streeter and Zephyr Teachout, 38–54. Boulder, CO: Paradigm Publishers, 2007.

Armstrong, Jerome. "The Journey With Trippi, Dean and DFA." *MyDD,* June 29, 2006. Accessed February 19, 2012. http://www.mydd.com/story/2006/6/29/12475/7402.

Bai, Matt. *The Argument: Billionaires, Bloggers, and the Battle to Remake Democratic Politics.* New York: Penguin Press, 2007.

Barber, Benjamin. "The New Telecommunications Technology: Endless Frontier or the End of Democracy." *Constellations* 4, no. 2 (1997): 202–228.

Benford, Robert D., and David. A. Snow. "Framing Processes and Social Movements: An Overview and Assessment." *Annual Review of Sociology* 26 (2000): 611–639.

Beniger, James. *The Control Revolution: Technological and Economic Origins of the Information Society.* Cambridge, MA: Harvard University Press, 1986.

Benkler, Yochai. *The Wealth of Networks: How Production Networks Transform Markets and Freedom.* New Haven, CT: Yale University Press, 2006.

Bennett, W. Lance. "Engineering Consent. The Persistence of a Problematic Communication Regime." In *Domestic Perspectives on Contemporary Democracy,* edited by Peter Nardulli, 131–154. Chicago: University of Illinois Press, 2008.

Berman, Ari. *Herding Donkeys: The Fight to Rebuild the Democratic Party and Reshape American Politics.* New York: Farrar, Straus and Giroux, 2010.

Bernstein, Jonathan. "The Expanded Party in American Politics." PhD diss., University of California at Berkeley, 1999.

Biddle, Larry. "Hitting Home Runs On and Off the Internet." In *Mousepads, Shoe Leather, and Hope: Lessons from the Howard Dean Campaign for the Future of Internet Politics,* edited by Thomas Streeter and Zephyr Teachout, 166–178. Boulder, CO: Paradigm Publishers, 2007.

Bimber, Bruce. *Information and American Democracy: Technology in the Evolution of Political Power.* New York: Cambridge University Press, 2003.

Bimber, Bruce, and Richard Davis. *Campaigning Online: The Internet in U.S. Elections.* New York: Oxford University Press, 2003.

Bimber, Bruce, Andrew Flanagin, and Cynthia Stohl. "Reconceptualizing Collective Action in the Contemporary Media Environment." *Communication Theory* 15, no. 4 (2005): 365–388.

Blumenthal, Sidney. *The Permanent Campaign: Inside the World of Elite Political Operatives.* Boston: Beacon Press, 1980.

Boulianne, Shelley. "Does Internet Use Affect Engagement? A Meta-Analysis of Research." *Political Communication* 26, no. 2 (2009): 193–211.

Bowker, Geoffrey C., and Susan L. Star. *Sorting Things Out: Classification and Its Consequences.* Cambridge, MA: MIT Press, 1999.

Brown, Robert E. "Conjuring Unity: The Politics of the Crowd and the Poetics of the Candidate." *American Behavioral Scientist* 54, no. 4 (December 1, 2010): 382–393.

Burch, Traci. "Can the New Commander in Chief Sustain His All-Volunteer Standing Army?" *Du Bois Review: Social Science Research on Race* 6, no. 1 (2009): 153–171.

Campbell, John. "Why Bush Won the Presidential Election of 2004: Incumbency, Ideology, Terrorism, and Turnout." *Political Science Quarterly* 120, no. 2 (2005): 219–241.

Carty, Victoria. "Multi-Issue, Internet-Mediated Interest Organizations and their Implications for US Politics: A Case of MoveOn.org." *Social Movement Studies* 10, no. 3 (August 2011): 265–282.

Carty, Victoria. *Wired and Mobilizing: Social Movements, New Technology, and Electoral Politics.* New York: Routledge, 2010.

Castells, Manuel. *Communication Power.* New York: Oxford University Press, 2009.

Chadwick, Andrew. "Digital Network Repertoires and Organizational Hybridity." *Political Communication* 24, no. 3 (2007): 283–301.

Chadwick, Andrew. "The Electronic Face of Government in the Internet Age: Borrowing from Murray Edelman." *Information, Communication, and Society* 4, no. 3 (2001): 435–457.

Chadwick, Andrew. "Web 2.0: New Challenges for the Study of E-Democracy in an Era of Informational Exuberance." *I/S: A Journal of Law and Policy for the Information Society* 5, no. 1 (2009): 9–41.

Chen, Katherine K. *Enabling Creative Chaos: The Organization Behind the Burning Man Event.* Chicago: University of Chicago Press, 2009.

Cillizza, Chris. "Critics Slam 'Demzilla': DNC Defends Vast Voter, Donor ID Project." *Roll Call,* June 4, 2003. Accessed October 25, 2011. http://www.rollcall.com/issues/48_99/-1820-1.html.

Coase, Ronald. "The Nature of the Firm." *Economica* 4, no. 16 (1937): 422–435.

Cohen, Marty, David Karol, Hans Noel, and John Zaller. *The Party Decides: Presidential Nominations Before and After Reform.* Chicago: University Of Chicago Press, 2008.

Cohn, David. "Drupal Nation: Software to Power the Left." Master's thesis, New York University, 2007.

Coleman, Stephen. "The Lonely Citizen: Indirect Representation in an Age of Networks." *Political Communication* 22, no. 2 (2005): 197–214.

Cornes, Richard, and Todd Sandler. *The Theory of Externalities, Public Goods, and Club Goods.* New York: Cambridge University Press, 1996.

Cornfield, Michael. "The Internet and Campaign 2004: A Look Back at the Campaigners." *Pew Internet and American Life Project,* 2005. http://pewinternet.org/~/media/Files/Reports/2005/Cornfield_commentary.pdf.

Davis, Richard. *The Web of Politics: The Internet's Impact on the American Political System.* New York: Oxford University Press, 1999.

Davis, Steve. "Presidential Campaigns Fine-Tune Online Strategies." *Journalism Studies* 6, no. 2 (2005): 241–244.

Delanda, Miguel. *A New Philosophy of Society: Assemblage Theory and Social Complexity.* New York: Continuum, 2006.

Delany, Colin. "After the Election, Will Obama's Online Army Target Congress?" *TechPresident,* July 30, 2008. Accessed February 19, 2012. http://techpresident.com/blog-entry/after-election-will-obamas-online-army-target-congress.

Delany, Colin. *Learning from Obama: Lessons for Online Communicators in 2009 and Beyond,* 2009. http://www.epolitics.com/learning-from-obama.

Delany, Colin. "Obama's Online Army Creaks into Action on Health Care Reform (Or, What a Difference a Year Makes)." *TechPresident,* September 2, 2009. http://techpresident.com/blog-entry/obamas-online-army-creaks-action-health-care-reform-or-what-difference-year-makes.

Denton, Robert E., Jr., ed. *The 2004 Presidential Campaign: A Communication Perspective.* Lanham, MD: Rowman & Littlefield, 2005.

Dulio, David A. *For Better or Worse? How Political Consultants Are Changing Elections in the United States.* Albany: State University of New York Press, 2004.

Earl, Jennifer, and Katrina Kimport. *Digitally Enabled Social Change: Activism in the Internet Age.* Cambridge, MA: MIT Press, 2010.

Edwards, Paul N. *A Vast Machine: Computer Models, Climate Data, and the Politics of Global Warming.* Cambridge, MA: MIT Press, 2010.

Exley, Zack. "Learn How to Do It Again in 2008." *The Huffington Post,* November 8, 2006. Accessed February 20, 2010. http://www.huffingtonpost.com/zack-exley/learn-how-to-do-it-again-_b_33675.html.

Farrell, Henry. "Bloggers and Parties: Can the Netroots Reshape American Democracy?" *Boston Review,* September/October, 2006. Accessed February 18, 2012. http://www.bostonreview.net.

Farrell, David M., Robin Kolodny, and Stephen Medvic. "Parties and Campaign Professionals in a Digital Age." *The Harvard International Journal of Press/Politics* 6, no. 4 (2001): 11–30.

Feld, Lowell, and Nate Wilcox. *Netroots Rising: How a Citizen Army of Bloggers and Online Activists Is Changing American Politics.* Westport, CT: Praeger Publishers, 2008.

Foot, Kirsten, and Stephen Schneider. *Web Campaigning.* New York: Oxford University Press, 2006.

Formisano, Ron. "Populist Currents in the 2008 Presidential Campaign." *Journal of Policy History* 22, no. 2 (2010): 237–255.

Fuller, Steve. *Science (The Art of Living).* Kingston, ON: Mcgill Queens University Press, 2010.

Galvin, Daniel J. *Presidential Party Building: Dwight D. Eisenhower to George W. Bush.* Princeton, NJ: Princeton University Press, 2009.

Ganz, Marshall. "Organizing Obama: Campaign, Organizing, Movement." Paper presented at the annual meeting of the American Sociological Association, San Francisco, California, August 2009.

Gibson, Rachel, and Andrea Rommele. "Changing Campaign Communications: A Party-Centered Theory of Professionalized Campaigning." *The Harvard International Journal of Press/Politics* 6, no. 4 (2001): 31–43.

Gould, Deborah. *Moving Politics: Emotion and ACT UP's Fight Against AIDS.* Chicago: University of Chicago Press, 2009.

Green, Jeffrey Edward. *The Eyes of the People: Democracy in an Age of Spectatorship.* New York: Oxford University Press, 2009.

Gronbeck, Bruce, and Danielle Wiese. "The Repersonalization of Presidential Campaigning in 2004." *American Behavioral Scientist* 49, no. 4 (2005): 520–534.

Grossman, Lawrence. *The Electronic Republic: Reshaping Democracy in the Information Age.* New York: Penguin, 1995.

Grossmann, Matthew. "Going Pro? The Professional Model and Political Campaign Consulting." *Journal of Political Marketing* 8, no. 2 (2009).

Haas, Gretchen A. "Subject to the System: The Rhetorical Constitution of Good Internet Citizenship in the 2004 U.S. Presidential Campaign." PhD diss., University of Minnesota, Minneapolis, 2006.

"Happy Days Are Virtually Here Again." *New York Times,* June 27, 2003. Accessed February 19, 2012. http://www.nytimes.com/2003/06/27/opinion/happy-days-are-virtually-here-again.html.

Harris, Heather E., Kimberly R. Moffitt, and Catherine R. Squires. *The Obama Effect: Multidisciplinary Renderings of the 2008 Campaign.* Albany: State University of New York Press, 2010.

Heaney, Michael. T., and Fabio Rojas. "Partisans, Nonpartisans, and the Antiwar Movement in the United States." *American Politics Research* 35, no. 4 (2007): 431–464.

Heaney, Michael T., and Fabio Rojas. "The Partisan Dynamics of Contention: Demobilization of the Antiwar Movement in the United States, 2007–2009." *Mobilization: An International Quarterly* 16, no. 1 (February 2011): 45–64.

Hindman, Matthew. *The Myth of Digital Democracy.* Princeton, NJ: Princeton University Press, 2008.

Hindman, Matthew. "The Real Lessons of Howard Dean: Reflections on the First Digital Campaign." *Perspectives on Politics* 3, no. 1 (2005): 121–128.

Hirschman, Albert O. *Exit, Voice, and Loyalty: Responses to Decline in Firms, Organizations, and States.* Cambridge, MA: Harvard University Press, 1970.

Howard, Philip N. *New Media Campaigns and the Managed Citizen.* New York: Cambridge University Press, 2006.

Issenberg, Sasha. "For Sale: Detailed Voter Profiles." *Slate,* January 30, 2012. Accessed February 19, 2012. http://www.slate.com/articles/news_and_politics/victory_lab/2012/01/the_co_op_and_the_data_trust_the_dnc_and_rnc_get_into_the_data_mining_business_.html.

Ivie, Robert L., and Oscar Giner. "American Exceptionalism in a Democratic Idiom: Transacting the Mythos of Change in the 2008 Presidential Campaign." *Communication Studies* 60 (August 10, 2009): 359–375.

Jamieson, Kathleen Hall. *Electing the President, 2004: The Insider's View.* Philadelphia: University of Pennsylvania Press, 2005.

Jamieson, Kathleen Hall. *Electing the President, 2008: The Insider's View.* Philadelphia: University of Pennsylvania Press, 2009.

Jaquith, Waldo. "The Demzilla Downfall?" *Waldo Jaquith Blog,* July 21, 2006. Accessed October 25, 2011. http://waldo.jaquith.org/blog/2006/07/demzilla-downfall/.

Jenkins, Henry. *Convergence Culture.* New York: New York University Press, 2006.

Jenkins, Henry, and David Thorburn. *Democracy and New Media.* Cambridge, MA: MIT Press, 2004.

John, Richard R. *Spreading the News: The American Postal System from Franklin to Morse.* Boston: Harvard University Press, 1998.

Johnson, Dennis W. *No Place for Amateurs: How Political Consultants Are Reshaping American Democracy.* New York: Routledge, 2007.

Johnson, Dennis W. *Campaigning in the 21st Century: A Whole New Ball Game?* New York: Routledge, 2011.

Kaid, Lynda Lee. *The Millennium Election: Communication in the 2000 Campaign.* Oxford: Rowman & Littlefield, 2003.

Kaid, Lynda Lee, and Anne Johnston. *Videostyle in Presidential Campaigns: Style and Content of Televised Political Advertising.* Westport, CT: Praeger/Greenwood, 2001.

Kallinikos, Jannis. *The Consequences of Information: Institutional Implications of Technological Change.* Northampton, MA: Edward Elgar Publishing, 2007.

Karlson, Rune. "Fear the Political Consultant: Campaign Professionals and New Technology in Norwegian Electoral Politics." *Party Politics* 16 no. 2 (2009): 193–214.

Karpf, David A. *The MoveOn Effect: The Unexpected Transformation of American Political Advocacy.* New York: Oxford University Press, 2012.

Kaye, Kate. *Campaign '08: A Turning Point for Digital Media.* CreateSpace Self Publishing, 2009.

Kazin, Michael. *A Godly Hero: The Life of William Jennings Bryan.* New York: Knopf, 2006.

Keiss, Daniel, and Philip N. Howard. "New Challenges to Political Privacy: Lessons from the First U.S. Presidential Race in the Web 2.0 Era." *International Journal of Communication* 4 (2010): 1032–1050.

Kelty, Chris. *Two Bits: The Cultural Significance of Free Software*. Durham, NC: Duke University Press, 2008.

Kenski, Kate, Bruce W. Hardy, and Kathleen Hall Jamieson. *The Obama Victory: How Media, Money, and Message Shaped the 2008 Election*. New York: Oxford University Press, 2010.

Kerbel, Matthew. *Netroots: Online Progressives and the Transformation of American Politics*. New York: Paradigm Publishers, 2009.

Kerbel, Matthew R., and Joel David Bloom. "Blog for America and Civic Involvement." *The Harvard International Journal of Press/Politics* 10, no. 4 (2005): 3–27.

Knorr Cetina, Karin. *Epistemic Cultures: How the Sciences Make Knowledge*. Cambridge, MA: Harvard University Press, 1999.

Knorr Cetina, Karin. "Objectual Practice." In *The Practice Turn in Contemporary Theory*, edited by Theodor R. Schatzki, Karin Knorr Cetina, and Eike von Savigny, 175–188. London: Routledge, 2001.

Knorr Cetina, Karin. "What Is a Pipe?: Obama and the Sociological Imagination." *Theory, Culture & Society* 26, no. 5 (2009): 129–140.

Koger, Gregory, Seth Maskett, and Hans Noel. "Cooperative Party Factions in American Politics." *American Politics Research* 38, no. 1 (2010): 33–53.

Kreiss, Daniel. "Acting in the Public Sphere: The Obama Campaign's Strategic Use of New Media to Shape Narratives of the 2008 Presidential Race." *Research in Social Movements, Conflicts, and Change* 33 (2012).

Kreiss, Daniel. "Developing the 'Good Citizen': Digital Artifacts, Peer Networks, and Formal Organization During the 2003–2004 Howard Dean Campaign." *The Journal of Information Technology and Politics* 6, no. 3/4 (2009): 281–297.

Kreiss, Daniel. "Open Source as Practice and Ideology: The 2003–2004 Howard Dean Campaign's Organizational and Cultural Innovations in Electoral Politics." *Journal of Information Technology and Politics* 8, no. 3 (2011): 367–382.

Kreiss, Daniel. "Taking Our Country Back? The Crafting of Networked Politics from Howard Dean to Barack Obama." PhD diss., Stanford University, Stanford, California, 2010.

Kreiss, Daniel. "Yes We Can (Profile You): A Brief Primer on Campaigns and Political Data." 64 Stan. L. Rev. Online 70, 2012.

Latour, Bruno. *Reassembling the Social: An Introduction to Actor-Network Theory*. New York: Oxford University Press, 2005.

Latour, Bruno. *Science in Action*. Cambridge, MA: Harvard University Press, 1987.

Latour, Bruno. "Where Are the Missing Masses? The Sociology of a Few Mundane Artifacts." In *Shaping Technology*, edited by Weibe Bijker and John Law, 225–258. Cambridge, MA: MIT Press, 1992.

Law, John. "Seeing Like a Survey." *Cultural Sociology* 3, no. 2 (2009): 239–256.

Levenshus, Abbey. "Online Relationship Management in a Presidential Campaign: A Case Study of the Obama Campaign's Management of Its Internet-Integrated Grassroots Effort." *Journal of Public Relations Research* 22 (July 2, 2010): 313–335.

Lievrouw, Leah A., and Sonia Livingstone, eds. *Handbook of New Media: Social Shaping and Social Consequences of ICTs*. London: Sage, 2006.

Lipton, Jacqueline D. "From Domain Names to Video Games: The Rise of the Internet in Presidential Politics." 86 Denver U. L. Rev. 693, 2009.

Livingstone, Sonia. "The Challenge of Engaging Youth Online: Contrasting Producers' and Teenagers' Interpretations of Websites." *European Journal of Communication* 22, no. 2 (June 2007): 165–184.

Lupia, Arthur, and Gisela Sin. "Which Public Goods Are Endangered? How Evolving Communication Technologies Affect the Logic of Collective Action." *Public Choice* 117, no. 3/4 (2003): 315–331.

Macomber, Shawn. "Letting Go." *The American Spectator*, February 18, 2004.

Mancini, Paolo. "New Frontiers in Political Professionalism." *Political Communication* 16, no. 3 (1999): 231–245.

Margolis, Michael, and David Resnick. *Politics As Usual: The Cyberspace "Revolution."* London: Sage, 2000.

McAdam, Doug, and Sidney Tarrow. "Ballots and Barricades: On the Reciprocal Relationship Between Elections and Social Movements." *Perspectives on Politics* 8, no. 2 (2010): 529–542.

McGerr, Michael E. *The Decline of Popular Politics: The American North, 1865–1928*. New York: Oxford University Press, 1986.

McKelvey, Fenwick. "A Programmable Platform? Drupal, Modularity, and the Future of the Web." *The Fibreculture Journal* 18 (2011). Accessed October 25, 2011. http://eighteen. fibreculturejournal.org/2011/10/09/fcj-128-programmable-platform-drupal-modularity-and-the-future-of-the-web/.

Medvic, Stephen K. "Professional Political Consultants: An Operational Definition." *Politics* 23, no. 2 (2003): 119–127.

Mele, Nicco. "A Web Activist Finds Dean." In *Mousepads, Shoe Leather, and Hope: Lessons from the Howard Dean Campaign for the Future of Internet Politics*, edited by Thomas Streeter and Zephyr Teachout, 179–191. Boulder, CO: Paradigm Publishers, 2007.

Michel, Amanda. "The Lessons of Generation Dean." In *Mousepads, Shoe Leather, and Hope: Lessons from the Howard Dean Campaign for the Future of Internet Politics*, edited by Thomas Streeter and Zephyr Teachout, 147–165. Boulder, CO: Paradigm Publishers, 2007.

Middleton, Joel A., and Donald Green. "Do Community-based Mobilization Campaigns Work Even in Battleground States? Evaluating the Effectiveness of MoveOn's 2004 Mobilization Campaign." *Quarterly Journal of Political Science* 3 (2008): 63–82.

Mouffe, Chantal. *Dimensions of Radical Democracy: Pluralism, Citizenship, Community*. New York: Verso Books, 1992.

Mumford, Lewis. *Technics and Human Development: The Myth of the Machine* (Vol. 1). New York: Mariner, 1971.

Neuman, W. Russell, Bruce Bimber, and Matthew Hindman. "The Internet and Four Dimensions of Citizenship." In *the Oxford Handbook of American Public Opinion and Media*, edited by Lawrence R. Jacobs and Robert Y. Shapiro, 22–42. New York: Oxford University Press, 2010.

Nielsen, Rasmus Kleis. *Ground Wars: Personalized Communication in Political Campaigns*. Princeton, NJ: Princeton University Press, 2012.

Nielsen, Rasmus Kleis. "The Labors of Internet-Assisted Activism: Overcommunication, Miscommunication, and Communicative Overload." *Journal of Information Technology and Politics* 6, no. 3/4 (2009): 267–280.

Nimmo, Dan D. *Political Persuaders: The Techniques of Modern Election Campaigns*. New York: Prentice Hall, 1970.

Norman, Donald A. *The Design of Everyday Things*. New York: Basic Books, 2002.

Norris, Pippa. *Digital Divide: Civic Engagement, Information Poverty, and the Internet Worldwide*. New York: Cambridge University Press, 2001.

Nuxoll, Kelly. "E-mail: Sign Your Own Name." In *Mousepads, Shoe Leather, and Hope: Lessons from the Howard Dean Campaign for the Future of Internet Politics*, edited by Thomas Streeter and Zephyr Teachout, 192–200. Boulder, CO: Paradigm Publishers, 2007.

Nye, David E. *American Technological Sublime*. Cambridge, MA: MIT Press, 1996.

Olson, Mancur. *The Logic of Collective Action*. Cambridge, MA: Harvard University Press, 1965.

"On the Download: Dean Internet Class of 2004—Where Are They Now?" *National Journal*, February 12, 2007. Accessed October 25, 2011. http://hotlineoncall.nationaljournal.com/ archives/2007/02/on_the_download_27.php.

O'Reilly, Tim. "Google, WalMart, and My.BarackObama.com: The Power of the Real Time Enterprise." *O'Reilly Radar*, December 27, 2008. Accessed February 20, 2010. http://radar.oreilly. com/2008/12/google-walmart-mybarackobama.html.

Panagopoulos, Costas. *Politicking Online: The Transformation of Election Campaign Communications*. New Brunswick, NJ: Rutgers University Press, 2009.

Pateman, Carole. *Participation and Democratic Theory*. Cambridge, UK: Cambridge University Press, 1976.

Plasser, Fritz. "Parties' Diminishing Relevance for Campaign Professionals." *The Harvard International Journal of Press/Politics* 6, no. 4 (2001): 44–59.

Plouffe, David. *The Audacity to Win: The Inside Story and Lessons of Barack Obama's Historic Victory*. New York: Viking Adult, 2009.

Podolny, Joel M., and Karen L. Page. "Network Forms of Organization." *Annual Review of Sociology* 24 (January 1, 1998): 57–76.

Polletta, Francesca. *It Was Like a Fever: Storytelling in Protest and Politics*. Chicago: University Of Chicago Press, 2006.

Polsby, Nelson. *The Consequences of Party Reform*. New York: Oxford University Press, 1983.

Postelnicu, Monica, Justin D. Martin, and Kristin Landreville. "The Role of Campaign Websites in Promoting Candidates and Attracting Campaign Resources." In *The Internet Election: Perspectives on the Web in Campaign 2004*, edited by Andrew P. Williams and John C. Tedesco, 99–111. Oxford: Rowman and Littlefield, 2006.

Powell, Walter W. "Neither Market nor Hierarchy: Network Forms of Organization." *Research In Organizational Behavior* 12, no. 1 (1990): 295–336.

Romano, Andrew. "Yes We Can (Can't We?)." *The Daily Beast*, January 2, 2012. Accessed February 19, 2012. http://www.thedailybeast.com/newsweek/2012/01/01/inside-president-obama-s-reelection-machine.html.

Rosenstone, Steven J., and John M. Hansen. *Mobilization, Participation, and Democracy in America*. New York: Longman, 1993.

Rosenthal, Steve. "Okay, We Lost Ohio. The Question Is, Why?" *Washington Post*, December 5, 2004.

Sabato, Larry J. *The Rise of Political Consultants: New Ways of Winning Elections*. New York: Basic Books, 1981.

Sabato, Larry J., ed. *The Year of Obama: How Barack Obama Won the White House*. New York: Longman, 2010.

Schudson, Michael. *The Good Citizen: A History of American Civic Life*. New York: The Free Press, 1999.

Seidman, Steven A. "Barack Obama's 2008 Campaign for the U.S. Presidency and Visual Design." *Journal of Visual Literacy* 29 (2010): 1–27.

Shapiro, Samantha M. "The Dean Connection." *New York Times Sunday Magazine*, December 7, 2003.

Shirky, Clay. *Here Comes Everybody*. New York: Penguin Press, 2008.

Skocpol, Theda. *Diminished Democracy: From Membership to Management in American Civic Life*. Norman: University of Oklahoma Press, 2004.

Skocpol, Theda. "United States: From Membership to Advocacy." In *Democracies in Flux: The Evolution of Social Capital in Contemporary Society*, edited by Robert Putnam, 103–136. New York: Oxford University Press, 2002.

Stanton, Alison. "The Dean Dozen." *Democracy for America Blog*, May 12, 2004. Accessed February 19, 2012. http://www.democracyforamerica.com/blog_posts/3902.

Star, Susan Leigh. "The Ethnography of Infrastructure." *American Behavioral Scientist* 43, no. 3 (November 1, 1999): 377–391.

Stark, David A. *The Sense of Dissonance: Accounts of Worth in Economic Life*. Princeton, NJ: Princeton University Press, 2009.

Streeter, Thomas, and Zephyr Teachout. "Theories: Technology, the Grassroots, and Network Generativity." In *Mousepads, Shoe Leather, and Hope: Lessons From the Howard Dean Campaign for the Future of Internet Politics*, edited by Thomas Streeter and Zephyr Teachout, 23–36. Boulder, CO: Paradigm Publishers, 2007.

Streeter, Thomas, and Zephyr Teachout, eds. *Mousepads, Shoe Leather, and Hope: Lessons from the Howard Dean Campaign for the Future of Internet Politics*. Boulder, CO: Paradigm Publishers, 2007.

Stromer-Galley, Jennifer, and Andrea B. Baker. "Joy and Sorrow of Interactivity on the Campaign Trail: Blogs in the Primary Campaign of Howard Dean." In *The Internet Election: Perspectives on the Web in Campaign 2004*, edited by Andrew P. Williams and John C. Tedesco, 111–131. New York: Rowan and Littlefield, 2006.

Talbot, David. "How Obama 'Really' Did It: The Social-networking Strategy That Took an Obscure Senator to the Doors of the White House." *Technology Review*, September/October 2008. Accessed February 19, 2012. http://www.technologyreview.com/web/21222/.

Tatarchevskiy, Tatiana. "The 'Popular' Culture of Internet Activism." *New Media & Society* 13, no. 2 (2011): 297–313.

Teachout, Zephyr. "Something Much Bigger Than a Candidate." In *Mousepads, Shoe Leather, and Hope: Lessons from the Howard Dean Campaign for the Future of Internet Politics*, edited by Thomas Streeter and Zephyr Teachout, 55–73. Boulder, CO: Paradigm Publishers, 2007.

Thomas, Scott. *Designing Obama*. Albany, CA: Post Press, LLC, 2010.

Thurber, James A., and Candice J. Nelson, eds. *Campaign Warriors: Political Consultants in Elections*. Washington, DC: Brookings Institution Press, 2000.

Tremayne, Mark, ed. *Blogging, Citizenship, and the Future of Media*. London: Routledge, 2007.

Trippi, Joe. "The Perfect Storm," *JoeTrippi.com*, May 2003. Accessed February 18, 2012. http://joetrippi.com/blog/?page_id=1378.

Trippi, Joe. *The Revolution Will Not Be Televised: Democracy, the Internet, and the Overthrow of Everything*. New York: Harper Collins, 2004.

Turow, Joseph. *Niche Envy: Marketing Discrimination in the Digital Age*. Cambridge, MA: MIT Press, 2006.

Turow, Joseph. *The Daily You: How the New Advertising Industry is Defining Your Identity and Your Worth*. New Haven, CT: Yale University Press, 2011.

Turner, Fred. *From Counterculture to Cyberculture: Stewart Brand, the Whole Earth Network, and the Rise of Digital Utopianism*. Chicago: Chicago University Press, 2006.

Turner, Fred. "Burning Man at Google: A Cultural Infrastructure for New Media Production." *New Media & Society* 11, no. 1/2 (2009): 73–94.

Vaccari, Cristian. "From the Air to the Ground: The Internet in the 2004 US Presidential Election." *New Media & Society* 10, no. 4 (2008): 647–665.

Vaccari, Cristian. "'Technology Is a Commodity': The Internet in the 2008 United States Presidential Election." *Journal of Information Technology and Politics* 7, no. 4 (2010): 318–339.

Wiese, Danielle R., and Bruce E. Gronbeck. "Campaign 2004 Developments in Cyberpolitics." In *The 2004 Presidential Campaign: A Communication Perspective*, edited by Richard E. Denton, Jr., 217–240. New York: Rowan and Littlefield, 2005.

Williams, Raymond. *The Long Revolution*. Hammondsworth, UK: Pelican Books, [1961] 1984.

Williamson, Oliver. *Markets and Hierarchies*. New York: Free Press, 1975.

Woolgar, Steve. "Configuring the User: The Case of Usability Trials." In *A Sociology of Monsters: Essays on Power, Technology, and Domination*, edited by John Law, 57–102. London: Routledge, 1991.

Yates, JoAnne. *Control Through Communication: The Rise of System in American Management*. Baltimore, MD: Johns Hopkins University Press, 1993.

# Index